The Shipwreck Research Handbook

by Gary Gentile

Bellerophon Bookworks

Copyright 2008 by Gary Gentile

All rights reserved. Except for the use of brief quotations embodied in critical articles and reviews, this book may not be reproduced in part or in whole, in any manner (including mechanical, electronic, photographic, and photocopy means), transmitted in any form, or recorded by any data storage and/or retrieval device, without express written permission from the author. Address all queries to:

Bellerophon Bookworks
P.O. Box 57137
Philadelphia, PA 19111

Additional copies of this book may be purchased from the same address by sending a check or money order in the amount of $25 U.S. for each copy (plus $4 postage per order, not per book, in the U.S. Inquire for shipping cost to foreign countries). Alternatively, copies may be purchased from the author's website, and paid by credit card:

http://www.ggentile.com

Picture Credits
All uncredited photographs were taken by the author. The front cover shows Pete Manchee on an unidentified sailing vessel in Lake Erie.

International Standard Book Numbers (ISBN)
1-883056-31-4
978-1-883056-31-5

First Edition

Printed in the U.S.A.

CONTENTS

Introduction - 9

Primary versus Secondary Research	9
Research Adventures	13
The Psychology of Research	13

Part One - 16
Published Sources

Publications with National Shipwreck Listings - 17

Encyclopedia of American Shipwrecks	17
New York Maritime Register	19
Lloyd's Weekly Shipping Index	20
Lloyd's Register Wreck Returns	21
Lloyd's Weekly Casualty Reports	21
Lloyd's Casualty Week	21
Merchant Steam Vessels of the United States 1790-1868	22
List of Merchant Vessels of the United States	23
Annual Report of the United States Life Saving Service	24
A Dictionary of Disasters at Sea During the Age of Steam 1869-1962	26
Canadian Coastal and Inland Steam Vessels 1809-1930	27
American Maritime Cases	28
A Guide to Sunken Ships in American Waters	29
Automatic Wreck and Obstruction Information System (AWOIS)	30
Non-Submarine Contacts	31

Volumes with Vessel Listings - 32

Lloyd's Register of Ships	32
Record of the American Bureau of Ships	36
Dictionary of American Naval Fighting Ships	36
The World's Fighting Ships (Jane's)	37

Contents

Books with Local Shipwreck Listings - 38

Atlas of Treasure Maps	39
Unfinished Voyages	39
Ship Ashore!	40
Perils of the Port of New York	40
Joan Charles Directories	40
An Oceanographic Atlas of the Carolina Continental Margin	42
Shipwrecks of South Carolina and Georgia	42
Cris Kohl's Great Lakes Shipwreck Books	42
Great Lakes Wreck Charts	43
Great Lakes Maritime History: Bibliography and Sources of Information	43
Official Records of the Union and Confederate Navies in the War of the Rebellion	43
Maritime Museums of North America, including Canada	45

Newspapers - 45

New York Times	48
Local Newspapers	49
The Newspaper Marketplace	50
Library of Congress	50
Microfilm Readers and Copiers	52
Newspapers on the Internet	56
Internet Newspaper Search Engines	59
Search Engine Idiosyncrasies	60
Search Techniques	62

Part Two - 66
Washington, District of Columbia

National Archives - 66

A *I* and a *II* and a . . .	67
Research Assistants	68
Getting Started	69
Historical Interlude	73
Back to the Present	75
Shuttle Bus	76
Unidentified Shipwrecks	77

Contents

Certificate of Enrollment	78
The Call Slip	79
Mail Order Research	82
Coincidences	83
The Central Research Room	84
Creature Comforts	86
Rules of Engagement	87
Self-Service Photocopiers	88
Photocopying Books and Ledgers	90
Photocopying Loose Documents	91
Special Cases	92
Photocopying Classified Documents	94
Photocopy Permutations	96
Bulk Copying	97
Central Desk Attendants	97
Alternative Copying Methods	98
Keeping Good Records	100
Done for the Day	101
Pull Times	102
After Hours	105
Segue to Archives Two	106
Archives Two Protocols	108
Multi-Level Research	110
Cartographic and Architectural Research	111
Microfilm	112
The Movies	113
Regional Archives	114
Serendipity	115
Back to the Regional Archives	115
Serendipitous Research	116
Archives Anecdotes	116

Naval Historical Center - 119

Getting There is Half the Battle	119
Touching All Four Bases	121
Navy Department Library	122
Ships History Branch	122
Operational Archives	123
The *Gentian* Report - Turnabout is Fair Play	125
Gone are the Good Old Days	127

Contents

Lame Excuse	131
Conspirators Unite	132
U.S.S. San Diego: the Last Armored Cruiser	132
Reverse Research	133
Control Freaks	134
The Witch Hunters	135
The Naval Hysterical Center	136
The Lion's Den	137
Poor Losers	138
The Castrated Operational Archives	140

Judge Advocate General - 141

Washington National Records Center	142
The JAGuar	144
The JAGged Edge of Stupidity	145
The Modern Capitalistic JAG	147

U.S. Coast Guard Historian's Office - 148

Library of Congress - 149

Transportation and Parking	150
Books Galore	150
Initial Checkpoint	152
The Jefferson Building	153
The Madison Building	154
The Adams Building	156
Copying Services	157
Librarians	157

Smithsonian Institution - 158

Part Three - 159
Maritime Museum Libraries

One is Not Enough	160
Attitude is Important	161
Philadelphia Maritime Museum	163
Independence Seaport Museum	165
The Mariners' Museum	168
Mystic Seaport Museum	170

Contents

Steamship Historical Society of America	171
Peabody Essex Museum	172
National Maritime Museum (San Francisco)	173
South Street Seaport Museum	174
Hart Nautical Collections	174
Maine Maritime Museum (formerly Bath Marine Museum)	175
Penobscot Marine Museum	175
Outer Banks History Center	176
Underwater Archaeology Branch of the North Carolina Office of State Archaeology	176
North Carolina State Department of Cultural Resources	177
South Carolina Institute of Archaeology and Anthropology	177
U.S. Naval Institute	177
Submarine Force Library and Museum Association	178
Historical Collections of the Great Lakes (formerly Institute for Great Lakes Research)	178
Great Lakes Historical Society	179
Wisconsin Marine Historical Society	180
Wisconsin Maritime Museum	180
Library and Archives Canada	181
National Maritime Museum (London)	181

Part Four - 182
Embarking on Research

The Internet Fallacy	182
Encyclopedia Salesmen on the Internet	184
Dive Websites	185
Here Today, Gone Tomorrow	186
Reading is Believing - Not!	186
Valid Internet Sources	188
The Future of the Internet	190
Snail Mail	191
E-mail	191
Alternative Internet Sources	192
Back to Basics	194

8   **Contents**

Insurance and Reinsurance	196
Bumps in the System	198
Mistaken Documentation	198
Unexpected Sources	200
Honesty in Reporting	202
A Final Word about Research Assistants	203

Part Five - 205
Picture Sources

Brevity Counts	206
Glossy versus Matte	208
Size Matters	210
Picture Source Overview	211
Great Lakes Vessel Picture Sources	212
Global Vessel Picture Sources	213
Getting the Picture	216
Copy Stand Work	216
Strobe for Copy Work	219
Film Camera for Copy Work	219
Lens for Copy Work	221
Black and White Film for Copy Work	222
Color Film for Copy Work	224
Digital Camera for Copy Work	225
National Archives Copy Work	226
Other Copy Work Protocols	231
Picture Postcards	233
Woodcuts and Steelcuts	236
Illustrated Newspapers	237
Oddball Picture Sources	239
Ownership Conundrum	242
Copyright Law	244
Copyright Image	245
Copyright Protection	245
Copyright Limitation	246
Public Domain	247

Primary Contacts - 250

Index	259
Books by the Author	273

Introduction

Shipwreck research can be the most exciting and the most frustrating of intellectual pursuits.

The exciting moments are those that occur when you discover that long-sought bit of information that no one to your knowledge has ever found: when you have secret erudition that fulfills a coveted quest for revelation. The frustrating times are those that result from long hours of fruitless effort that leave you bleary-eyed and dissatisfied.

It has long been said that enlightenment is priceless. This is ever more true in today's information society, in which the possession of a single datum – perhaps about enemy movements, or about a criminal on trial, or about a plaintiff's position in civil litigation – can make a profound difference in the outcome of an action.

The hunt for facts about the past has reached epic proportions – not only in purely academic studies but also in everyday life. The pursuit of knowledge for its own sake bequeaths abstract rewards that money cannot buy. And so it is with shipwreck research.

Shipwrecks are slowly becoming recognized as worthy of documentation. One can learn a great deal about human activity by studying the circumstances that surround a shipwreck: heroism, cowardice, tragedy, negligence, and the inevitable submission to the overwhelming forces of nature, to name a few. Vessels are lost as a result of accident, arrogance, stupidity, war, and a myriad other reasons. People live and die by unavoidable caprice, or by dint of the will to survive (or the lack of such will). All this and more one can learn about mankind's battle against the sea.

Primary versus Secondary Research

There are two kinds of research: primary and secondary. Which kind of research you pursue depends upon your goals or the depth of your interest: in other words, your research objectives.

Most people who want to know something about a shipwreck do not want to spend much effort or money in the process of acquiring the knowledge. They merely want to read about it. This does not constitute research.

Students in high school and college, and writers of popular nonfiction, generally conduct what is known as "secondary research." For example, a student writing a term paper might obtain his information from published sources such as books and magazines, compile this information in the body of his paper, and cite his sources at the end. Many magazine and newspaper articles are composed in a similar fashion (although generally without citing sources).

In essence, the accumulated facts are not any that were previously unknown or unavailable to the world at large. If anything is new in the paper or article, it is the order or the presentation of the facts: in other words, the manner in which the data are organized for the purpose that was intended.

This process constitutes bona fide research for students because usually the object of the assignment is not to learn something new about a specific topic, but to learn the *process* of research: how to do it, where to look, and so on. The teacher wants to know that his students are familiar enough with a library to locate books that contain information about the subject matter, and can effectively utilize *The Readers' Guide to Periodical Literature*. (On the other hand, a student working toward a master's degree or a doctorate must do primary research.)

Many people who think of themselves as researchers are content with doing secondary research. Basically, this means reading the results of someone else's research: generally, research that has been published in books, magazines, or newspapers. In my opinion, except in the case of students noted above, this hardly constitutes research because it produces no new

Introduction

facts. It merely acquaints the so-called researcher with facts that someone else uncovered. This kind of "research" involves little or no endeavor – unless you have to track down a book title or magazine article in a library.

Primary research is a quantum leap beyond secondary research. This means locating unpublished historical documents: prime sources of information such as official investigations, courts of inquiry, interviews with survivors, log books, construction documents, and so on. Some primary sources may have been published in limited quantities: ship registers, Congressional records, steamboat inspection reports, annual Life Saving Service books, and so on. Unfortunately, all too often, the only contemporary accounts that have survived the paper purges and space limitations are local newspaper articles.

In the 1980's, Richard von Doenhoff, a research assistant at the National Archives, told me that of all the documents that have ever been created, less than 3% have been saved. When I mentioned this recently to Barry Zerby, another research assistant at the National Archives, he told me that von Doenhoff was being generous. Zerby thinks that less than 2% have been saved. Another research assistant at the National Archives agreed with Zerby's assessment. What this means for the primary shipwreck researcher is that there is very little likelihood that he will find the document he seeks.

In most cases, the documents that have been archived constitute *governmental* records such as those noted above. That is because, historically, the government has been in the business of preserving its own records: part of the check and balance system of an informed democracy. Almost *no* private documents have been saved. By private documents I mean company files, corporate records, individual diaries, and so on.

For example, a great deal could be learned about shipwrecks from the records of a commercial salvage outfit. But salvage outfits are in the business of conducting salvage, not in saving historical records. After a certain number of years – or perhaps upon completion of a job and payment for services – a salvage outfit is likely to have discarded old files in order to make office space available for new files. This is like you getting rid of unneeded paperwork when you change premises, or have to make room for another baby.

Some of these records may have been donated to museums. For example, the construction records of the Newport News Ship Building and Dry Dock Company were donated to The Mariners Museum in Newport News. Similarly, the records of the New York Ship Building Company were donated to the Philadelphia Maritime Museum (now called the Independence Seaport Museum). In relation to the previous paragraph, the records of the Thomas A. Scott salvage company were donated to the Mystic Seaport Museum. These museums have archived the records in their possession and have made them available to the public.

Some insurance companies may have kept records for a hundred years or more. For example, the Insurance Company of North America maintains an archive in which original insurance claims and payouts are kept. When I first met Drew Maser, he worked as an accountant at INA and had easy access to the company's archive. He photocopied documents from World War One casualties on which we were diving. But nowadays the company has restricted access to its archive, and it is unlikely that an individual who does not work for the company could gain access to these documents. Other insurance companies may maintain old records, but as they are not museums that cater to visitors and researchers, access to their archived records may be difficult or impossible to obtain.

Except for the instances noted above, the vast majority of other company records were probably discarded long ago: in the same manner in which you probably threw out your old tax records when the mandatory retention period expired, and you no longer

Introduction

had to worry about being audited for those years. Who would believe – or even care – if records might someday be useful to a far-distant future historian. Nonetheless, one never knows what holdings a corner museum might have in its basement: unknown perhaps even to the museum's own staff members.

Research Adventures

Shipwreck research is an adventure. As with any adventure, it begins with a single step that leads from one source to another.

Shipwreck research is also drudgery. It has highs and lows: a few moments of exhilaration that punctuate long times of nonproductive dreariness. But then, if shipwreck research were easy, everyone would be doing it and it would not be as much of an adventure.

There are no college courses on shipwreck research, and no published tutorials. *The Shipwreck Research Handbook* is unique: the one and only comprehensive guide to the methodology and pitfalls of researching shipwrecks. I learned this arcane skill by trial and error – mostly error. The reader of this volume will gain the advantage of the author's thirty-seven years of shipwreck research.

The Psychology of Research

The most important rule of shipwreck research is this: Never, *ever*, under any circumstances admit that you are a wreck-diver to a librarian or research assistant, *especially* one in a maritime museum. The shipwreck research neophyte might believe that by attributing to a shared interest he can curry some favor that will encourage the research assistant to extend extra courtesy or effort in his behalf. This may happen. But the researcher might find instead that the assistant will give him the cold shoulder, put roadblocks in his way, or resort to outright obstructionism.

Although recognition of this pathology is counterintuitive, the beginner will soon learn that not everyone admires those who put their lives at risk by diving on shipwrecks, and who then develop a curiosity to learn more about those wrecks. Some research assistants abhor wreck-divers, castigating them as wreck rapers or destroyers. I don't profess to fully understand this psychological distemper, but it seems to stem from a mistaken belief that wreck-divers belong to a subhuman species whose sense of adventure precludes them from possessing intellectual inquisitiveness, and that they have no right to educate themselves about shipwrecks.

It is nearly as counterproductive to mention possible publication. Some maritime museum librarians appear to have formed the neurotic belief that they were hired to archive records for future generations at the expense of accessibility to the present generation. Other research assistants seem to believe that their job is to protect those records from the gaze of invaders who might profit by access to them. Yet other assistants behave as if they actually *own* the records that they were hired to archive and make available to the public. I call this misanthropic territorial imperative the "junkyard dog complex."

A junkyard dog is an aggressive pet whose purpose is to protect a junkyard from thieves and trespassers when the premises are closed for business. At first, the dog barks at only those interlopers who attempt to enter the junkyard after hours or at places along the fence that are remote from the gate. After a while, the dog barks at all passers-by on the other side of the fence. Then the dog barks at bona fide customers who enter the gate in the normal manner. Finally, the dog barks at everyone but the junkyard owner. It may even attack people. The dog has lost sight of its original purpose. It now presumes that the junkyard belongs to *it* and not to the owner, and that every visitor is trespassing on its private domain.

Ask for information. Do not explain why you want the information. If pressed, state simply that you are interested in the wreck in question. Most librarians and research assistants will not ask the reason for your interest. Usually they do not care. The job for which they are being paid is to find relevant documents. Most are professionals, and work to the best of their ability to find those documents.

Sometimes a research assistant has an off day, or has risen on the wrong side of the bed. His dedication may be temporarily lacking. If you do not stress your concern with sufficient passion, he may believe that your interest in the subject is trifling, and that a minimal amount of effort is necessary to satisfy your request.

The name of the game with research assistants is psychology. Those who are reluctant to help must be convinced that it is their responsibility to do so. Don't be pushy, but don't be lackadaisical either. Be persistent.

As I once wrote in a magazine article: Only those who seek, will find.

I would like to dedicate this book to all the people who have assisted me with my research efforts throughout the years. They helped me to find what I sought.

Part One
Published Sources

Although commercial publications are generally considered to be secondary sources, there is nothing wrong with utilizing such sources in the beginning of your research: as a starting point to get the ball rolling. At the same time, some books are official publications: that is, they were published by government agencies or by non-government entities that had access to primary materials.

Another type of book that you may find useful in place of primary sources is one that was published shortly after the occurrence of events that are recorded in the book. For example, one volume in my collection is *The Mariners' Chronicle* (whose explanatory but prodigious subtitle reads, "Containing narratives of the most remarkable disasters at sea, such as shipwrecks, storms, fires and famines, also naval engagements, piratical adventures, incidents of discovery, and other extraordinary and interesting occurrences"). This book was published in 1835. It chronicles shipwrecks for which the primary sources may longer exist. If that is the case, while a particular account may not be a primary source in itself, that account may constitute the most primary source still extant.

In this chapter I will describe those books and publications that are the most useful – if not indispensable – in taking the first step toward accomplishing your research objective. I will describe *how* these published sources can be used. And in some cases I will provide examples of how these publications have been helpful to me in ascertaining the names of shipwrecks, learning the dates of catastrophe, locating wreck sites, identifying shipwrecks, providing historical information, and so on.

No such list can be exhaustive. Thousands of books

National Shipwreck Listings

have been published about shipwrecks. I have several hundred in my personal collection. When I began my avocation in shipwreck research, I purchased the most valuable books for my reference library – so I would not have to run to a public library or maritime museum every time I wanted to look up a potential shipwreck. The casual researcher may not feel the need to possess each and every book that he references. But the ardent researcher is advised to procure a few basic books for his "wreck room" bookshelf in order to facilitate initial research.

Publications with National Shipwreck Listings

Encyclopedia of American Shipwrecks, by Bruce D. Berman (1972)

The title is a misnomer. The book is a directory rather than an encyclopedia. Nonetheless, this is the *Bible* of shipwreck research, and a must-have for every serious shipwreck researcher. It is the first book I reach for whenever I hear the name of a shipwreck that is unfamiliar to me.

I have thumbed and highlighted my first copy so often that twice I have had to reinforce the binding with tape, because the signatures were separating from the spine. I still have it, but I also have three other copies in better condition: kept in various locations. I never go on a research trip without one. I carry the oldest copy with me, so my loss will not be great if I misplace the book or if it is stolen.

The book lists 13,000 shipwrecks off the coasts of the United States, including the Great Lakes. It is separated into six geographical areas for local reference. Each section is arranged alphabetically by vessel name. Each single-line entry has seven data columns: name, type of vessel, tonnage, date of construction, date of loss, cause of loss, and place (including comments, if any).

If you hear the name of a shipwreck and its general location, you can quickly flip through the pages in order to ascertain its existence. For "flipping" purposes, the soft cover is preferable to the more durable hard cover. If the shipwreck is listed, then you know for certain that the vessel was wrecked. Column five then provides the second most important item of information about a shipwreck: the date of loss. Armed with these two facts, you have a better than even chance of obtaining additional information from other sources.

Because a shipwreck is *not* listed does not necessarily imply that a vessel of that name was not wrecked. Some shipwrecks are inexplicably missing from the directory, yet can be found in other sources that Berman must not have referenced. Yet credit must be given to him for the sheer scope of the compilation. A non-listing means that you have to work harder to ascertain the shipwreck's existence. And, perhaps, the shipwreck truly does not exist.

The book is not perfect. No book is. The mistakes are few and far between, and generally are minor in nature: more than a typographical error, but not of major importance unless the inaccuracy is in the date. Berman did not provide the sources of his information.

If you know – or want to know – the location of a shipwreck, you can scroll down the place column and scan left for the date and name. For example, when I was researching, say, *Shipwrecks of North Carolina*, I highlighted the rows of every shipwreck that was listed off that State. Similarly, if you have dived on a shipwreck that is unidentified, and can approximate the age of the wreck from its construction and observable condition, you can compile a list of potential candidates by using the same method. You can then cull your contenders by the date of loss. For example, a wooden-hulled paddle wheel steamer that is completely collapsed is not likely to have sunk during World War Two, and a nearly intact modern freighter that is equipped with a diesel engine is not likely to have sunk prior to 1900.

National Shipwreck Listings

My advice is this: get a copy today, then get another copy tomorrow.

New York Maritime Register (June 10, 1869 to at least 1948)

This weekly newspaper is the next place I look to confirm shipwreck information. Once you know the name and date of a shipwreck, you can go to the issue following the date of the casualty and scroll through the listings in the Disasters column, which was initiated on August 21, 1869. This column mentions all vessel casualties, not just vessels that were totally wrecked: minor collisions, temporary strandings, engine breakdowns, and so on.

News traveled slowly in the old days, so a casualty might not appear for a week or two after the accident. In the twentieth century, a wreck might be listed the day after the accident.

When windjammers dominated oceanic travel, vessels in the Disasters column were classified by rig: Steamships, (full-rigged) Ships, Brigs, Brigantines, Barks, and Barkentines. Within the classification they are listed alphabetically. If you don't know the type of vessel, be sure to look under each classification. Steamships are obvious, but otherwise you might not see your shipwreck listed under Ships because it was a bark. After a decade or so, all vessels were lumped together and listed alphabetically, with the rig given in parentheses after the name of the vessel.

Each entry includes a short paragraph about the nature of the disaster. It is important to look in succeeding issues for follow-up items. If a wreck was being salvaged, brief reports about ongoing progress may be given. You might find that all of a vessel's rigging was removed before the vessel was abandoned; or how much of the cargo was recovered; or that the wreck was sold at auction; or that the hull was refloated, repaired, and returned to service.

How far ahead to keep searching depends upon the tidbits that are provided. I followed one wreck for a year before the salvors terminated their efforts, but that was an exception. Usually several weeks or at most a month or two is sufficient.

NYMR was widely distributed to subscribers in the maritime industry: ship owners, underwriters, freight consignors, and so on. Most of the news dealt with vessel arrivals and departures. There were also advertisements.

Few original issues have survived. Those that did are in museums, bound into volumes containing six months each. The Independence Seaport Museum took it upon itself to have its collection microfilmed: an expensive process that was funded by a private grant. The ISM then recouped some of its investment by selling complete sets of microfilm to other museums. I know that The Mariners Museum and the Mystic Seaport Museum have copies, and likely there are others. The problem with these microfilms is that the ISM was missing the volume that contained July through December 1939, so those months were not microfilmed.

A staff member at the Mystic Seaport Museum told me that they have their own run of paper copies that not only includes the missing months of 1939, but which continues to 1948. The ISM collection ends in 1941. I do not know when the NYMR actually ceased publication.

By order of the U.S. Navy, the Disasters section was suspended as of September 4, 1918, due to U-boat activity off the American eastern seaboard. The Navy did not want German agents to read about the effectiveness of the U-boat campaign. The Disasters section was resumed on October 30, 1918. I presume that the Disasters section was suspended again on March 11, 1942, when Secretary of the Navy Frank Knox initiated another ban on the release of merchant ship casualties for the same reason.

Lloyd's Weekly Shipping Index (1880's ? to 1916 ?)

This weekly maritime newspaper was identical in format and content to the *New York Maritime Register*.

National Shipwreck Listings

I have never seen a full set so I don't know when it commenced and ceased publication. Perhaps full runs are available in England. It goes back at least to the 1880's. The Independence Seaport Museum has a scattering of issues to 1916. Other museums may have other issues. When I have compared the entries in the LWSI with entries in the NYMR, I have found them to be nearly identical, and sometimes verbatim. Occasionally there were minor differences: one snippet printed in one that was not printed in the other.

I would not state categorically that the two newspapers are redundant as far as the Disasters section is concerned (the only part of the newspapers that I have ever paid attention to), so if you are researching a wreck on which information is meager if not otherwise nonexistent, then certainly look in both of these newspapers. Otherwise, if you have access to one, you don't necessarily need to look up the wreck in the other.

Lloyd's Register Wreck Returns (1890 to present)

This weekly directory consists of single-line entries that provide no information other than the factuality of a wreck: name and date of casualty. Usefulness is limited to confirmation that a vessel was indeed wrecked. A separate section provides statistics that show the number of vessels that were lost from each country. Some are available from The Mariners Museum.

Lloyd's Weekly Casualty Reports and *Lloyd's Casualty Week* (July 1950 to present)

This quarterly maritime pamphlet lists only accidents, without any ancillary material such as that which is included in the *New York Maritime Register* and the *Lloyd's Weekly Shipping Index*. The Mariners' Museum has bound issues from July 1950 to July 2, 1993 (after which the title was changed from LWCR to LCW) and from July 1993 to present. Each entry provides a descriptive paragraph similar in content to the NYMR and the LWSI, so it is every bit as useful. With respect to availability of official wreck reports, it picks up pretty much where the newspapers leave off, with only a short holiday in between.

Each issue is indexed for easy reference. Because publication was quarterly, multiple entries for an accidents are grouped together chronologically unless follow-up entries carried into the subsequent quarter.

Merchant Steam Vessels of the United States 1790-1868, by William C. Lytle and Forrest R. Holdcamper, updated by C. Bradford Mitchell (1975)

This book is commonly called the Lytle List, or the Lytle-Holdcamper List. The authors compiled the directory from vessel enrollments, in order to make up for the lack of steam vessel listings prior to 1869, at which time the government commenced annual publication of the *List of Merchant Vessels of the United States*. It supposedly lists every steamship and steamboat, but I have found that one or two vessels were missing from the directory. Otherwise it is considered complete.

Vessels are arranged alphabetically. Each single-line entry provides the date and place of construction, tonnage, first homeport, and ultimate disposition.

This handy directory of vessels in existence in the early days of steam is made handier by the inclusion of a loss list that is nearly half the length of the primary directory. The inference is that a large majority of steamships and steamboats were "lost" as opposed to being abandoned or dismantled after they outlived their usefulness. The lost list is also arranged alphabetically. It provides the date, place, and circumstances of loss.

During the time period that is covered by the book, most of the vessels were steamboats that plied the nation's inland waterways: rivers and lakes. Stranding was the most prevalent reason for a vessel's loss, although fire and boiler explosions accounted for a fair number of casualties. The vast majority of these vessels were paddle wheel steamers: typically, stern wheel river steamers such as Mississippi River boats.

Most of the remainder were coastal steamers: typically, side wheel steamships. Few were screw steamers,

National Shipwreck Listings

and few were transoceanic steamers.

New copies are available from the Steamship Historical Society of America.

List of Merchant Vessels of the United States (1868 to present)

These annual volumes were published by the Treasury Department, Bureau of Navigation. They supposedly list all registered vessels, including sailing vessels, steamships, motor vessels, and unrigged vessels (barges). Some vessels are inexplicably unlisted. With the proliferation of yachts in the 1900's, the government published a separate set of annual volumes that covered only yachts (sail, steam, and motor). Navy vessels were listed prior to the turn of the twentieth century, as well as other government vessels such as those belonging to the Quartermaster's Department, Revenue Cutter Service, Lighthouse Establishment, and so on. Government vessels were phased out in the twentieth century, from which point only merchant vessels were listed.

MVUS is an excellent place to confirm the existence of a particular vessel, and to ascertain the enrollment number that distinguishes it from other vessels of the same name. Single-line statistics include tonnage, dimensions, place of construction, and current homeport.

Beginning in 1906, a loss list was added. This list is invaluable for confirming a vessel's demise, and for ascertaining the date and place of loss. The loss list purportedly furnished entries for vessels that were lost in the preceding year. This was not always the case. MVUS used the fiscal year, which ran from July 31 to June 30. Thus a vessel that was lost after June 30 in the previous calendar year would not be listed in the following annual volume, but in the succeeding volume. Sometimes a lost vessel was not entered on the lost list for two years or more. The most bizarre case that I have found was that of the *F.C. Pendleton*. This vessel was lost in 1925, but was not reported lost until fifteen years later, in 1940. I have no idea why.

For reasons that I have been unable to fathom, occasionally a loss was *never* entered, so that the absence of an entry in the loss list cannot be construed as negative proof that the vessel was not lost. It seems as if a vessel could be carried on the extant list and not entered on the loss list until the paperwork was processed: that is, when the final certificate of enrollment was endorsed by the owner and submitted to the government. Because endorsement required an act of volition on the part of the owner, lazy or irresponsible owners may have been slow in compliance with the rules. Perhaps those that went out of business never complied. Some vessels disappeared from the extant list – and simply disappeared, with no future entries.

Fiscal year publication ended with the 1939 volume. No volume was published in 1940. After resumption in 1941, MVUS commenced to use the calendar year. No loss lists were included during the war years, because of the ban on publishing merchant vessel losses that enemy agents could read. When the loss list resumed in 1945, it accumulated many of the losses that occurred during the previous four years. Several years were required before backdated losses were accounted for. No volumes were published between 1982 and 1988.

In the early 1970's, when I began all-out shipwreck research, I photocopied the MVUS loss lists so that I would not have to run to the museum every time I wanted to look up a shipwreck.

Annual Report of the United States Life Saving Service (1872 to 1915)

Every year the LSS published the results of its lifesaving efforts from the previous fiscal year (July 1 to June 30). The books are separated into several sections whose format varied slightly throughout the publishing history of the reports. Generally, each volume opened with an explanatory section that described tools, techniques, and other informative material about the Life

National Shipwreck Listings

Saving Service in general. A few of the most dramatic rescue operations were described in detail.

The LSS was divided into geographical districts. Each district has a section in which assistance rendered was listed chronologically. Each entry has columns that provide pertinent information such as the name of the vessel to which assistance was rendered, the name of the station (or stations) that rendered assistance, the date of the casualty, the number of lives lost and saved, and a brief description of the circumstances.

Each volume is indexed for easy reference.

The annual report was compiled and condensed from hand-written station logs that were maintained by the Keepers (as the people in charge of the stations were known). The station log often contained more detail than what appeared in the published report. If a researcher requires in-depth information about a particular shipwreck, I advise you to track down the hand-written log. Not all the logs are extant, and those that were saved have been dispersed throughout the country. They may be found in libraries, museums, or archives that are located close to the station locale.

By way of example, I found the logs of stations along the northern coast of New Jersey at the New York Public Library. In this particular case, and because I knew the names and casualty dates of the shipwrecks that I wanted, I did not have to visit the library to obtain photocopies of the log entries that I wanted. For a nominal fee, a librarian found the entries, photocopied the pages, and mailed the copies to me. It was then left to me to decipher the decorative cursive writing style that was typical of the times.

Research assistants at the National Archives may be able to suggest which facilities possess the station logs you want. Otherwise, ask around.

An Act of Congress authorized the Life Saving Service in 1872. In 1915, the Life Saving Service was merged with the Revenue Cutter Service to form the United States Coast Guard. Life Saving Service stations became Coast Guard stations. The Coast Guard discontinued the policy of publishing annual reports. The National Archives has microfilms of Coast Guard casualty reports, but each entry is only a three by five card on which the bare essentials were printed, primarily name and date. The cards were not microfilmed in any kind of order, seeming to have been shuffled prior to microfilming, so that you have to scroll through rolls and rolls of microfilm in order to find a particular entry – which may not even exist.

The station log system appears to have been discontinued; or, perhaps the logs were trashed. I have never found any Coast Guard station logs anywhere, nor are research assistants at the National Archives aware of any in existence.

A Dictionary of Disasters at Sea During the Age of Steam 1869-1962, by Charles Hocking (1969)

This two-volume set is nearly 800 pages in length. Vessels are listed alphabetically: A to M in Volume One, N to Z in Volume Two. A reprint edition was published in a single volume. It was followed in 1989 by *Modern Shipping Disasters 1963-1987*, by Norman Hooke. The latter book is not as useful to shipwreck researchers only because not very many vessels of wreck-diving interest have been lost in "modern" times, thanks to the advent of sophisticated shipboard safety features such as radar and loran.

Because the book was published by Lloyd's of London, and was compiled from the conglomerate's massive insurance records, the information is extremely accurate. Each entry starts with the vessel's vital statistics: owner at the time of loss, date of construction, name of builder, tonnage, dimensions, and propulsion characteristics. This is followed by a brief description that always includes the date, place, and manner of loss. An entry may be as short as one sentence or as long as several paragraphs, with one multi-sentence paragraph being typical.

Sailing vessels and engine-powered vessels are

National Shipwreck Listings

included. Despite the global inclusiveness that is suggested by the title, the entries are weighted heavily for the two world wars, and outside of the wars by British vessels. If a vessel of any nation was lost during World War One or World War Two, by either marine casualty or by enemy action, it most assuredly will be listed. If the vessel was registered to a British homeport, it is extremely likely to be listed. Otherwise, inclusion is sporadic. Foreign vessels (that is, vessels foreign to British registry) are less likely to be included unless they were lost in British waters.

A U.S. registered vessel that sank off the eastern seaboard is less likely to be included than a British registered vessel that sank in the same area. The reason has to do with insurance. As explained below in the listing for *Lloyd's Register*, inclusion is based upon coverage from a company that was listed with Lloyd's of London. A vessel that was not insured (or reinsured) with Lloyd's is not likely to be included. Many U.S. vessels were underwritten domestically. Most foreign vessels (that is, foreign to both the U.S. and Great Britain – Norwegian, Spanish, Brazilian, for example) were insured by Lloyd's, so they are likely to be included wherever they sank in the world.

Hocking's book has been posted on the Internet. It disappeared for a while, then reappeared. At the time of this writing it was available. Currently, the homepage shows the letters of the alphabet, each of which is a link to a list of the vessels that start with that particular letter. The list is arranged alphabetically. Clicking on a vessel name takes the viewer to a scan of the page in the original book on which the vessel appeared.

Canadian Coastal and Inland Steam Vessels 1809-1930, by John M. Mills (1979)

Published by the Steamship Historical Society of America, which has new copies available, this is a companion volume to *Merchant Steam Vessels of the United States 1790-1868* (described above). This alphabetical directory itemizes all known Canadian steamships that exceeded seventy-five feet in length. Like the Lytle list, each entry includes the vessel's official number, rig, tonnage, dimensions, place and date of construction, and ultimate disposition.

American Maritime Cases (1923 to present)

These hefty annual volumes are not about shipwrecks in particular, but, as the title implies, about maritime casualties in general. According to its promotional literature, the books cover "significant maritime decisions rendered by United States (Federal and State) courts. It also reports legislative action, administrative law decisions, arbitration decisions, Maritime Law Association of the U.S. source material and other items."

Despite the broad scope, the set is valuable to shipwreck researchers primarily for those cases which involved vessels in collision, because lawsuits usually resulted. Each volume is indexed by vessel name. You won't find these books in the average public library, but any good law library should have a complete set.

I was lucky. When I intervened as an amicus curiae in the *Lusitania* case, I was represented by maritime attorney Phil Davey. He had a full set in his conference room. He let me go through them and photocopy the cases that dealt with vessel collisions along the eastern seaboard. It took me a day and a half.

The best thing about maritime court cases is that they divulge the nitty-gritty. The main witnesses are generally the officers of the watch: those individuals who had the best view of the impending collision, and who were the ones most responsible for trying to avoid it. The facts that are brought to light during the examination of the witnesses come right from the horse's mouth. Perspectives may differ, but they can be weighed against each other irrelevant of the opinion of the court.

Trial transcripts, statements, and exhibits are not included in the coverage of the case, only the final decision. But in rendering an opinion about how the circumstances related to law, the court usually enumerated the facts, sometimes in exacting detail.

Furthermore, the citations will lead you to the district court that heard the case, thus enabling you to know where to access the original court documents, should you be so inclined. All court documents are public records. You may not be able to obtain these records through the mail, but you will know which city has the documents in possession.

A Guide to Sunken Ships in American Waters, by Adrian Lonsdale and H.R. Kaplan (1964)

This book was compiled by two Coast Guard officers who had access to official records. Shipwrecks are separated into geographical ranges. Within each section, shipwrecks are listed *not* alphabetically but by approximate descending latitude (from north to south), sometimes with confusing overlaps. Only a few hundred of the most well known shipwrecks are listed, and then with hardly any information other than the date of loss and possibly the circumstances.

The book is pretty much a compilation of the Wreck Information List of 1945, and the Navy Wreck List of 1957. The latter list is a regeneration of the former, with a few updates and revisions. Neither list was ever published, although they are available in printed form from the National Archives and the Library of Congress. Much of their information formed the basis of the Automated Wreck and Obstruction Information System (AWOIS), which see below. These two lists are riddled with errors that Lonsdale and Kaplan did not attempt to correct. Some shipwrecks are listed as unknowns, some names are misspelled, and position accuracy is general: perhaps 1 to 3 miles.

Although the book is replete with copied misinformation, at one time it was the only published source of the information that it contained. It has now been superseded by a host of more reliable publications. Nonetheless, it was a classic in its time.

Automated Wreck and Obstruction Information System (1981 to present)

This directory is separated into fifteen sections that encompass the entire United States, including the Great Lakes, Alaska, and Hawaii. AWOIS is an outgrowth of hydrographic surveys that were conducted during World War Two. In 1981, hydrographic surveys from the war and afterward were collected under the guidance of the National Ocean Service to create a centralized catalog that could be updated continuously with information from new surveys.

Each listing includes several fields that provide such statistics as classification (wreck or obstruction), name (if a wreck), and position information. A descriptive box provides background data such as survey date, origin and history of the listing, and pertinent details such as the height of the wreck or obstruction, wire-drag notes, and authenticity and accuracy of the data.

Historical information is meager: the name of the wreck, date of loss, and perhaps the reason for the vessel's loss.

Position information is given in four grades – high, medium, low, and poor – with high meaning that a diver examined the site or that a side-scan sonar target was integrated with an onboard GPS unit. Medium means that the location is approximate. Low and poor mean that the object was never located or was included strictly for historical reasons or perhaps from unidentified or incomplete surveys.

Initially, researchers could obtain printouts of either an individual listing, a geographic area within specified parameters, or a complete section – and then only after writing or phoning the NOS office. The NOS now operates under the National Oceanic and Atmospheric Administration (NOAA), which has made AWOIS available online. Researchers can either view each section on the AWOIS website, download entire sections, or print desired entries.

I used to have hardcopies of all the sections on the eastern seaboard, but I tossed out the paper versions

National Shipwreck Listings

(which took two feet of shelf space in loose-leaf binders) and replaced them with downloads which I store on my computer for quick and constant access without having to be on the Internet. The database is searceable.

Some of the wreck locations are right on the money. Others are nonexistent. Nonetheless, AWOIS has its uses.

Non-Submarine Contacts (1968)

This classified document is nearly impossible to obtain. It publication was restricted for military applications to those with a "need to know." After hearing of its existence, I requested a copy from the Defense Mapping Agency, which compiled the list. The reply I received was neutral: the DMA neither confirmed nor denied the existence of any such list. Perhaps the list was merely a rumor. I persisted by writing to several government agencies, none of which professed to have any knowledge of the list.

At a diving conference in the mid-1980's, I met a man who told me that he worked for the DMA. I said, "Oh, then you have access to the Non-Sub Contact list." He stared at me expressionlessly without acknowledging my question. I switched subjects because I realized that he was not going to admit to the existence of information that was classified.

Several years later, I met a civilian who said that he had acquired a photocopy of the list through an anonymous government contact. I told him of my intense interest in obtaining a copy. Several weeks later, the postal service delivered a large manila envelope that had no return address. The person did not want the package to be traced to him in case it fell into the wrong hands.

As far as I have been able to ascertain, the list was compiled as a Cold War strategy to identify known wreck sites in order to distinguish them from Russian nuclear submarines that were lurking off the coast of the United States. I do not know the origination of the list, or how the wrecks were identified, but I presume that it was done by comparison with official records of shipping losses, particularly war losses.

The directory is arranged by descending latitude (from north to south). Each single-line entry provides the shipwreck's name and tonnage, and gives its location in latitude and longitude. The position accuracy is too general to enable a diver to pinpoint the sites, which gives me pause to wonder about how useful the list could have been for its intended purpose. It is helpful as an historical reference in that it confirms vessel losses and their approximate locations, but little else.

In effect, the list proved to be somewhat of a disappointment as a shipwreck research tool. Most of the information is more readily available elsewhere.

Rumor has it that the original list undergoes a continual process of revision. With subsequent all-inclusive military mapping of the seafloor by means of sophisticated electronic surveillance techniques, recent generations of the list must have grown geometrically in size and should specify positions with GPS precision.

Volumes with Vessel Listings

Lloyd's Register of Ships (1768 to present)

Contrary to popular belief, Lloyd's of London is not an insurance company. It is a consortium of individual underwriters, each of whom posts a large bond and possesses minimum capital assets in order to engage in the insurance business under the Lloyd's banner. The name originates from Edward Lloyd, a man who had no connection with insurance but who owned a coffee house in London, England, in which people who were associated with the shipping industry started to meet, in 1688, in order to discuss their business.

Informal airings eventually became formalized in the 1700's. In the latter part of the century, participating underwriters formed a committee and moved to new premises. In the 1800's, the British Parliament officially recognized Lloyd's as an important adjunct to the

Volumes with Vessel Listings

maritime insurance industry, which was still the consortium's primary interest. By the 1900's, Lloyd's of London was firmly entrenched as *the* maritime insurance marketplace in the world (even though membership subscription was strictly British, albeit with agents in other countries).

From the very beginning, underwriters kept lists of the vessels that they insured, as a routine method of monitoring their business. In due course, these lists were shared and collated in order to reduce insurance fraud by ship owners who insured aged or decrepit vessels with more than one underwriter in order to multiply their indemnity when the vessel was accidentally or intentionally wrecked. Lloyd's inaugurated an inspection and classification system that adjudged a vessel's seaworthiness. These measures evolved into the *Lloyd's Register of Ships* (*Lloyd's Register* for short): a directory that was published and updated annually.

The *Lloyd's Register* is not a directory of every vessel in existence. It is a directory only of those vessels that were insured by Lloyd's of London. For that reason, many vessels that were registered in the United States will not be found in the *Lloyd's Register*, either because they were insured by domestic underwriters, or because they were uninsured.

The information that is provided in the register has changed throughout the centuries. Early editions provided minimal statistical data. Later editions expanded the coverage for entries.

Toward the end of the 1800's, the statistical information that was given for each vessel included the enrollment number, type of vessel (steamship, schooner, bark, and so on), hull material (wood, iron, or steel), tonnage (gross and net), dimensions, name and location of builder, name and location of owner, homeport, rig or type of machinery, previous names, inspection dates, and sometimes such items of interest as the number of boilers, number of decks, type of wood planking, and so on.

The back of each volume has directories of vessel

name changes, compound names, underwriters, ship builders, and ship owners. In the middle of the 1900's, these secondary directories were published as a separate volume, because the ship register was already too heavy to handle.

Rarely, the date of a vessel's loss may be printed in red in one of the right-hand columns: month and year only, such as 10/90 (October 1890).

Normally, a vessel is listed for every year of its existence. There are exceptions, such as when its insurance coverage was interrupted (which almost never occurred), or when a vessel was sold to another company that chose to insure it outside of Lloyd's, or chose not to insure it because it was old and not worth the cost of the premium. Occasionally a vessel was uninsurable: that is, the vessel was so decrepit that no underwriter was willing to take a chance that it would survive the next voyage.

Generally, a vessel was deleted from the register when the vessel was lost or abandoned. Thus you can sometimes infer the year in which a vessel was wrecked by looking through every annual register until the name disappears. Again, there are exceptions.

The most common reason for delisting a name was a name change. For example, if a new owner changed a vessel's name, the vessel would appear in the subsequent edition under its new name. The directory gives a vessel's previous name or names, so you can backtrack a vessel's history of name changes. Tracking forward may not be so easy.

Early editions contained no mechanism for determining a vessel's new name other than scanning every one of the thousands of entries for previous names: a laborious and time-consuming process that no one but the most dedicated or insane researcher would undertake. In the 1900's, Lloyd's added a section that listed vessels whose names had been changed since the previous volume. The list is arranged alphabetically by the vessel's name in the previous volume, with the new name in the adjacent column.

Volumes with Vessel Listings

If you are tracking a vessel forward to the year of its demise, you might find that a vessel name was delisted because its name was changed, and not because the vessel was wrecked or abandoned.

The most important item of information about a specific vessel is its enrollment number. While a vessel's name may change several times throughout its career, its enrollment number remains the same. The enrollment number is equivalent to a vehicle identification number, or VIN. Armed with this number, you can wade through all the vessels that have identical names, and single out the one that is the vessel that you are researching.

Each of the aged and crusty volumes of the *Lloyd's Register* weighs more than five pounds. Initially, whenever I pulled one off the shelf, I had a tendency to support some of the weight by resting the heel of the spine on my belt buckle. The covers are coated with a chemical that simulates lampblack. This flaking black chemical rubbed onto my shirt, staining it noticeably, sometimes permanently. I soon learned to place the book on the floor or on a nearby table while thumbing through the pages.

Another reason for placing the book flat on a convenient surface is its fragility. These registers must be treated carefully. Some of these books are extremely worn from longtime usage. The crumbling spines may be coming apart literally at the seams. In some cases the leaves have separated from the gluing. The stitches were made of string, and some of these strings may be broken or unknotted so that entire signatures have separated from the binding. The paper may be so dry and brittle that the outer edges snap off at the slightest touch, leaving a pile of flecks.

Use extraordinary care when flipping over a volume so that the pages face down on the glass plate of a photocopy machine.

Record of the American Bureau of Ships (1869 to present)

This annual volume is a directory of U.S.A. vessels that were examined by the American Bureau of Ships. Like Lloyd's, the ABS devised a classification system for insurance purposes. By way of example, a vessel that was classified A1 would could obtain a lower insurance premium than one of a lower classification. A vessel's classification might be reduced from its previous rating on account of age.

Not all vessels that were issued certificates of enrollment by the U.S. government were examined by the ABS, so that not every U.S.A. vessel is listed. Those that are not listed may be found in the *List of Merchant Vessels of the United States* (see above).

Entries are nearly identical to those in the *Lloyd's Register*. Everything in the previous section is true for the *Record*; there is no need to repeat the information here.

Dictionary of American Naval Fighting Ships (8 volumes published individually between 1959 and 1981)

Known as DANF (pronounced dan-ef), these volumes are more like encyclopedias than dictionaries. Major warships are arranged alphabetically. Each entry provides general statistics such as type of vessel, tonnage, dimensions, speed, complement, armament, date and place of construction, dates of launching and commissioning, and ultimate disposition. Then comes a history of the warship, which might be anywhere from several paragraphs to several pages, depending upon the importance of the warship and its peacetime and wartime engagements.

Minor warships are spread haphazardly throughout the set by Navy classification. Information may be meager, or might consist of only a single line entry that is little more than an acknowledgment of existence.

DANF was prepared over the course of several decades by civilian staff members at the Naval Historical Center, and by historians in the Ships History Branch, all of whom had unlimited access to original Naval documents. Despite the wealth of information at the fingertips of the researchers, the entries are rife with errors and inaccuracies. Some of these mistakes are niggling and inconsequential, but others are significant.

The Ships History Branch requests suggestions for corrections, but if I were to spell out all the errors that I have discovered throughout the years, I would not have time to write my books. This is not to state that DANF is not an admirable job, only that its usefulness is limited to research applications that do not require strict adherence to factual detail. I also find it annoying that certain meaningful though detracting events are not mentioned in a warship's career. For example, incidents in which a warship rammed and sank a merchant vessel were expurgated from the history: a sanitizing process of deceit by means of concealment.

I purchased the eight-volume set soon after it was available in its entirety, in 1981. I have lost count of the number of times that I have pulled a volume off the shelf to check a reference. Despite the caveats in the previous paragraph, the books have been invaluable to me and to my global research objectives.

Nowadays it is no longer necessary to buy this expensive set of books. The content is available on the Internet and is maintained by the Navy Historical Center. In its first Internet generation, pages were simply scanned from the published volumes. Now there is an ongoing project to append the original material, revise poorly written text, and correct the multitudinous errors. I suspect, however, that no effort will be made to introduce events that were bowdlerized.

The World's Fighting Ships, by Fred T. Jane (1898 to present)

This annual directory of worldwide warships is better known as *Jane's Fighting Ships*. Each issue lists major warships by country. Minor warships are not listed. Entries include some statistics such as type of vessel, tonnage, dimensions, and general characteristics. A picture usually accompanies the entries for each class of warship, but not of every warship within the class.

The following annual directors are of tangential interest. I have listed only those dates that I have actually seen. Other years may exist.
Mercantile Navy List (of British Registered Steam Vessels) 1857 to1955
Underwriters' Registry for Iron Vessels (1862 to 1885)
Talbot Booth's Merchant Ships (1939 to 1979)
Merchant Yachts of the United States (1904 to present)
American Yacht List (1884 to 1901)
Lloyd's Register of American Yachts (1901 to 1989)
Manning's Yacht Register (1901 to 1902)
Lloyd's Register of Yachts (British and Foreign) 1884 to 1980)
Hunt's Universal Yacht List (of British Yachts) 1884 to 1891

Books with Local Shipwreck Listings

There are many commercial books that contain lists of shipwrecks. They provide varying amounts of data: at the very least the name of the vessel, the date of loss, and the place of the casualty. Some of these books may include additional snippets of information as well.

Although these books count as secondary sources whose authority and veracity rest with the reputation of the author, they can nonetheless save a researcher a great deal of time by furnishing the basic information that is needed to proceed through the morass of official documentation. A one-line entry can act as a jumping off place – and sometimes it can be very much more.

The following list is by no means exhaustive. Local and maritime libraries have numerous titles that may lead you toward your goal. I mention these titles

Books with Local Shipwreck Listings

because it is worthwhile knowing about them, and will help to get a researcher started on an otherwise complicated endeavor. Except for the first title, the list is arranged geographically from north to south along the U.S. eastern seaboard, then in the Great Lakes, and finally along the Pacific coast.

Atlas of Treasure Maps, by F.L. Coffman (1957)

I mention this title only because I do not want anyone to waste his time by referencing such a poorly researched book: one that is replete with so much erroneous material. Misinformation can be more damaging than no information, because it will lead you to start from wrong assumptions. This atlas of putative treasure wrecks is supposed to provide accurate position information. It stands to reason that if anyone actually possessed the precise locations of real treasure troves, he would not publicize his knowledge.

To give you a sense of the book's ridiculous entries, Coffman lists the *R.P. Resor* as a treasure wreck. This tanker was torpedoed by a German U-boat in World War Two. Its only treasure was black gold in the form of crude oil, most of which burned away as the tanker drifted in flames for two days. The wreck is a popular dive site that I have visited often. Coffman puts it fifty miles away from its actual location.

This book is only for the gullible. I put it right up there with Lieutenant Harry E. Rieseberg's fictitious treasure salvage books.

Unfinished Voyages, by John Perry Fish (1986)

After several popular accounts of shipwrecks in the New England area, the book is appended with an extensive chronological listing of maritime casualties dating from 1606 to 1956. If you are trying to find or identify a wreck in the area of coverage, its name, date, and location are probably given in the appendix. Fish's work is fully authenticated.

Ship Ashore!, by Jeannette Edwards Rattray (1955)

This book covers maritime disasters off Montauk and eastern Long Island between 1640 and 1955. Popular accounts are followed by an appendix of vessel losses off these New York coastal communities.

The Perils of the Port of New York, by Jeannette Edwards Rattray (1973)

This companion volume to the preceding entry comprises maritime disasters from 1614 to 1972. The area of coverage is the Hudson River outflow through the Mud Hole to the Hudson Canyon, or the northern waters off New Jersey and the waters south of Long Island, New York. Popular accounts are followed by an appendix of vessel losses that are arranged chronologically.

I have found the loss list useful on several occasions. In one memorable case, after Paul Hepler discovered a shipwreck off the New Jersey coast in 1976, I conducted a survey of the site. By examining the engine and by observing the state of hull collapse, I determined that this steamship was of pre-1900 vintage, and that it had probably sunk before 1900. When I perused Rattray's loss list for my estimated time frame, I found an entry whose location closely approximated the position of the wreck. The suspect vessel was the *Macedonia*.

Armed with the name and the date of loss, I checked the index of the *New York Times*. There was an article about the *Macedonia* and her collision with the *Hamilton*. The article gave the location and the distance from shore, both of which matched perfectly with the position of the wreck.

Joan Charles Directories

The exhaustive "diwrecktories" of Joan Charles are invaluable aids to modern researchers. Each title is geographical in nature, and is separated into sections whose cross-indexing multiplies the usefulness of the book. The first section is the largest, and consists of a

Books with Local Shipwreck Listings

chronological listing of every vessel that was lost in the area of coverage during the titled time frame. Following each date is the source document by name. She then gives the name of the vessel and a brief description of the disaster. Every casualty is fully documented and traceable.

Sometimes she provides a few particulars of the more interesting shipwrecks. But this is not nearly as important to researchers as the source materials: newspaper articles that are annotated by the newspaper's name, date of issue, and the page on which the article appeared. Page by page and column by column, she meticulously scanned thousands of local and sometimes obscure newspapers in the preparation of each volume. She used the *Annual Report of the United States Life Saving Service* as an additional source. And she used other esoteric journals, gazettes, and colonial records.

The two Mid-Atlantic volumes include a short chronological listing without descriptive annotations. This section is useful for quick skimming or browsing. This section is not included in subsequent State-named volumes.

The next section groups vessel losses by locality. Within the locality, each entry provides the name of the vessel and the date of loss. Once you know the date, you can then refer to the first section for source annotations.

The final section is an index that is arranged alphabetically by vessel name. Again, each entry provides the place and date so you can refer to the first section for source annotations.

Thus there are three ways of locating any particular vessel: by date, by location, and by name. Whichever item of information you possess will lead to the primary source annotations.

Here are the volumes that she has published so far:

Mid Atlantic Shipwreck Accounts to 1899 (1997)
Mid-Atlantic Shipwreck Accounts II to 1914 (1999)

New Jersey Delaware Pennsylvania Shipwreck Accounts 1705 to 1950 (2003)
Virginia and Maryland Shipwreck Accounts 1623 to 1950 (2004)
North Carolina Shipwreck Accounts 1709 to 1950 (2004)

An Oceanographic Atlas of the Carolina Continental Margin, by John Newton, Orrin Pilke, and J.O. Blanton (1971)

This single sheet of paper is the size of a nautical chart. Shipwreck locations are plotted, while a legend provides vessel names and dates of loss. The locations are only approximate, as they are based upon historically supported positions.

Shipwrecks of South Carolina and Georgia, by E. Lee Spence (1984)

This book on local shipwrecks is appended with Spence's List, a chronological directory of shipwrecks dating from 1520 to 1865. The list is incomplete. Piecemeal portions were published in later books, each portion incomplete and overlapping portions that were published elsewhere. As far as I know, Spence's List was never published in its entirety in a single volume.

Shipwrecks are arranged chronologically. Vessels are not cross-indexed by name. The only way to locate a shipwreck by name is to scroll through the dates.

Each entry includes the date of loss and the name of the vessel. The entry is fully annotated with the sources from which the information was obtained, and usually multiple sources, so that one can then access the primary sources for detailed information. Sources include national and local newspapers, and the thirty-one-volume set of *Official Records of the Union and Confederate Navies in the War of the Rebellion* (see below).

Cris Kohl's Great Lakes Shipwreck Books

Most of these consist of accounts rather than directories. Nonetheless, several of his books are formatted in such a way that the accounts are brief enough to qualify as expanded listings. Because each of the many entries provides the name of the vessel, date of loss, and statistical data, some of his shipwreck guides can double as a starting point for delving into local newspapers and archival sources for more detailed information. The text is amplified by the addition of numerous pictures.

Kohl's work is meticulously and extraordinarily well researched so that it is difficult if not impossible to find an error that is not typographical.

Here are the volumes that lean more toward directories:

The 100 Best Great Lakes Shipwrecks, Volume I (1998)
The 100 Best Great Lakes Shipwrecks, Volume II (1998)
The Great Lakes Diving Guide (2001)

Great Lakes Wreck Charts

This is a set of five charts, one for each lake, which in addition to charting the historic locations of shipwrecks, includes a legend which provides the names of wrecked vessels and the dates of their loss.

***Great Lakes Maritime History: Bibliography and Sources of Information,* by Charles E. Feltner and Jeri Baron Feltner (1982)**

This book is not a directory of shipwrecks but, as the subtitle suggests, a bibliography of shipwreck research sources. The book is split into sections for each lake, state, and so on. Although it is now a quarter of a century old, the sources are still valid and the insights are timeless.

***Official Records of the Union and Confederate Navies in the War of the Rebellion* (31 volumes published individually between 1884 and 1922; some volumes consist of more than one book, but are paginated sequentially)**

The U.S. government spent nearly forty years in compiling, typesetting, and printing this 31-volume set of official orders, dispatches, reports, correspondence, and memoranda. The set contains a wealth of information about Navy vessels and activities, all originating from primary sources. If you are researching vessels that sank during the Civil War, or that served in any military capacity during the Civil War, there is undoubtedly some mention of them here.

Activities are arranged chronologically starting with Series I, Volume 1 through Volume 27. Each volume is indexed. Series II consists of three volumes, of which Volume 1 is exceptionally useful for the section entitled "Statistical Data of Union and Confederate Ships." This section provides background information on construction, acquisition, armament, disposition, and so on; plus statistical data such as tonnage and dimensions.

An Index volume consists of a comprehensive index to the entire set. Each entry in the Index provides the Series number and Volume number of the subject. For example, a vessel entry might be given thus: I, 7, 9; II, 1. This means that the vessel is mentioned in Series I, Volume 7; Series I, Volume 9; and Series II, Volume 1. To find page numbers, you then look up the vessel in question in the index at the back of each volume.

Complete sets cost thousand of dollars and occupy about eight feet of shelf space. Most large libraries and maritime museums possess complete sets.

The complete set is also available on a single CD. I bought mine for $80. The trade-off for instant access is a search engine instead of an index.

In keeping with standard grammatical practice, vessel names are italicized in the indexes. This makes it easy to distinguish entries for *Virginia* (the Confederate ironclad) from Virginia (the State). The search engine makes no such distinction. When you type "Virginia" in the find block, the search engine finds every mention the word without informing you which finds relate to the vessel and which relate to the State. In this case, you have a monumental task of checking each and every entry in order to cull the wheat from the chaff.

***Maritime Museums of North America, Including Canada*, by Robert H. Smith (1990)**

As the title implies, this book is a reference guide to more than 600 museums that specialize in maritime topics. This information can be useful if you wish to pursue avenues of research that do not exist in major archives and museum libraries. Listings include contact information, directions, hours of operation, admission policies, and so on.

In 2002, the original book was updated, expanded, and reissued as three volumes:

Smith's Guide to Maritime Museums of North America – Part 1: Canadian Maritime Provinces, New England/Mid-Atlantic.

Smith's Guide to Maritime Museums of North America – Part 2: Southern Gulf Coast.

Smith's Guide to Maritime Museums of North America – Part 3: Mid-West/Canada/West Coast including Hawaii.

Newspapers

Over the years, I have been involved in a number of incidents that were reported in the newspapers. In only one instance was the account described accurately. All the other incidents were related erroneously.

I was misquoted. Words were ascribed to me that I never said. Events were embellished or grossly exaggerated. Parts of some stories were complete fabrications. One account was so distorted that I did not recognize the event on which it was based, even though I was featured and was intimately involved in the outcome.

Thus it is with great trepidation that I remark that newspapers constitute primary sources of information that a researcher cannot afford to overlook. My hope – my prayer – is that correspondents of yesteryear were more honest and sincere in their profession than their counterparts today, and that they embraced their work with integrity that appears to be absent in modern times. But I have little basis for believing that this is true.

It is not uncommon for two accounts of the same event to differ. Sometimes this occurs because different correspondents interviewed different eyewitnesses, or obtained their information from different sources. Dissimilar accounts are not necessarily contradictory. Indeed, they may be complimentary, with one newspaper providing coverage that was not provided by another. This is the researcher's yearning: to compile from a variety of sources a cohesive account that is greater than the disparate parts on which the integrated account was based.

Research is sometimes described as plagiarizing from a number of sources instead of plagiarizing from one. I take exception to this disparaging definition. Real historians do not create or rewrite history – they compile it. They cannot produce narratives without drawing on contemporary sources of information. It is only when they change or ignore those sources that they dishonor their profession.

It is a fundamental truth that an historian is only as good as his source material. An historian cannot be blamed if his sources were wrong or ill informed. For this and other reasons, I invariably put quote marks around passages that I abstract from newspapers, and sometimes from other and more reliable sources as well. The reasons for doing this are several.

First and foremost, alerting my readers that I am quoting verbatim lets me off the hook should the information prove to be incorrect. This technique enables me to take advantage of questionable sources with appropriate caveats. If I rely on multiple sources that differ slightly, I make note of that fact instead of manipulating the data. For example, I might write, "The number of lives lost was twelve (or fourteen, or fifteen; sources differ)."

On more than one occasion I have used two official and reliable sources, each of which I would accept as gospel, but which disagreed with each other. Again, I

Newspapers

quote both sources and let the reader decide which (if either) might be correct.

My research philosophy has always been: when in doubt about the veracity of a source, quote it.

Second, rather than paraphrase a contemporary account, I sometimes quote it even though I believe in its accuracy. Generally I do this because the account was written so clearly and concisely that I could not improve upon it. To alter it would devalue it.

Third, I sometimes quote old-time passages in order to preserve the flavor of the quaint writing style, which conveys a value all its own and which is distinct from the information that the passage contains.

If I have an official source – say, a Court of Inquiry, a Life Saving Service write-up, or an investigation conducted by the Steamboat Inspection Service – I give it more weight than I give to the newspapers. By the same token, newspaper articles sometimes provide information that is not given in official documents. One item that comes to mind is the employment of given names of people who were involved in an incident, whereas official reports often refer to participants only by surname.

Another research philosophy of mine is: use as many sources as possible when reconstructing an historical event. Even if the sources contradict each other, each source may have certain critical value. Sometimes this value is coverage of an event from a different perspective. For example, official interrogations may focus strictly on the *cause* of a disaster, whereas newspaper interviews may focus more on the *human* element.

It is largely in this latter regard that newspaper articles can complement official reports.

All too often, newspaper articles are the *only* source extant. Remember what I wrote in the Introduction: that less than 2% of all the documents that have ever been generated have been saved. Far too many official reports have been lost, discarded, misfiled, or never archived in the first place. This dearth of reliable primary source material places reliance on newspapers for historical documentation. I shudder at the thought, but that is the truth of the matter.

New York Times (1857 to present)

The newspaper that I have found the most useful in my research is the *New York Times*. This is not because that newspaper was better written or more inclusive than any other newspaper, but because it was indexed. The early indexes were slender and hand-written, but the annual index for each year in the twentieth century is more than three inches thick.

In the early 1970's, when I first started planning my lifelong shipwreck research ambition, I photocopied every page of every section in every index that related to merchant and naval disasters, from the newspaper's inception in 1857 all the way to 1945. After World War Two, major maritime casualties were few and far between.

Headings changed throughout the newspaper's history. In some years shipwrecks were listed under Accidents: Shipping. In other years they were listed under Shipping: Accidents. Then again they could be listed under Shipping: Disasters. War and naval casualties were listed separately.

I three-hole-punched the photocopied pages and placed them chronologically in a loose-leaf binder that was two inches thick. With my own handy desk reference, I did not have to dash off to the library every time I wanted to see if a shipwreck was covered. I could gratify my curiosity as soon as the thought was ideated. To make my work easier, I highlighted every shipwreck in which I was interested. When I wanted to see the actual article, I could make my research list at home and at my leisure, then hand it to the librarian immediately upon arrival at the library. The librarian pulled the appropriate microfilms, and I could set down to business quickly and efficiently to make the most effective use of my library time.

Local Newspapers

The *New York Times* did not cover every maritime disaster: not by a long shot. It covered those that were of local interest to its subscribers in New York and New Jersey. Secondarily, it covered those that were of major importance worldwide: disasters to vessels that were large or well known, or that resulted in a great number of fatalities. Disasters to lesser vessels were covered briefly or not at all.

For more extensive coverage, I had to access newspapers that were published and distributed close to the scene of the disaster. My newspaper research took me to public libraries from Providence, Rhode Island to Atlantic City, New Jersey to Virginia Beach, Virginia to Savannah, Georgia; and to college libraries from Wilmington, North Carolina to Myrtle Beach, South Carolina, to name a few. I had to go wherever the newspaper microfilms were archived.

Whereas 98% of official documents have been trashed, nearly every newspaper has been saved from extinction courtesy of the nation's public libraries. This is due not only to their interest to the general public, but to their large circulation. Only a handful of copies of an official report may have been printed, whereas thousands or tens of thousands of issues of a newspaper may have been circulated.

Fortunately for historians of today and of future generations, libraries are in the business of preserving newspapers and making them available to their members. Libraries generally subscribe to all the local newspapers, and some of the major metropolitan newspapers as well.

As you can imagine, these fat reams of newsprint occupied an awful lot of space on the shelves. Eventually, libraries moved the older newspapers to basement stacks or storage boxes, in order to make room for newer editions in the reading rooms. About the time that most libraries were becoming overwhelmed with pulp, someone thought of the idea of putting newspapers on microfilm.

The photography process was expensive, but the rewards far outweighed the capital investment. A whole stack of newspapers could be copied onto a single spool of microfilm. And so it began.

The Newspaper Marketplace

Once the newspapers were microfilmed, most of the hard copies were discarded. Not all the old newspapers found their way to the trash dump or fed raging bonfires, though. Many were salvaged by entrepreneurs who warehoused them for eventual resale in the collectibles market.

I have spent many thousands of dollars to purchase hundreds of these antique newspapers in my quest for wreck related items – but more on that in the chapter about Picture Sources. For now, suffice it to say that there are a number of merchants who have vast collections of original newspapers for sale. A Google search on the Internet will find most of them. Others auction their wares on eBay.

There are daily and weekly newspapers available from as long ago as the late 1700's. If you find an article on microfilm, there exists the possibility that you can locate the original newspaper.

Library of Congress

Except for the *New York Times*, I have conducted most of my newspaper research at the Library of Congress in Washington, DC. This great repository possesses microfilms of newspapers from all over the country. Not every newspaper has been archived, and of the newspapers it archived it may not have every issue. But by and large, the congressional library is your best chance of finding a slew of old newspapers in one central location.

Since no newspapers other than the *New York Times* are indexed, there is no guarantee that you will find anything written about the shipwreck you are researching. You have to put in a call slip, wait an hour before the microfilm is pulled from the storage stacks,

Newspapers

then load the spool onto a reader, and scan each page on and subsequent to the date of disaster.

News traveled slowly in the old days, especially in the 1800's. When a shipwreck was discovered on a storm-ridden beach, or when pitiful survivors were landed in port after a wreck that occurred at sea, initial communication to an editor's desk was made by means of telegraph. If the event were deemed newsworthy, the editor would dispatch a correspondent to the scene. Most strandings occurred at remote shore locations, perhaps on uninhabited outer banks that were not bridged to the mainland. The correspondent had to travel to the strand by carriage or horse and buggy, then take a rowboat to the island offshore. There were no paved highways, only dirt roads and rutted trails through the forest. The correspondent might take a day or two to reach his destination, spending nights at isolated inns. He then had to track down and interview survivors or lifesavers. By the time he returned to the city, wrote the article, had it set in linotype, and got the presses rolling, a week might have passed.

Keep this in mind when scanning antebellum newspapers. News traveled faster toward the latter decades of the century; the time lag was reduced to days. As seclusion waned with the encroachment of civilization at the turn of the century, an article might appear on the day after disaster. In the 1900's, an evening edition could have an article about a wreck that happened that morning.

If you do not find an article in the local newspaper that is closest to the scene, try looking in a newspaper from a neighboring community that may be larger and might have wider circulation.

After you find a related article, you should scroll through the next several days for follow-up pieces. I have often found that, in the rush to get sensational news into print before competitors, the initial article was somewhat inaccurate because it was based partly upon hearsay instead of upon interviews with witnesses. Subsequent articles correct the misinformation, and add detail that was not available for the first printing. Some events were covered for several days as more news dribbled in, or if the event was sensational enough to sustain reader interest.

Be careful of skipped days. Just because you do not find another article in the next issue does not mean that news of the event did not appear several days later. You may even learn that the wreck was refloated. When to stop looking is a guessing game. If this kind of research sounds a lot like drudgery, that is because it is.

The downside to the Library of Congress is that it has the oldest, most decrepit, and worst maintained microfilm readers and copiers that I have ever encountered. They constantly malfunction, they often print illegible copies, and they do not reimburse you for substandard printouts. If you do not like what you get, pay more money while you adjust the focus and exposure for another copy.

Microfilm Readers and Copiers

While I am on the subject of microfilm, let me make an aside to discuss its usage, so you will not think that your experiences are the only bad ones.

As I mentioned in the previous section, microfilm readers and copiers often leave much to be desired. In some facilities, such as the main branch of Free Library of Philadelphia (called the Central Library), you must preview microfilm on a reader. After you find the article you want, you rewind the microfilm, and take the spool to a librarian, who then puts the spool on a copier, finds the page you want, and makes the copy. In other branches, the process differs only in that you are permitted to operate the copier yourself without the assistance of a librarian; but you still have to preview the microfilm on a reader before loading the spool onto the copier. In at least one branch, if the microfilm reading room is not overly crowded, and there is no waiting line for the copier, the librarian might let you view the microfilm directly on the copier – but that depends on which librarian is on duty at the time, and which side of the bed he or she got up on.

Several years ago, millions of dollars were spent on renovating some of the branches of the Free Library of Philadelphia. New carpets were installed, new decorations were added, and beautiful ornately carved wooden paneling was hung on the interior walls to hide the peeling paint. Great emphasis was placed on imagery and façade. But the ancient first-generation microfilm readers, which were always breaking down and taken out of service, were not replaced with modern ones. Researchers now have a pleasant environment in which to get frustrated with broken down equipment.

In other libraries, instead of having separate readers and copiers, every unit is a copier. You find the article you want, press the print button (or insert the appropriate amount of change), and print your own copy. Some facilities do not have coin-operated copiers; they trust you to pay your total bill at the end of your microfilm session.

In most facilities, a time limit is placed on microfilm readers whenever too many people want to use them. In a few facilities, once you grab a reader it is yours to keep until you are done with it.

I have yet to find an ergonomic microfilm reader. If reading microfilm sounds easy, wait until you try it before you venture an opinion. Reading microfilm is backbreaking and eye-straining work. Microfilm readers must have been designed by physically challenged mechanical engineers or aliens from another planet: beings who have bodies that differ radically from that of normal humans.

I have never found a way to sit comfortably in front of a microfilm reader or copier. The base of the unit is usually solid so you cannot slide your legs under the platform as you would do at a table. This forces you back away from the screen. By shrinking an entire page to the size of the screen, the text is so small that you cannot read it from a distance. You have to lean forward in order to decipher the miniscule text.

Most readers and copiers have the screen higher than eye level. This means that you have to crane your neck upward, instead of the more natural position of looking down, say, at your computer screen.

Microfilm must be advanced past a magnifying lens onto a take-up spool. Some machines are operated manually by means of a hand wheel that has to be cranked. It may take several minutes to reach the end of the spool, then several more minutes to rewind the microfilm. More modern and expensive machines have variable speed electrical controls. In either case, you have to extend your arm to the control mechanism in order to advance and rewind the microfilm. This adds another twist to your backbone and muscles. The extended arm fatigues quickly, and soon becomes painful.

Chairs add to the physical discomfort because they were recycled from trash dumps after they were bent and broken beyond repair. The lamps that illuminate the microfilm are often inadequate. Glare from ceiling lights makes the screen difficult to read except at an angle. You have to bend and weave your spine into unnatural attitudes.

After several minutes of these painful postures, the back begins to ache as if it were being bent like a pretzel, or stretched on a torture rack from the Spanish Inquisition. Suffer these torments for hours on end, as I have often done, and you can sympathize with my complaints.

Aiding and abetting these dimwitted design flaws is the additional defect in the aspect ratio of the viewing screen. Although microfilm readers were primarily intended for viewing newspapers, which are rectangular in shape and generally twice as tall as they are wide, the screens are square. If the machine is equipped with progressive magnification, you can reduce the image size far enough so the whole page is displayed on the screen – but then the text is too small to make out. If you increase the image size to the point of readability, you cannot see the entire page – you have to scroll up

Newspapers

and down and from side to side.

Adding intellectual insult to physical injury, some newspapers were badly microfilmed: the images were either overexposed, underexposed, or out of focus. The microfilm photographers were either shoddy or indifferent, and did not have enough pride in their work to film the images carefully.

On machines that are poorly maintained, the focusing lens may be out of whack so that it will focus on only part of the page, leaving the rest of the page illegible. In that case, you have to scroll the microfilm until the text that you want to read passes under the lens's focal point. In this regard, sometimes I have had to make two or three copies – each one focused on a different part of a page – in order to make one legible version of a full column article.

In an effort to save money, some facilities still cling to their aged wet process copiers. They were state-of-the-art decades ago, but have long since been replaced with dry process copiers. Wet process paper is dispensed from a roll. The ink smears and the paper curls. Eventually, the ink may fade to the vanishing point. For longevity, wet process copies should be photocopied on a dry process photocopier.

Coins are required to operate old-style microfilm copiers. Some give change; some do not. Some operate only on exact change, and not a nickel more.

Up-to-date facilities use a copy card. This is a plastic card that is the size and shape of a credit card. You purchase copy credit from a human cashier or from a bill-collecting machine by turning cash into electronic money which is registered on the card. You insert the copy card into a slot the same as you would do at a gasoline filling station. When you make a copy, the machine deducts the cost of the copy from the credit on your card. When the card is reduced to zero credit, you regenerate the card with more cash.

The copy card system is far more convenient than buying dollars worth of dimes. I have a card case full of copy cards for the various facilities in which I work.

One last tidbit while I am discussing microfilm research – and this goes for any kind of archival research: do not do research when you are hungry or thirsty. When you are distracted by hunger pangs or a parched throat, you will not be concentrating effectively on your research. You will tend to rush things, in order get done so you can get a drink or catch a bite to eat. Rushing equates to missing information. An article might be right in front of your eyes, yet because you are squirming and scanning mechanically, and not actually comprehending what your eyes are passing over, you could easily miss the very item that you are looking for.

The same goes for elimination processes. Do not hold it in – squirt when necessary.

It is worth your while to take a few minutes to eat, drink, and relax, then return to the task at hand fully refreshed and reinvigorated. Take it from one who knows.

Newspapers on the Internet

Nowadays there is an easier way to research shipwrecks in newspapers than by traipsing all over the country the way I had to do it. Several companies have entered the market by making scanned newspaper pages available online. Some of these companies have literally millions of individual page scans that can be viewed on a subscriber-only website via computer hookup to the Internet. The service is not free. Indeed, some are so expensive that only rich universities and well-funded libraries can afford the hefty access fees.

The convenience is unbelievable. Imagine sitting in the comfort of your own home, with your feet propped up on your desk, sipping a cup of coffee, while you search thousands of national and local newspapers for contemporary shipwreck articles. Better yet, copy costs are so minimal as to be practically non-existent: nothing more than toner and a sheet of paper from your very own printer.

For lack of an existing term, I will christen these companies Internet Newspaper Providers.

Newspapers

The best one that I have used so far is called ProQuest. The version to which I had access for a while had two sections: one with five major metropolitan newspapers for the entire span of their publication, and one with obscure local newspapers according to availability. The city sheets included the *New York Times*, the *Washington Post*, the *Boston Globe*, the *Chicago Tribune*, and the *Los Angeles Times*. Local newspapers were catch as catch can, but it was amazing to me how many backwoods town rags had been published during the past two centuries, much less how many survived library purges and holocausts: every burg, hamlet, and village from Lower Jebip to Upper Podunk. I am exaggerating of course, but you get the point.

Other online newspaper services exist. I have not tried them all. NewspaperArchive.com, for example, concentrates on small local newspapers, whose usefulness can be inestimable in finding articles about local or statewide events that the major metropolitan newspapers neglected to cover in their devotion to national and international news. Competition seems to be growing, with the result that these Internet newspaper services are constantly expanding their databases. More and more newspapers are becoming available every day, every hour, every minute.

These Internet Newspaper Providers have enabled me to find articles that never in a million years would I have found otherwise. This time I am *not* exaggerating. Well, hardly. The point is, while many newspapers printed identical information because the articles were obtained from a wire service, some added new material that helped to flesh out a story – and some wrote their own articles. Remember what research is all about: collecting snippets of information from here and there, and collating them all into a comprehensible and cohesive whole.

Now the question is: how do you obtain access to these fee-oriented, subscriber-only websites? As an individual, you cannot. Or, if you can, the cost might be prohibitive for the amount of research you want to do.

The easiest and least expensive way is through a college or public library. These study organizations make newspaper websites available as a free benefit to students, staff, members, and alumni. Money to pay for the service comes from tuition, grant, or municipal funding. Access to the service is generally made through on-site library computers, but some libraries enable their patrons to access the service from their home computers by the assignation of a membership code number.

Access is limited in a number of ways. For example, anyone can visit any branch of the Free Library of Philadelphia and utilize the facilities on site. To borrow books, or to gain Internet access from home, you must be a card-carrying member of the library. Membership is free, but you must be a resident of Philadelphia. Membership is not available to residents of the rest of Pennsylvania, or to residents of any other State.

When I wanted to research shipwrecks off Boston, I found that the Philadelphia library did not subscribe to an Internet newspaper service that included Massachusetts newspapers. The library subscribed to a service that was provided by Ebsco Host Research Databases, and included only regional newspapers and only as far back as 1980.

When I checked with the Boston Public Library, I found that, although its Internet newspaper service included some Massachusetts newspapers for certain date ranges, it had membership restrictions much like the Philadelphia library: membership was restricted to residents of the State (although it was not restricted only to residents of the city).

This catch-22 was compounded by the fact that neither city library had *full* Internet newspaper service. The Boston library subscribed to ProQuest, but in order to save money, the library did not subscribe to the full service, instead choosing only a portion of the service that included a few local newspapers.

Worse yet, in some cases the Boston library package was limited in date range. For example, its newspa-

Newspapers

per service package did not include the *Boston Globe* between 1924 and 1979 inclusive, only before and after. Thus a Massachusetts resident with a library card can view *Boston Globe* newspapers between 1872 and 1923, and between 1980 and the present, but not during that sixty-six year hiatus.

If you do not belong to an organization that subscribes to a full Internet service, try to find someone who does (like a university student): someone who will let you borrow his membership code number so you can do your newspaper research from home.

Internet Newspaper Search Engines

One awesome advantage to using an Internet newspaper service is that you can search all the newspapers that the provider has on file, and at the same time. This beats scrolling through roll after roll of microfilm on the off chance that the shipwreck you are researching received coverage. Not only can an Internet Newspaper Provider inform you which newspapers covered your topic, but you can open the relevant page as a PDF file as fast as your Internet service connection speed will allow.

On the other hand, finding a shipwreck is not as easy as it sounds. Search engines are not like indexes. When I use the *New York Times* index, and look under the category for shipping accidents, vessel names are italicized and every italicized name refers to a vessel. Search engines do not work that way. They have no way of restricting your search to vessels.

Search engines search for words and word combinations.

Let me give you some examples from my recent shipwreck researches. The *Asa H. Purvere* was a distinct enough name that nearly every mention of this combination of words that was returned in a global search referred to the vessel in question. I even learned that Asa H. Purvere, the man for whom the vessel was named, died on November 17, 1879, and was buried in the Wellfleet Pleasant Hill Cemetery. In all likelihood, I never would have stumbled across the demise of the eponymous skipper by usual research means. This gratuitous item of information added an interesting anecdote to the story that I would not have been able to include otherwise.

This same situation did not hold true when I searched for the *Coyote*. My global search returned thousands of hits about the rampant prairie wolf problem in western States. Separating the wheat from the chaff would have been an enormous undertaking, because nearly every article was chaff – and perhaps that elusive grain of wheat did not exist, if no newspaper covered the scuttling of the *Coyote*.

By refining my search to 1932, I still had scores of screens full of chaff about wild canines and the damage they were doing to the environment. When I refined the date range to January, I was able to locate that grain among the chaff, but only after scrolling through a number of screens.

Note that some Internet Newspaper Providers display entire pages of a newspaper, while others separate the articles so that each article is displayed as a standalone.

Search Engine Idiosyncrasies

Each search engine works differently, and not every one works perfectly all the time. Glitches occur. One Internet Newspaper Provider automatically highlighted my search word after the PDF file was downloaded. Others did not, leaving me no recourse but to read an entire page of miniscule print in order to find the word. Sometimes a search engine led me to a page on which my search word did not appear. I don't know why.

Even less understandable is the reason why a search engine would *not* find a page that contained a word that I specified on a previous search, despite the fact that I managed to stumble onto that page from a different direction, by using another search word that accidentally put me on the right page. Whenever this has happened, I have carefully retyped my original search word into the search line, double-checked that the spelling was correct, and tapped Enter. Still the search engine would not take me to the page on which that word appeared, even though I was actually looking at the page from the previous search, and seeing the word in real time. No matter how many times I repeated the process, the search engine would not find that appearance of the word. Again, I don't know why. It is one of those mysteries of computer science that no one can understand, not even the computer experts who wrote the programs.

Another peculiarity about search engines is that they do not perform consistently. For example, if you search for a word or a phrase in quotes, Google will return those hits that fit your search criteria. If you do it again several minutes later, or a day later, you might find that the number of hits has changed, that the order in which the hits are displayed is different, that hits that you saw on the first search are no longer displayed, or that hits are displayed that did not appear the first time.

This quirky inconsistency is frustrating to say the least. It means that you cannot rely on repeatability when conducting search engine searches. What causes such erratic behavior in a supposedly immutable computer application is another mystery of computer science. Caprice is supposed to be a human fallibility, but search engine aberrations make me wonder sometimes how close to artificial intelligence these computer programs are becoming.

I suppose one might equate search engines to indexes by noting that not every word in a book is found in the index: only the important words, or those words that the author thought his readers might want to look up. But I don't think that analogy is valid. A search engine is not supposed to be selective.

Another foible of search engines is their occasional inability to find a phrase on a global search that it *will* find on a refined search. To make up an example, suppose I were looking for the wreck of the *Coyote.* If I type

"Coyote" into the search engine, it should find every appearance of the word. As I noted above, the amount of chaff is enormous, so I could try to refine my search by searching for two words: "Coyote" and "steamer," or "steamship."

Hopefully, this ploy would trick the search engine into returning only those pages on which both words appear. The words might be in different articles – one on ocean-going vessels and one on carnivorous American mammals – but at least there would be some refinement and considerably less chaff. The main problem with this gambit is that an article about the scuttling of the *Coyote* might not specify that the vessel was a steamer or steamship, in which case the search engine would not return a hit for the very article for which you are searching.

You must be careful not to use a combination of words that might exclude the object of your search. Or, taking another tack, try using different combinations of words that will refine your search but will exclude most of the chaff. Instead of using "steamer" or "steamship" as a refinement technique, try "ship" or "wreck" or, in this case, "Massachusetts" or "Boston Harbor."

But here is the unexplainable quirk that I foreshadowed three paragraphs above: sometimes a search engine will find a pertinent article with a combination of search words such as "Coyote" and "harbor," but will *not* find that article by searching for *only* "Coyote" or "harbor." This makes no sense and is contrary to Boolean logic, but there it is.

Search Techniques

The two most important keystrokes to know when you are searching a page of text on a computer are "Control F." These are the keys for the find mechanism. Alternatively, to open the find mechanism by means of the cursor, use your mouse or trackpad to move the cursor to the Toolbar at the top of the page, select the Edit menu near the left, and scroll down to Find. When the dialogue box appears, type the word that you want

Newspapers

to find in the Find What space, and tap Enter on the keyboard or click Find Next in the dialogue box. The find mechanism will highlight the first occurrence of the word. Repeat the Find Next procedure to highlight subsequent occurrences of the word.

This may not work on PDF files if the page is interpreted as a picture file instead of a text file, but it works most of the time.

When I searched for the *Mohave* for 1928, I got a wealth of hits about the Indian tribe. A search for the *Pottstown* for 1944 returned fields of chaff about the town in central Pennsylvania. When I searched for the *Wathen* (the tug that was towing the barge *Pottstown*), I was directed to obituaries for people whose surname was Wathen. *Mars* gave me loads of articles about the planet, but none about the tugboat. *Delaware* was lost among mentions of the First State. Do not even think about searching for a wreck named *New York* unless you have all eternity to search. And unless you already know the precise month and day, forget about the *Romance* that stranded on a ledge in 1936.

Different Internet Newspaper Providers offer different ways of refining a search other than by date range. Some allow you to select certain newspapers. Others let you choose newspapers from a specific State, or from a geographical area. You can try adding additional search words in combination with the name of the vessel, such as "shipwreck" or "wreck" or "schooner" or "tug" or "barge." You can try incorporating combinations of vessel names if the casualty was caused by collision. But if an article was published without the use of your inclusionary criteria, the search engine will skip over it.

You can try searching for "the *Coyote*," as vessel names are usually preceded by the definite article. While Google will confine hits to both words in sequence, many search engines do not recognize "small" words such as articles and prepositions because their usage is too common. You will still turn up numerous pieces about *Canis latrans* pelts.

Employ quote marks to search for a phrase, or else

the search engine will find pages on which all the words appear but not necessarily in the order that you specified. For example, if you search for Harding Ledge without enclosing the words in quotes, you might find newspaper pages on which President Warren Harding is mentioned in one place, and swallows on a cliff ledge are mentioned elsewhere. Refine your search thus: "Harding Ledge."

Most search engines do not recognize individual letters as part of a search string. For example, a search for the *W.A. Marshall* in quotes (as "W.A. Marshall") will find every instance of the word "marshall" without the inclusive initials. It will find *W.A. Marshall*, too, but the appearances of the vessel will be buried in mounds of chaff.

Most search engines are not case sensitive (that is, they do not distinguish between uppercase or capital letters and lowercase or small letters), and most do not recognize punctuation. As I already mentioned, they do not recognize italics either, but that is largely irrelevant as most correspondents were not familiar enough with grammatical usage to employ italics for vessel names.

By way of example, a search for the *King Philip* might turn up chaff like this: "Although he wanted to be king, Philip thought otherwise." Permutations that you could never dream of will occur.

Some search engines permit the use of exclusionary words. If so, search for the *Baleen* by adding –whale (minus whale). In this instance, the search engine will find pages with the word on which the word "baleen" appears, but will exclude those pages on which the word "whale" also appears. But be careful when you do this. Every page on which the word "whale" appears will be omitted, not only if it is printed in a separate article from the one about the *Baleen*, but also if the writer mentioned in an article about the *Baleen* that the name was derived from the straining material on the upper jaw of a plankton-eating cetacean.

If you get too many hits, be creative. If you do not get enough, or do not get any, try another Internet

Newspapers

Newspaper Provider – or go back to the tried and true microfilm method.

The possibilities are endless. That is the nature of shipwreck research.

Part Two - Washington District of Columbia

The nation's capitol is not only the seat of democratic government; it is the holy receptacle and sacrosanct repository of archival material that embodies the official history of the United States of America.

It is necessary that the representatives of the people have immediate access to historic documents in order to assist them in the performance of their duties. This is the rationale for having comprehensive libraries and archives in one centralized area.

No shipwreck researcher can conduct bona fide primary research without visiting or at least corresponding with the facilities that are located in the District of Columbia.

National Archives

There is no greater facility in the country for conducting primary shipwreck research than the National Archives. Known officially as the National Archives and Records Administration (NARA), I think of it simply as *the* Archives.

When the National Archives opened for business, in 1935, the building was large enough to house all the records that had been designated for holding in perpetuity. Over the years, as records were accessioned from various governmental agencies, the stacks and storage areas got so crowded that the internal spacing arrangements had to be reorganized in order to hold the growing accumulation of documents. Eventually, the stacks became so crowded that the building was bursting at the seams.

The 1990's saw the construction of a new National Archives building, this one located outside of DC in College Park, Maryland. After it opened, in 1994, I overheard one Archives employee describe the new building as "an architectural conceit." He meant it disparagingly, but there is no doubt in my mind that the ultramodern building provides a wonderful ergonomic working environment, for researchers as well as for staff members. It is also one of the most beautiful buildings in the world, inside as well as outside.

By comparison, the original Archives building, with its fluted columns and archaic design, looks more like the Roman coliseum than an esteemed warehouse for invaluable and irreplaceable documents. It is gradually being retrofitted, but it will always look like an antique edifice from yesteryear, and its operational climate is only slightly better than barnlike.

To distinguish one from the other, the two buildings have been numerically Latinized: the downtown facility is now called Archives I; the new College Park facility is called Archives II.

A *I* and a *II* and a . . .

I have a personal dislike for Roman numerals. This antipathy has nothing to do with the fact that I struggled through four years of Latin in high school. My prejudice is based upon the difficulty of interpreting numerals that are, in fact, letters. Undoubtedly, I am not the only one who has grappled with the letter twister MCMLVIII. To translate this as 1958, you not only need to know what numbers the letters stand for, but you need to add and subtract letters in your head.

In all my writings I have scorned the usage of Roman numerals as my way of advancing the evolution of language exclusively to the Arabic system, which is far easier to understand and calculate.

In the present instance, I can also apply ease of recognition. I and II are too easily confused with one another in print. In skimming over text, a reader is likely to read Archives I for Archives II, and vice versa (a phrase that is borrowed from Latin because its meaning is so precise and avoids confusion, and because – like the French déjà vu – it has no exact and succinct English equivalent).

From now on, I will write Archives I as Archives One, and Archives II as Archives Two.

Research Assistants

Of all the librarians and archivists I have met throughout the years, the people who work at the National Archives are without a doubt the most knowledgeable, most professional, most helpful, and generally the most personable. They know their job and they take great pride in doing it to the best of their ability. If they feel that they lack adequate knowledge to handle your specific research objective effectively, they will confer with others who may be more knowledgeable about the location and content of records that may fit your needs.

I can't count the number of times that a research assistant tracked me down in the Central Research Room in order to obtain additional information about my request for records, or to clarify a point about my inquiry, or to explain why certain records were being pulled pursuant to my request, or to suggest alternative or additional avenues of approach, or to inform me what he or she had found thus far, and ask if that might be helpful in any way. They are the quintessential professionals, giving new and enlightened meaning to the word.

These research assistants are dogged in tracking down records. Perhaps they feel that anyone who traveled all the way to DC on a workday deserves their greatest endeavor, but it often seems to me as if they feel that the fate of the world hinges upon their finding all the relevant documents. Their knowledge and persistence generally pays off in spades. On more than one occasion they have taken me into the stacks – the most holy of places where researchers are usually not allowed to go – to look through boxes that might contain the information I wanted.

A research assistant will never ask why you want information about a specific vessel, any more than a librarian will ask why you want a certain book. You

National Archives

don't have to justify your research. It doesn't matter if you're writing a book, or working for hire, or are just plain curious. Theirs is not to reason why, theirs is just to identify records.

The National Archives recognizes a hierarchy in its research staff: from archivist to specialist to technician. These designations may not be apparent to visiting researchers because staff members do not wear insignia. Depending upon availability at the time of your arrival, anyone from the three classifications may assist you.

An archivist holds the highest position. He or she knows the records and filing system better than a specialist or technician, and probably worked his way up through the ranks as he increased his knowledge base. A specialist is one level below an archivist: he is less knowledgeable than an archivist, and more knowledgeable than a technician. A technician occupies the lowest level but is by no means ignorant. He probably learned the ropes as a puller.

The archivist, specialist, or technician identifies which records to pull. The puller is a person you will probably never see. He works in the background, and is usually the one who actually pulls the boxes of records out of the stacks, places them on a cart, and delivers them to the Central Research Room (Room 203).

For the sake of simplicity, hereafter I will refer to all three hierarchic classifications by the generic term "research assistant."

Getting Started

In order to introduce you to the system, let me take you on a hypothetical tour of your first visit to the National Archives. The procedure is slightly different between Archives One and Archives Two. Let's start with Archives One, located in downtown DC on Pennsylvania Avenue between 7th and 9th Streets, Northwest.

This is actually the rear of the building. The front of the building faces Constitution Avenue, but that

National Archives

A rare moment on Pennsylvania Avenue when there was no traffic except for one standing vehicle. The researcher's entrance to the National Archives is the dark vertical rectangle beneath the base of the fluted columns, in the middle between the lampposts. The shuttle bus stop is around the corner to the left.

entrance is for tourists who wish to see the Declaration of Independence, the Constitution of the United States, and other historical documents, or who wish to take a tour of the museum. The research entrance faces the U.S. Navy Memorial and the convenient Metro subway station across the street.

The Archives opens for researchers at 9 a.m. Upon entering the lobby, the first thing you need to do is go through a metal detector and send your briefcase and outer clothing through an x-ray machine, along with any metallic objects that are in your pockets – just as you would do at an airport.

Do *not* send unprocessed film through the x-ray machine. Have it examined visually. I don't care what they tell you, x-rays will always do some damage to your film, especially if it is high-speed film. When they say that low-speed film is not damaged by x-radiation, what they mean is that the damage is usually not noticeable. Keep in mind that x-radiation has a cumu-

National Archives

lative effect. If a roll of film is x-rayed multiple times, the accumulated dosage will degrade the film until it *does* become noticeable.

This can happen if you don't shoot all your film, and you pass through a number of security checkpoints, say, by returning to the Archives or by making a series of trips by air. This applies not only to film in your camera, but more so to extra film that you may carry for future use. If a roll of film is x-rayed often enough, the pictures may look foggy or overexposed. Plane travelers beware.

After you are given the okay, collect your belongings and proceed to the guard stand. I am personally offended by the fact that the guards carry side arms. I think that an automatic pistol is an excessive show of force for a research facility. The prominent display of handguns is not a response to recent terrorism. National Archives guards have always been armed. In any case, I very much doubt that a guard would shoot someone on suspicion of stealing an archival document.

Present a valid photo identification card to the guard. A current driver's license or passport will suffice. For reasons that I cannot understand, and for which no one can offer a reasonable explanation, an expired ID is not acceptable. This is absurd. A license that has expired means only that your driving privileges have been temporarily suspended. An out-of-date passport means that you cannot re-enter the country (and may have difficulty entering a foreign country). Neither one means that your identity has expired. Your identity expires only when you, well, expire. The same absurdity holds true with respect to airport security.

Print and sign your name on the sign-in sheet, along with the time of your arrival and the purpose of your visit. In the column under Address, print your home address. On subsequent visits, you will print your researcher identification number instead of your address.

The guard will ask if you have any original documents in your possession. If you do, you need to produce them now, or else you may have trouble leaving the building.

The guard will also ask if you have any cameras, computers, or other devices. If you do, show them to the guard so he can copy the types, brands, and serial numbers on an equipment receipt. Keep this receipt in your possession at all times inside the building. You will need to show it to the guard upon departure. If you lose the receipt, your equipment may be confiscated. Equipment receipts are valid for only 90 days, after which you must obtain a new one.

You must repeat this procedure every time you enter the building, even if you leave only for a cigarette or food or a breath of fresh air. During the cherry blossom season in the spring, the DC air can smell refreshingly fresh and scented.

The guard will hand you a visitor's pass. This pass is a laminated card that you can either clip to your shirtfront or wear around your neck on a chain. You must wear this number card at all times within the building. You will turn in the card upon your departure.

If this is your first time at the Archives, the guard will direct you to the Customer Service Center on the Ground Floor, where you will register for your researcher identification card. The process is painless and takes only a few minutes. If you feel the need to appear decent before your photograph is taken, visit the restroom and comb your hair or apply makeup. Present your driver's license or passport to the clerk. Your contact information will be entered on the Archives database. A digital camera will be used to snap your picture. A machine will print your photo research card: a plastic laminated card that is the same size and thickness as a credit card. You are done.

Now you may roam throughout those parts of the building that are open to authorized personnel. If you want to look at microfilm, you can go directly to the Microfilm Research Room, which is now located at the back of the Ground Floor. (It used to be on the Fourth

National Archives

Floor, in Room 410.) More than likely, you will first want to speak with a research assistant of the Navy/Maritime Team at the west side of the floor. The Ground Floor is now called the Research Center.

Print and sign your name on the sign-in sheet, along with the time of your arrival and the purpose of your visit. Print your researcher identification number in the column under Address. Proceed to the right into the room of the Navy/Maritime Team. Desks in the center of this room are reserved for researchers who need assistance. The perimeter of the room is occupied by cubicles for staff members. Attract the attention of a staff member, introduce yourself, and explain the nature of your visit. You will then be directed to a research assistant who specializes either in Navy records or in Maritime records (which used to be called Old Coast Guard records), but only within certain time frames.

Depending upon the nature of your research, you may have to speak with two research assistants: one assigned to Navy records and one assigned to Maritime records.

Historical Interlude

The split in the holdings has created a logistical problem for researchers, making research more difficult today than it used to be. In the old days (the 1970's, 1980's, and early 1990's), all the Record Groups were housed in Archives One.

The offices of the archivists of the Old Coast Guard (now Maritime) Record Groups were located in a room on 19E, while the offices of the archivists of the Navy Record Groups were located in rooms on 19W and 20W. E stands for East Wing; W stands for West Wing. Picture the internal arrangement of the building as a horseshoe, with the arch facing toward you and the opening facing away from you. In this configuration, the left extension of the horseshoe represents the East Wing; the right extension represents the West Wing. The lobby is at the arch. The arch isn't really an arch, but a long flat corridor that extends from 7th Street to 9th Street.

The stories in the rear of the building (on the researcher's side) are called Floors. The stories in the front of the building (the tourist's side) are called Tiers. To reach the room on 19E, I had to take one of the two lobby elevators to the 4th Floor, or walk up four flights of stairs (past the Mezzanine). Then I proceeded east to the end (at 7th Street), turned right, passed through a doorway, and walked along a hallway in the left extension to the East Wing elevator bank at the front of the building. This elevator bank was sealed off from the tourist area, which comprised the "inside" of the horseshoe. Both wings consisted of offices and storage rooms. Although I had not changed levels, the 4th Floor had become the 7th Tier. I took the elevator to the 19th Tier, then proceeded to the office and signed in.

After speaking with a research assistant in the Old Coast Guard division, and filling out call slips (I'll explain that later), I headed for the offices of the research assistants of the Navy division on 19W. Because of the horseshoe arrangement, I could not go directly from the tip of one extension to the tip of the other. I had to retrace my steps down the elevator to the 7th Tier, go north to the rear of the building, which then became the 4th Floor, traverse the corridor all the way to the 9th Street end, turn left through the doorway, proceed along the hallway to the West Wing elevator bank at the front of the building, where again I was on the 7th Tier, then go up to the 19th Tier.

After signing in and speaking with the Navy division research assistant, I sometimes had to go up to a room on 20W, because the Navy records were divided into different operational divisions. I had to sign in at each room. Once I filled out call slips for the various Navy records, I then had to go to the Central Research Room on the 2nd Floor in order to view the documents that I had requested. I got there by retracing my route down the elevator to the 7th Tier, walking north along the hallway and through the doorway onto the 4th Floor at

National Archives

the rear of the building, then proceeding to the main elevator bank, and going down either the elevator or the steps. The steps were faster.

Depending upon how much time had passed since I turned in my call slips from the Old Coast Guard division, I might sign in the Central Research Room right away – to see if any of my materials had been delivered – or I might take the elevator up to the Still Picture Branch, in order to make more efficient use of my time while I was waiting for records to be delivered.

The Still Picture Branch was located on the 21st Floor, but the elevator went only as high as the 18th Floor. I had to walk through a number of crowded offices and climb the last three flights of stairs.

In those days, I certainly got my exercise doing research.

Back to the Present

You might think that nowadays the research regimen has gotten easier, with the Navy records office and the Old Coast Guard records office having been merged into a single office called the Navy/Maritime Team, which is centrally located. Afraid not. Instead of being located in different wings, these records are now located in different buildings that are more than ten miles apart (as the crow flies).

With the opening of Archives Two, some Navy Record Groups and some Coast Guard Record Groups were transferred to College Park. The divisions were temporal, splitting for the most part at World War Two. For example, to quote the primary records that I have accessed throughout the years, Archives One retained RG 26 (Records of the U.S. Coast Guard War Casualty Section – World War Two), RG 41 (Bureau of Marine Inspection and Navigation), and RG 45 (Naval Records Collection of the Office of Naval Records and Library – Subject Files 1911-1927), while Archives Two now holds Record Group 38 (Armed Guard Engagement Reports, War Diary of the Eastern Sea Frontier, and Reports and Analyses of U.S. and Allied Merchant Ship

Losses, 1941-1945).

If you want to see warship deck logs prior to 1941, go to Archives One. For warship deck logs after 1940, go to Archives Two. Deck logs that are less than thirty years old are held at the Naval Historical Center.

These temporal divisions have changed throughout the years, and are in a constant state of flux as holdings are gradually transferred from Archives One to Archives Two. No one knows what the future holds. As a precaution, I suggest that you call the Archives and speak with a research assistant prior to your planned visit, in order to ascertain which facility has the Record Groups that you are most likely to want to access.

Shuttle Bus

The National Archives provides free shuttle service between the archive facilities. The service is intended for staff members, but researchers may take the bus as long as seats are available. The shuttle bus departs from each building every hour on the hour, starting at 8 a.m. and ending at 4 p.m. The trip takes about fifty minutes.

If you miss the bus, you have to wait an hour for the next one. Don't miss the last bus, or hope that it isn't overcrowded and you get left behind, because then you will have to find alternative means of transportation to your starting point. Taxicabs are expensive.

I have taken the shuttle bus a number of times. The first and last trips can be crowded, but never have I not found a seat. The bus is mostly empty in the middle of the day.

There is mass transit service between Archives One and Two. From Archives One, enter the Metro subway station across the street and take the Green Line to Prince George's Plaza, then transfer to the R3 bus; the bus will stop at the front door of Archives Two.

From Archives Two, catch the R3 bus to Prince George's Plaza, and take the Green Line to the Archives/Navy Memorial station.

The R3 bus does not operate on Saturday. For a

National Archives

more circuitous route between buildings, you can ride the Red Line to the Glenmont station and catch the C8 bus to Archives Two; you can take this route in reverse to travel from Archives Two to One.

If this sounds confusing, all Metro stations post color-coded system maps that are simple to decipher.

Unidentified Shipwrecks

To a certain extent, the researcher is at the mercy of his research assistant. By that I mean that the research assistant is responsible for knowing which Record Groups are most likely to contain the documents that you want, and where within that Record Group you should initiate your search.

On the other hand, the researcher is responsible for explaining in detail the kind of information he is seeking. *You must do your homework.* Learn as much as possible about your shipwreck before making the pilgrimage to the National Archives. If you arrive unprepared, with little or no foreknowledge about your subject matter, the research assistant may not be able to help you. Or, he may be forced to suggest avenues of research that are so global that you could spend hours or days sifting through mountains of chaff in order to find a few scattered grains of wheat.

It is possible to find records of vessels for which you do not know the name, but the process is laborious and the outcome is uncertain. Consider the discovery of an unidentified nineteenth-century steamship off the coast of New Jersey. Recovered hardware items were of American manufacture.

After Trueman Seamans recovered a case of Missisquoi Spring bottles, his wife Nike ascertained that the company stopped bottling spring water in 1870. Jon Hulburt recovered a door latch with a patent date of March 29, 1869. The Seamans and the Hulburts visited the National Archives. When they informed the research assistant of the date parameters, he suggested that they scan the relevant years in the records of the Steamboat Inspection Service. Jon's wife Judy found the identifying entry: the coastal freighter *Brunette* sank on February 1, 1870 after a collision with the *Santiago de Cuba*.

This is the textbook case of shipwreck validation that so rarely occurs in such circumstances. On one hand, the Seamans and the Hulburts were lucky. But on the other hand, they demonstrated initiative and perseverance that ultimately resulted in success. In this situation, the researchers provided the research assistant with crucial information that enabled him to suggest where to begin their research.

As the name implies, the Steamboat Inspection Service inspected American vessels that were propelled by steam engines. It did not inspect vessels of foreign registry. It also investigated accidents in which American steamships were involved, or on which casualties occurred. The Service was created in 1852. After various reorganizations under different U.S. departments, the U.S. Coast Guard assumed its functions during World War Two.

The inspector wrote a report on his investigation, and filed this report with Service headquarters. Unfortunately for historians, the early investigative reports were not saved. The only records remaining are annual *lists* of these reports, which are organized by district, and a three-by-five card index file on which were typed the bare particulars of the incident.

By the way, Joe Milligan took a different tack. He scanned the listings in *Encyclopedia of American Shipwrecks*. He saw that a steamship named *Brunette* sank off Manasquan on the date given above, then got full particulars of the collision from contemporary newspapers. There is more than one way to skin a cat – or to conduct shipwreck research.

Certificate of Enrollment

In most cases, a researcher already knows the name of the vessel that he wants to research. It is equally as important to know *which* vessel of that name that he wants to research. Once again, a researcher

National Archives

must do his homework. Many vessels went by the same name; and many vessels changed names throughout a long career under different owners.

The National Archives possesses an extensive and nearly complete collection of Certificates of Enrollment for practically every vessel that was ever registered in the United States. If I wanted to track an American vessel's enrollment history, I would ask for this history by the name and dates of the vessel: that is, the date of its construction and the date of its demise. Better yet is to have the unique enrollment number, which can be obtained from the *Lloyd's Register*, the *Record* of the American Bureau of Ships, or the *List of Merchant Vessels of the United States*. This information will enable the research assistant to know which file history to pull, and where to look for it.

As a precautionary note, unless this particular vessel's enrollment history has already been requested at some time in the past, in which case an Archive staff member would have created a folder in which to file the vessel's collated documents, the process of locating and pulling each Certificate of Enrollment could take several hours, or even a couple of days. I once asked for a vessel's enrollment history on Tuesday, and was told to return for it on Thursday.

A vessel's first Certificate of Enrollment should provide the vessel's owner, location, and statistics of the vessel such as tonnage and dimensions. Subsequent Certificates will annotate the reasons for the change in enrollment (new name, new owner, new homeport, changes in the vessel's occupation or tonnage, and so on). The endorsement on the final Certificate should note the reason for the end of enrollment (sunk, sold foreign, dismantled, and so on). Researchers beware: many enrollment histories are incomplete or contain spotty information.

The Call Slip

The research assistant will ask to see your research card. This is redundant because you could not have gotten past the guard without it, unless it was your first time in the Archives and you bypassed the card application process.

Be that as it may, once you have provided the research assistant with all the information that you have on the vessel in question, and you have informed him what kind of information you are seeking, he will commence an onsite search of his finding aids. These finding aids are loose-leaf binders whose pages describe the holdings within the various Record Groups. They also inform the research assistant of the location of the boxes in which documents are stored.

Sometimes the research assistant will hand you a binder and suggest that you to look through it for descriptions that fit your search criteria. At other times, he may indicate which Record Group holdings are likely to contain the requested information, and instruct you on how to fill out a Reference Service Slip, better known as a call slip. No pens are allowed. You must use a pencil that is provided. Call slips measure six inches high by eight inches wide. Each call slip is filled out in quadruplicate, courtesy of three sheets of carbon paper. The four slips are color-coded: white, pink, green, and yellow.

You must fill out a call slip for each and every box of documents that you want to have pulled. If two boxes are numbered consecutively, you may use one call slip for both.

On the call slip you print the date, your name, your researcher identification number, and the location information taken from the finding aid. The location information will be something like this: RG 24, Stack Area 470, Row 40, Compartment 19, Shelf 3. In the box for Record Identification, you would print (as I did in this case) "Deck Log for AM 69 (*Curlew*) in Boxes 9 and 10." This informs the puller exactly where in that vast building complex he will find the *Curlew's* deck log for the dates I wanted. I appended a note on the call slip for myself: "1944 April 5. Rescued *Spring Chicken* off Virginia."

National Archives

If you are requesting a number of boxes from the same Record Group and location, the research assistant may fill out the location information on the first call slip, then leave it to you to fill out the rest. I have filled out as many as fifty call slips at a sitting. It took an hour. I was allowed to have only twenty-four boxes pulled at one time, because that is the number of boxes that fit on a cart. I had to return later to turn in the rest of my call slips.

It is important for you to understand that the research assistant does not *know* if the information you want is in the boxes that were requested. It is likely that of the tens of thousands of boxes in the stacks, he has seen the inside of only a small percentage. His job is to point you in the right direction by indicating the most likely boxes in which to look.

For example, in writing *Track of the Gray Wolf* in the late 1980's, I had to research some 150 vessels that were attacked by German U-boats. I relied heavily upon RG 26 – Records of the U.S. Coast Guard War Casualty Section (World War Two), Boxes 3 and 4 (Statements of Survivors of Vessel War Casualties). The standard file box holds around 1,000 sheets of paper. This portion of my research required skimming some 2,000 pages of text that were jammed into the boxes in no order whatsoever.

The statements were shuffled like a deck of cards. There were no statements from the survivors of some vessels, and statements from a number of survivors of other vessels. If there were statements from more than one survivor of one particular vessel, they might *not* be filed together or even in close proximity. They might even be filed in different boxes.

Since I was doing bulk research, this lack of systemization was not necessarily an impediment. But if you were looking for the statement of a survivor from one particular vessel, you would have had to skim every page in both boxes – and then you might not have found the statement that you wanted.

This is why the National Archives cannot generally

furnish information to researchers pursuant to mail order requests. Their task would be prodigious. On the other hand, if you wanted the final Certificate of Enrollment of a vessel for which you knew the name and official number, the Archives could obtain and photocopy the relevant document with relative ease.

Mail Order Research

One time a research assistant showed me a letter of complaint that he had received from a mail order researcher. The researcher had requested specifically dated pages from a vessel's deck log. The research assistant duly complied with the researcher's request, photocopied the pages in question, and sent them to the researcher along with a bill for the service. The researcher complained that the pages were blank.

While it was true that the deck log pages were blank, copies of those pages were what the researcher had requested. In certain cases, negative information can be nearly as valuable as positive information. Knowing that the vessel was out of service at that time may have been useful to know. The research assistant did not know why the request had been made – perhaps, he may have surmised, it was to establish that the vessel was out of operation during that time. His was not to wonder why; his was to honor the request.

This is why mail order research often fails to achieve the goals of the researcher. The only way to conduct global research is to browse through file boxes that contain hundreds if not thousands of documents. Consider this scenario: a research assistant once suggested that I look through a general correspondence file. What was delivered to the Central Research Room was a cart containing fifteen file boxes of documents. In five minutes I ascertained that the correspondence all related to supply requests or personnel data for a Naval base, but nothing that related to vessels. I turned in the cart. A staff member would never have had the time to scan these thousands of documents in response to a mail order request.

Coincidences

Consider another scenario: I was working with one research assistant while a nearby researcher was working with another assistant. The researcher had flown all the way from California, and took lodging at a local hotel, in order to conduct research that he could not conduct through the mail. When the research assistant identified the file boxes that the researcher requested, he found that they had already been pulled for another researcher the day before. Once pulled, boxes might not be refiled for several days, depending upon the workload of the pullers.

The best advice that the research assistant could offer was to ask people in the Central Research Room if they were working with those files, and wouldn't mind sharing them.

The chances of this happening are small. I once asked for the original Certificate of Enrollment of the *Dora*, from 1859. At that period in time, the Certificates were not issued as individual form sheets on which the enrolling clerk filled in the blanks, but were written by hand in an oversized bound ledger. These Certificate registrations were not entered in any particular order: they were written into the ledger at the request of the shipping agent who was next in line. The particular ledger that I wanted had already been pulled.

I thought: What were the chances that another researcher would be in the Archives at the same time I was there, to request a Certificate of an obscure vessel from 1859, and from the same ledger in which the *Dora* Enrollment was entered?

I put that item on the back burner. When I returned to the Archives a couple of months later, I filled out a new call slip for the *Dora* Certificate. Again the research assistant informed me that the ledger had already been pulled. This coincidence was beyond the bounds of reason: a statistical anomaly. I asked the assistant to double check that the ledger actually existed. He did, and found a recently dated call slip in place of the ledger.

In this instance, I would have been better off sending a mail order request, and paying the research and copy fee.

Because of the amount of time that I have spent at the National Archives, and the sheer abundance of research that I have done, I suppose that coincidences like this are bound to happen sooner or later.

On another occasion, when I pulled a folder out of a box, I saw a marker tab wrapped around several sheets of paper. A research assistant uses a marker tab to designate pages that he wants a puller to photocopy pursuant to a mail order request. The name on the tab was Sheard. Brad Sheard was a long-time friend. I recognized the name of the wreck that he was researching by mail.

At home, I wrote him a letter and asked him why he was researching that wreck at the National Archives. In his reply, he asked how the heck I knew what he was researching. Facetiously, I told him that I knew everything about local shipwreck research. This kept him wondering until I met him on a dive boat several months later, at which time I told him the truth.

The Central Research Room

After you turn in your call slips, go to the Central Research Room to await the delivery of your documents. You may have to wait for an hour to an hour and a half, depending upon how busy the pullers are at the time.

Items that are *not* permitted in the room are hats, coats, jackets, purses, handbags, briefcases, knapsacks, pens, markers, books, papers, and cell phones. The armed guard at the station inside the doorway will not let you enter if you have any of these items in your possession. The Archives provides lockers in which to store your personal belongings during your visit. The lock is operated with a quarter, but the quarter is returned when you turn the key in the lock.

The clothing restrictions apply because there have been authenticated cases of people stealing original documents by secreting them in large pockets or in the

National Archives

lining of heavy outer clothing. The same is true of purses, handbags, and briefcases. If you think you might be cold, wear a sweater.

Inside the Central Research Room, you will find a table on which pencils, paper, and marker tabs are furnished. Each sheet of ruled paper is distinguished by a hole that is punched in one corner. When you make notes, do not have the paper on top of any documents; place the paper on the desktop next to the documents. This is so the pencil does not leave impressions on a document through the notepaper.

The Archives has done away with the sign-in sheet at the guard station. Hand your research card to the guard, and he or she will swipe it. The guard knows at all times how many researchers are in the room, and who they are. You must have your card swiped when you leave the room, even if you are just going out for a drink of water.

You may take a small number of notepapers with you into the room. You must first show them to the guard, who will determine that they are merely notepapers and not original documents. He will direct you to have the papers stamped by a staff member at the central desk. Without this stamp, your papers will be confiscated upon your departure. The guard will inspect every sheet of paper that you take from the room.

A central desk attendant will staple your papers in an upper corner, then stamp the back of the last sheet in the stack. He will date and initial the stamp by hand. You may then ask if any documents have been delivered in your name.

The attendant will look through the stack of pink call slips that are arranged alphabetically by surname. If there are none in your name, you will be asked to wait. In the meantime, you can choose a workstation to your liking, and collect pencil, paper, and marking tabs.

A workstation is a section of a long desk which is separated from adjacent and opposite sections by short glass partitions. Each workstation is equipped with a lamp and a duplex electrical outlet. The lamp is necessary because the ceiling arches thirty feet overhead. Sunlight suffuses into the room through tall windows that stretch along the outer wall. The woodwork of the ceiling and walls is wonderfully ornate.

If your documents still have not been delivered, you have nothing to do but daydream. You are not permitted to bring a book with you to read. If you want to read, you must sign out of the room, go downstairs to your locker, bring a book back up to the hallway outside the Central Research Room, and read while waiting for your documents.

When your documents arrive, an attendant will announce your name in a loud voice that carries throughout the room and out into the hallway. If you are reading, you must return the book to your locker before entering the Central Research Room. The guard will scan your research card. Sign for your documents at the central desk.

If you are signing for a ledger or a single box, it will be stowed on a shelf behind the central desk. If there are a number of ledgers or boxes, an attendant will retrieve them from a storage area down the hall, and bring them to you on a cart. Wheel the cart to your workstation.

You are finally ready to begin the real work of research.

Creature Comforts

To repeat what I wrote a few pages back, you need to be comfortable in order to do good research. By comfortable I don't mean sitting in a padded easy chair, although that would be nice if one were available. I mean comfort on a more basic level.

First and foremost, you can't squirm like a worm on a hot tarred road. If you are distracted by the need to urinate, or worse, you won't be observant in reading documents. You might miss an important iota completely. Visit the restroom as soon as the urge arises. You used to be able to use the restrooms that are located a couple of hundred feet along the hallway outside of Room 203, but these have now been closed to the public. Now you have to go down to the Ground Floor, and to the public restroom that is located outside the locker room.

Your workstation must be cleared before you are allowed to leave the room. This means that you may not leave loose documents, file folders, or boxes on the desktop. You must pack everything away and put the materials on your cart – unless you had only one ledger or file box, and did not have a cart, in which case you may leave the ledger or file box on the desktop.

You can't concentrate if your throat is parched, or if your stomach is grumbling with hunger pangs. I have found that if I try to work through lunch, in order to gain an extra half hour of research, I usually can't pay as close attention as I should to the documents that I am supposed to be scanning. Instead, I have a tendency to skim quickly through text, and might miss things.

In the long run, it is better to appease your appetite than to suffer quiet discomfort in the belief that you are being more productive.

Short breaks will serve you better in the end than hour after hour of reading text or viewing microfilm.

Get a good night's sleep before a day of research. If you are drowsy or not well rested, your eyes will move mechanically across lines of text, but your mind will not comprehend what your eyes are seeing.

Rules of Engagement

From the cart you may take only one box at a time. From the box you may remove only one folder at a time. You must place a marking tab between folders in the box from which you removed your folder. Lay the folder flat on the desktop and open it. The documents inside are seldom if ever in any order. Nonetheless, you must maintain the original disorder while perusing documents for relevant information. If you are spotted violating any of these rules, a central desk attendant will chastise you for doing so.

One time, after hours of reading through miniscule text, my back was aching from sitting on the hard wooden chair and leaning forward over ledgers. I sat back in the chair and pulled the ledger onto the edge of the workstation, with the bottom resting on my legs, so that the ledger was resting at an angle. An attendant appeared at my side immediately, and told me to lay the ledger flat. They are afraid that a researcher might drop a ledger and damage it, or let a folder fall onto the floor and get the loose disarranged papers rearranged.

By the same token, you may not rest documents on your lap, or hold them off the desktop in the air, or put them on the floor.

More often than not, archival documents adhere to each other and are difficult to separate. Some sheets are so thin that you cannot finger the edge of one without fingering two or more. It's like flipping the pages of a paperback book while wearing boxing gloves. You are not allowed to lick or otherwise moisten your fingers in order to separate sheets of paper. Be patient and deal with it.

If – and I do mean if – you find a document that has relevant information, there are a number of ways in which you can copy that information. You can make handwritten notes. This process may be long and laborious if there is a great deal of text that you need to transcribe. Furthermore, you may make a mistake, or you may leave out a crucial word, or you might learn later that you needed other information that was printed elsewhere on the page.

In order to avoid these pitfalls, I photocopy everything. That way I can always refer to the entire document should the need arise for clarification. Over the years and at great expense I have photocopied tens of thousands of pages – enough to fill more than three four-drawer filing cabinets.

Self-Service Photocopiers
Researchers are not allowed to bring their own photocopy machines into the Archives.

National Archives

There are four photocopiers in the Central Research Room for researchers to use. These machines used to be coin operated. I would always start by buying a couple of rolls of dimes from the Cashier on the Ground Floor. In the 1990's, a Copy Card scanner replaced the coin mechanism. The researcher paid fifty cents for the card, then put as much money on it as he thought he would need. You could not reclaim unused money that was left on the card. I just saved the leftover for my next visit.

The Copy Card was the size and shape of a plastic credit card. Each copier was equipped with a card scanner: a separate metal box that was connected to the copier by means of an electrical cable. When you stuck the card in the slot on the card scanner, the device scanned the amount of money that remained on the card, and displayed the number digitally. Whenever you pressed the Copy button, ten cents were deducted from the usable amount. When the card ran out of money, the copier would not operate.

You could then have the Cashier add more money to the card – the preferred method if you needed a receipt. For convenience, the Central Research Room is equipped with an automated regenerator. You could place your card in the appropriate slot on the regenerator, feed paper bills into another slot, and the machine would add the amount to your card.

The regenerator accepted bills in the denominations of $1, $5, $10, and $20. It did not give change like the bill acceptor on the Metro. The bill acceptor was exceptionally sensitive. It would not accept bills with any slight crease or smidgeon of dirt or, sometimes, just because it didn't like the bill.

In the 2000's, the Copy Card was abandoned for a better system. With the advent of the bar-coded researcher identification card, the new card doubled as a Copy Card. There was also an increase in the copier charge: first to fifteen cents per copy, then to twenty cents, and currently to twenty-five cents. The cost of doing research is continually becoming more expensive.

Photocopying Books and Ledgers

Only rarely are restrictions placed upon the photocopying of documents. The only problem that I have ever encountered is with bound volumes. The Archives will not allow books or ledgers to be placed flat down on the glass plate of a photocopier. This protocol is based on the premise that flattening the covers might damage the spine or split the binding – very real concerns, as many archival books and ledgers are old and decrepit.

Even if you can prove that the book will lie flat on its own account, attendants will not allow you to photocopy interior pages (although you may photocopy the covers and spine). They are afraid that in the process of flipping over the book, you might bend or crease some pages, or drop the book and damage it. Most documents in the Archives are one-of-a-kind archival documents that are being saved for posterity. Damage, no matter how slight, can become cumulative with usage over time. It makes sense to protect them.

I have a different theory. By photocopying documents, they are no longer one-of-a-kind. The more copies that are made, the less rare the information becomes. Should an item become lost, stolen, or misfiled, there exists the possibility that the information can be recovered from a researcher's copy.

Archivists have lost sight of the fact that the information *on* a document is generally more valuable than the document itself; that the primary reason for preserving a document is to preserve the information that it bears. The document itself is merely the holder of information.

There are exceptions, such as the Declaration of Independence and the Constitution of the United States, which are noted above, but these exceptions are rare. For the most part, a document is an item made of cellulose pulp whose substance may possess some slight importance to the history or forensic science of paper manufacturing processes, but whose ink is arranged in ways that may make it fabulously significant. In my opinion, the information is more important

National Archives

than the paper on which it is printed.

This perspective exemplifies the quintessential difference between an archivist and an historian. An archivist preserves documents, while an historian preserves history.

My views notwithstanding, throughout most of my research career, I have had to transcribe the text on ledgers onto notepaper. On very rare occasions, an archivist would consent to making a photocopy himself, if I were willing to pay for the service and could wait to have the photocopies sent to my home at a later date.

In the 1990's, the Archives installed overhead scanners that researchers could use to copy pages of books. The bed of the scanner has a flexible groove to accept the spine of a book, and the floating base plate tilts downward. You can open the covers and lightly hold the pages flat with your fingers. The light source is located above. The process is equivalent to taking a picture with a strobe or flashbulb, and printing the resultant image.

The downside is the cost: seventy-five cents per page when photocopies cost ten cents. Now the cost is a dollar fifty per page. The saving grace is the paper size: 11 inches by 16 inches – large enough to copy both facing pages of a standard sized book.

Photocopying Loose Documents

Most documents in file folders are loose. Sometimes several sheets are stapled or clipped together. Occasionally, sheets are hole-punched and secured to a binder by means of metal prongs that are inserted through the holes and bent flat.

Some documents are flimsies. A flimsy is an exceptionally thin sheet of paper that is gauzelike and almost transparent; it was used to make carbon copies.

All these documents may be photocopied, but there is a precise procedure that must be followed in doing so.

Let's say that you open a folder on your workstation. The folder is filled with documents, or sheets of paper. The papers lie on the right side of the folder. You pick up each sheet, flip it over sideways, and lay it face down on the left side of the folder – the same as you would do if you were turning the pages of a book. You come to a document that you would like to photocopy. You place a marker tab around this document.

A marker tab is a folded strip of paper that measures one inch in width by about thirty inches in length. The length is folded in the middle so that each leg measures about fifteen inches. You slip the sheet into the marker tab so that the open ends of the tab protrude beyond the end of the folder. Without rearranging the documents, place the document back where it belongs, and close the folder.

You carry the folder and the box to the central desk. You open the folder to the document in question. You ask if it is okay to photocopy the document. The attendant will examine the document. If it is an ordinary sheet of paper that is in acceptable condition, it will pass this initial inspection. The attendant will read the heading and location label on the box. Under ordinary circumstances, photocopying will be okayed.

You carry the folder and the box back to your workstation. You leave the box at the workstation, and carry the folder to a self-service photocopier that is not in use. You place the folder on the table next to the machine, open the folder to your tabbed document, remove the document from the tab – but leave the tab in place so you know where to return the document to its proper place. Make your copy. Return the document to its proper place, remove the tab, return to your workstation, and proceed to view the rest of the documents in the folder.

This is a time consuming process. Before going to the central desk for approval, look through the entire folder and tab every document that you want to copy. This will make more efficient use of your time.

Special Cases

Occasionally, a central desk attendant will deny

National Archives

you the privilege of photocoping a document. Some documents are deemed too fragile to photocopy: the pulp paper may be crumbling or falling apart merely by handling it, much less flipping it over onto the glass face of a copier. The ancient ink may be so faded that archivists and central desk attendants are afraid that heat from the scanner tube will cause additional fading, making the text illegible.

The fragility of a document is subjective. A document that one attendant believes is too brittle or delicate to photocopy, another and more easy-going attendant may allow you to copy with the admonition to be careful. If one attendant turns you down, wait for a shift change and try again.

Oversized documents may be too large to fit on the scanning glass. I don't know what this has to do with anything, because I have copied such documents one end at a time. Nonetheless, attendants may decide not to let you photocopy such a document. One time, when I was copying an extra long document, an abrasive attendant scolded me for folding the paper. I informed her that the paper had already been folded, and in fact would not have fit in the folder had it not been folded. When I showed her the aged fold, she repeated her reprimand and walked off in a huff.

Documents that *you* are not allowed to photocopy can still be copied, but only by a staff member who has been specially trained to handle fragile materials. You may not be able to have the document copied that day; you may have to tab it and submit a copy request.

Other documents that you may not be permitted to copy are blueprints, charts, maps, and large drawings. A cartographic and architectural research room has special equipment to handle such copying jobs. If a staff member cannot do the job, or if the Archives is not equipped to meet your special requirements, the Archives has authorized certain vendors to make copies for you. Be warned: vendors are expensive.

Photocopying Classified Documents

Some documents may not be copied "as is" because they contain stamped or typewritten words such as Confidential, Secret, or Top Secret. In the old days this was never an issue because – in accordance with the thirty-year rule – an Act of Congress sweepingly declassified all such documents from both world wars, and made them available to the public without restriction.

Throughout the 1970's and early 1980's, I copied numerous documents from World War One that had originally been classified, and no one said a word about it. In 1976, the thirty-year ban expired on World War Two classified documents. My collection is filled with copies of previously classified documents.

For some reason that I am unable to fathom, some time in the 1980's the Archives got a bug about releasing photocopies of once classified documents that had not been individually stamped with a declassification notification – despite the global declassification that was granted by Congress. The date on a document was adequate to signify its automatic declassification. Nonetheless, the Archives developed a phobia about letting these documents pass through its doors into the outside world.

Technically speaking, in order to meet the criteria of its own convention, the Archives should have gone through all of its holdings and placed a declassification stamp or sticker on each and every newly declassified document. However, there are literally millions of such documents. It would have taken hundreds of years and billions of dollars to complete such a task.

Instead of letting well enough alone, the Archives invented a stopgap solution: a central desk attendant would stamp each classified document as it was presented for permission to photocopy, then date and initial the stamp. This useless expedient took time, which equated to a loss of productivity for researchers in the collection of information.

There was an interesting sideline to this senseless procedure. It made me supremely aware of how many documents I was copying that had never been copied – else they would have already been stamped. It goes to show how precious little primary shipwreck research was being conducted, if any. I almost never found a stamped document.

In the 1990's, someone or some committee in the Archives suddenly realized that by stamping and initialing classified documents, they were altering and disfiguring the document. This is a definite no-no in archival protocol. They had to devise a new scheme that did not affect the document's integrity by defacing it. The present system then came into vogue.

Affixed to the glass face of every photocopier in the National Archives is a clear plastic sticker on which is printed in black, "Photocopied at the National Archives." This identifier enables guards to quickly ascertain that the sheet of paper is a copy and not an original document. In addition to this, the photocopiers use only legal-sized paper, which is 14 inches in length instead of 11 inches.

For classified documents, the Archives created another clear plastic sticker on which is printed a standard declassification notation, to which the central desk attendant adds the source information taken from the label on the file box. A length of clear tape is stuck to the back of the sticker, and the sticker is then placed face down on the glass next to the other plastic sticker.

By this means, the photocopy leaves the Archives with a declassification notation.

The Archives is fooling only itself. Legal-sized paper does not fit in my filing cabinet unless it is folded. A folded sheet occupies twice as much space in the drawer as a single sheet. Most of the documents that I copy are standard size. So the first thing I do when I return home from a trip to the Archives is to pull out my flatbed paper trimmer and slice the blank three inches off each sheet of paper. Since I make the copies with the Archives stickers at the blank end, the reproduction notice and declassification sticker go into the trash. Then I file the papers in the proper shipwreck folders.

Photocopy Permutations

If several documents are clipped together, it is a simple matter to remove the paperclip for copying purposes. You must take care to reclip the documents in the original order, not to leave any documents out of the reclipped stack, and not to add documents that do not belong in the clipped stack. Always return the paperclip to its original location, which is marked by the indentations in the sheets.

If several documents are stapled together, you have two choices. You can fold the documents so that only the sheet that you want to copy is placed against the glass. Fold the sheets back one at a time to copy successive sheets. This method is fast but not without complications. If the stack of documents is thick, the end of the sheet that is nearest the staple will not come in contact with the glass, and will therefore be out of range of the scanner's focal point. The text may be blurred or out of focus.

If you press down hard next to the staple, you may be able to bring the text into focus, but you might also crease the paper. Some sheets already have creases because they have previously been copied by this method.

Alternatively, you can ask a central desk attendant to remove the staple. You are not permitted to remove the staple yourself. Attendants used to use a staple remover, but they now believe that this may damage the paper, especially if it is old or flimsy. Instead, they use a pointed metal pry – like a nail file in appearance – with which they straighten the prongs. Then they slide the pry under the top of the staple and lift it out slowly, so that the holes made from the prongs are not torn or enlarged.

Before returning the documents to you for copying, the attendant will fold a small rectangle of stiffened paper over the edge of the stack, and clip it in place. The rectangle of stiffened paper prevents the paperclip from leaving impressions on the documents. Remove the new paperclip at the copier, then replace it after making your copies. Once done, the paperclip replacement is permanent.

If the documents are hole-punched and secured to a binder, the central desk attendant will generally let you straighten the prongs yourself, and remove the topmost documents in order to reach those that you wish to copy. Be careful to replace the documents in order before reassembling the binder.

Bulk Copying

There are limitations on usage of the photocopiers in the Central Research Room. If it's a slow day, and no one is waiting to use a copier, you can copy till your heart's content. But as soon as a line forms – even if the line consists of only one person – then a central desk attendant will announce that there is a three-minute limit on copiers. At the end of three minutes, an attendant will ask the person who has been using a copier the longest, to quit and get at the end of the line. As long as there is a line, the time limit remains at three minutes.

This situation is annoying for all concerned. If there is a line, tab documents and continue your research instead of standing in line for a copier. Wait until the rush is over, then copy your tabbed documents all at once.

If you find that there are a large number of documents that you would like to photocopy, you can make special arrangements to use the Archives bulk copier in a separate room. You may have to make these arrangements a day in advance, but if the bulk copier is unoccupied, or if there are holidays between appointments, you may gain access shortly after submitting your request. Documents to be photocopied still have to be examined by an attendant for suitability.

Central Desk Attendants

After you have perused all your documents, return the cart to the central desk. You can have these documents held for up to three days, for later reference, or you can turn them in with finality. You can then ask the attendant if there are any other call slips in your name. If so, you can start the process over again.

The attendants are there to assist you. If you have trouble with a copier, or when it runs out of paper, ask an attendant for assistance. They will be glad to help.

The attendants are also there to enforce the rules of engagement. Like State troopers, most of them are courteous but not very friendly. When they are not minding the desk, they rove around the room and stare over people's shoulders to ensure that they are complying with all the rules and regulations.

Some of them delight in reproving people for minor infractions. With these attendants, courtesy ends and gruffness begins when they catch you bending a rule. Some attendants have developed rules of their own that are not National Archives rules, yet they enforce them just the same. They give you a hard time when you ask to copy documents, or they watch over you at the copier. They might even rebuke you for mishandling documents when you are in fact exercising care.

These are the attendants who abuse their authority because they can get away with it. You'll learn who they are very quickly. Avoid the sticklers who have personal grudges. If you need permission to copy documents, wait until they are away from the central desk before approaching it. If you see them approaching you, either at your workstation or at the copier, stop what you are doing, and do nothing until they pass. They are looking for the slightest excuse to admonish you on your putative misconduct. Don't give them any.

Alternative Copying Methods

You are permitted to take a laptop computer into the Central Research Room. Make sure you have your equipment receipt with you at all times, for you will have to produce it upon leaving the room with your equipment. This is to prevent someone from stealing another person's equipment. Many people take notes on a computer instead of on paper. I can type much faster than I can write, and my typing is easier to read than my cursive.

I am a fanatic about backups. Too many times during my writing career my computer has malfunctioned and lost data. Save your data frequently throughout the day by pressing Control S. Better yet, go to the File tab at the top left of your screen, and do a Save As under a different name (or add a version number to the original name). That way, if your file is corrupted, you have another file which has most of your data.

Better yet, periodically copy your files onto a memory stick. That way, if your computer crashes, you still have the results of a hard day's work.

Certain types of scanners are permitted in the Central Research Room. To quote the Archives restrictions, "The copying surface (platen) must be the same size or larger than the record; the scanner must not cause friction, abrasion, or otherwise damage records; light sources must not generate heat on the records; and equipment surfaces must be clean and dry before being used. Drum and automatic feeder scanners are prohibited."

You may also bring cameras into the Central Research Room. Flash photography is prohibited – because archivists and central desk attendants are afraid that the intense flash of light might damage fragile paper or ink – so bring high-speed film instead of a strobe. Better yet is a digital camera. I have had great success with making digital images of documents, then printing hard copies at home.

A mid-range digital camera will have a close-focusing feature. If I anticipate taking pictures, I choose a workstation near a window. I take a picture of the entire page; then, if necessary, I take close-up pictures of sections of the page so that the sections overlap and can be pieced together.

A digital camera can also be used to photograph documents that are fragile or oversized, because the restrictions that apply to those documents have to do with handling, not with copying. I now use my digital camera to photograph pages in books, instead of using the expensive overhead scanner. These copies are essentially free (except for paper and toner, which are incidental), so I save a great deal of money.

You are allowed to bring a tripod or camera stand into the Central Research Room, but not a copy stand. These tools enable you to work quickly and easily. Once the camera is set for the proper distance from the document, you don't have to waste time and energy on focusing. This beats having to bend over the document with your camera in your hand, swaying while you try to get the image in focus and at the proper distance in order to capture a picture of the page in its entirety.

Bring extra batteries and memory cards if you expect to take a lot of pictures.

Keeping Good Records

I reiterate: a researcher is only as good as his research assistant, or the one who is assigned to him that day.

Once I visited the Archives on a day when all the regular research assistants were out. One of my requests was for annual reports of the Life Saving Service. These volumes used to be on a shelf in the Old Coast Guard office, where they were readily accessible to researchers and research assistants. In those days, I was allowed to photocopy a few pages for free on the staff copier. Then the higher-ups decided that the set needed to be boxed and stored in the stacks at Archives Two. Now, in order to see these books, I have to travel to a different city and fill out a call slip. When I get them, I am no longer allowed to photocopy pages on the flatbed copier as I used to do; I have to use the expensive overhead scanner.

My problem on this day was worse. The substitute research assistants could not find the books. They went so far as to inform me that they did not exist in the Archives holdings. Had I been a novice researcher, and had I not already requested these books on numerous occasions, I would have shrugged it off and accepted

National Archives

their counsel.

I knew otherwise. I had requested the books several months previous. The substitutes disagreed, but I was persistent. They scoured the Archives computerized listings; they went through the sign-in sheets that were filed on the Archives database to see when I last visited the facility; they even took me into the staff room in order to join a general discussion among other research assistants about the existence and possible location of these books. None of them knew anything about these annual volumes.

I swore that I requested these books all the time. I described them, and I described the boxes in which they were stored. Finally, late in the afternoon, they found my previous call slip on which the location was given, and they pulled the books from the stacks. We all learned something that day.

Research assistants are not infallible. I always relied on them implicitly to find what I wanted. Perhaps I had become complacent because this situation had never arisen. I did not appreciate until then the necessity to record all citations for future reference. I just figured that the next research assistant would know where to look. If this situation should recur, I can inform the research assistant to look in RG 287, Stack 150, Row A, Compartment 68, Shelf 3, T24.1 boxes T653-658, and hope that the books have not been moved.

It is equally important to record the Record Groups, titles, and locations of records that you researched, and to keep notes on what you found in those records. If they proved useful, you might want to refer to them again. If they were useless, you want to remind yourself that you already looked through them and didn't find anything of value.

Done for the Day

Once your research is completed, or if a central desk attendant announces that the National Archives will soon be closing, it is time to turn in your records and gather your materials.

Return your pencil, marking tabs, and any unused notepaper. Hand your research card and all your documents to the guard. The guard will look at each and every sheet of paper to determine that you are not trying to sneak out with any original documents.

One time a guard discovered that of the hundred or so photocopies that I had made that day, one did not carry a declassification stamp. The entire bundle was confiscated. I was not allowed to keep any of the photocopies because they all had to be turned over to an archivist for approval. I was told that they would be mailed to me. In the event, they beat me home, since I spent the rest of the week doing research in DC.

Assuming that you successfully pass muster with the Central Research Room guard, you can then reclaim your personal belongings from your locker. In the lobby, another guard will inspect your baggage, your documents, and your electronic devices. Make sure to have your equipment receipts readily accessible.

You have just completed a successful day's research. Or have you?

Pull Times

Over the years, as researchers have proliferated, the National Archives has done its best to make research as difficult, inefficient, and time consuming as possible. The process of conducting research becomes more restrictive with each passing day. Practically every time I visit the Archives, some procedure has been tightened to make research more laborious and inconvenient, or some new policy has been implemented to make researchers waste more of their time.

In working assiduously toward the achievement of this goal, the Archives has now instituted an impediment known as pull times. Whereas records used to be pulled as soon as the research assistant checked the call slips for accuracy, now records are pulled only according to an inflexible and inexpedient time sched-

National Archives

ule: 10:00 a.m., 11 a.m., 1:30 p.m., and 2:30 p.m.

While this system reduces the workload for pullers, and indirectly reduces the workload for research assistants, it severely limits the amount of research that a researcher can do in a day.

As if this were not bad enough, researchers are allowed to have records pulled from only one Record Group for each pull. If the research assistant identifies file boxes from five Record Groups that may contain information about your project, you can see only four of them that day.

The reality is even worse. Let's say that you arrive at the Archives in the morning, go through the metal detector and x-ray machine, sign the book at the guard station, get a new equipment receipt for your digital camera, store your belongings in a locker, visit the restroom, sign in at the desk of the Navy/Maritime Team, and wait for the research assistants to finish identifying records for other researchers. You explain the nature of your research. You spend time looking through finding aids. You fill out call slips. You hand your call slips to a research assistant. He looks them over, adds location information, okays them with his initials, and places them in the pull box.

By now the time is one minute after 10 o'clock. The research assistant advises you that you have missed the 10 o'clock pull, and will have to wait for the next pull, at 11 o'clock. It takes an hour or more for the puller to retrieve your records from the stacks, so you have two hours in which to twiddle your thumbs. Finally, after noon, your records are delivered. You spend some time in going through the file boxes. Perhaps you find some useful information; perhaps you don't.

You turn in your cart and return to the Navy/Maritime Team office. All the research assistants are out to lunch. You wait around until someone returns to help you. You repeat the morning procedure, and identify some more records that might be responsive to your needs. You fill out call slips. By now, 1:30 has come and gone. You have missed the first afternoon pull, and must wait for the 2:30 pull to turn in your call slips.

Around 3:30 your cart is delivered. You quickly ascertain that the boxes contain no information that relates to your project. You are at a dead end. You can return to the Navy/Maritime Team office and speak with a research assistant, but it is already too late to have any more records pulled that afternoon. You are advised to come back some other day.

Your net gain for the day is zero, zilch, nothing, nil, nada.

Compare this to the early days that I described above. Sure, I had to put on considerable mileage by traveling between the offices in 19E and 19W. But without scheduled pull times, records were retrieved continuously and immediately upon request. Without restrictions on the number of Record Groups that I could access, I could line up a whole day's work. I could also return to the offices at any time and ask for additional records.

Records were delivered to the Central Research Room on an ongoing basis. Once I sat down at my workstation, I could plan on a constant flow of records to peruse throughout the day. Except for brief breaks, I could accomplish nearly eight solid hours of research. My pants pockets were stuffed with plastic bags that held crackers or bread, slices of pepperoni, and bite-sized chunks of cheese. I nibbled a mouthful at a time by looking around and seeing that no guards or attendants were looking in my direction. I left the room only to cycle liquids (some in, some out).

Research was never easy, but it has become a more formidable task than the twelve labors of Hercules. Archives policies need cleaning more than the Augean stables. The present system subverts the efforts of dedicated staff members, and is counterproductive for researchers who travel long distances at great expense for the opportunity to unearth significant moments of the nation's rich history.

The National Archives keeps suggestion boxes located strategically throughout its facilities. Time and

National Archives

again I have dropped notes in these boxes, calling attention to the stupidity of the pull time system. Apparently the suggestion boxes are just for show, for no one has paid any mind to the logic of my comments about how strong a deterrent the pull time system is against successful research.

After Hours

The main problem for part-time researchers is that nearly all research facilities are open only during business hours on weekdays. People who have full-time occupations must give up a day's work – and consequently a day's pay – to conduct primary research. Although the National Archives may seem like an exception to this rule – by offering occasional evening hours and by opening its doors on Saturday – these extended hours are deceptive.

Days with extended hours have changed throughout the years. Never were there more than two days per week with extended hours. On those days, the Central Research Room stays open until 9 p.m. This means that you can keep looking through records after 5 o'clock on extended days, and all day on Saturday.

The gimmick is this: you cannot have records retrieved from the stacks during these extended hours or on Saturday. No research assistants or record pullers are on duty – only attendants at the central desk.

On those weekdays that have extended hours, another pull time is scheduled for 3:30 p.m. This extra pull enables researchers to access five Record Groups in one day. Otherwise, your research is limited to examining records that you already had pulled and put on hold. To do research on Saturday, you have to go to the Archives on Friday afternoon in order to have records pulled and held.

These extended hours options are not much help for out-of-towners with jobs.

When the Archives stays open late, the Microfilm Research Room is also open late. This is largely self-service research, although knowledgeable staff members are always on duty to assist researchers in using the finding aids, locating microfilms, loading the readers, and printing copies.

Segue to Archives Two

The best way to reach the downtown DC building is by Metro. If you are driving to Washington, park your vehicle in a suburban Metro station parking lot, and take the subway into town. Depending upon where you start, you may have to transfer to a different colored line. Exit at the station named Archives/Navy Memorial. Seats are at a premium during rush hour, when you are competing with commuters, but the ride is smooth and effortless. Reverse your route to return to your point of origin.

Traffic in DC during the commuter rush is like it is in any other big city: slow to no go. Parking near the building is practically impossible unless you arrive at oh-dark-hundred. Some street parking is available, but because of meter restrictions, you have to keep running outside to move your vehicle to another spot. You are not allowed to leave your vehicle in the same spot beyond the allowable time limit, even if you put more money in the meter; your vehicle will be either ticketed or towed.

If the parking garages are not full, bring an extra arm and leg to pay the fee.

For out-of-towners who are driving from the north to the downtown facility, an excellent option is to park at Archives Two in College Park, then take the free shuttle bus to Archives One.

If you are flying into the DC area and must take lodging at a hotel, make long-term loan arrangements with your bank prior to departure, or take a second mortgage on your house.

By contrast, Archives Two is like an island paradise. Personally, I will be glad when all the holdings that I commonly access are transferred to the new facility. The building is sequestered in a vast rustic area

National Archives 107

that is thickly forested with hardwoods. Autumn foliage rivals a painter's palette for color.

Parking is free in the underground garage or in the weather above it. On those rare occasions when the garage is full, overflow parking is available along the meandering driveway that connects the building with the highway.

Hotels can be found within a couple of miles of the building, at rates that are far more affordable than downtown hotels.

I generally bring a lunch, but both Archives One and Two have cafeterias and coffee shops for staff members and the public. If you bring your own lunch, you are allowed to eat it in the cafeteria. In Archives One, the cafeteria is located in the basement. In Archives Two, the cafeteria is located on Level 1 (the ground floor).

It is worth going to Archives Two just to see the building.

The protruding section of glasswork is the lobby. The researchers' entrance to Archives Two is through the glass doors in the middle. Researchers work in the structure to the right. Everything else contains storage areas and administrative offices. Buses drive around the tree-filled circle. The parking garage is behind the camera.

Archives Two Protocols

Working at Archives Two is not much different from working at Archives One. After going through the metal detector and x-ray machine, and showing your research card to the armed guard, you enter a huge lobby that is reminiscent of a scene from a futuristic science fiction movie. This ground floor is called Level 1. Archives Two does not require researchers to wear a visitor's pass or badge.

If you do not already have a researcher identification card, you can obtain one in the Researcher Registration room a few feet to the right. In this same room you must have your notepapers stamped and dated.

From the central desk in the lobby, you must obtain an equipment pass if you have any cameras, computers, or other devices. In its wisdom, Archives Two does not recognize equipment passes from Archives One – although it does recognize your research card (and any copy credit that is embedded in it).

Take the extraordinarily long flight of stairs down to the basement, which is called Level B, where the locker room is located. Store your personal belongings. Then climb the stairs back up to the lobby. Now you must go through a guard station, or security checkpoint. The guard will scan your research card, and examine your notepapers and equipment.

Proceed to the elevator bank. The Cashier is situated adjacent to the elevators. Ride an elevator car or walk up the steps in the fire escape to the appropriate level. The Textual Research Room is located on Level 2. This vast room is equivalent to the Central Research Room *and* the Navy/Maritime Team office combined. Instead of running back and forth between floors and rooms, as in Archives One, you could spend your entire day in this one room (except for breaks).

Restrooms and water fountains are located right outside the door, opposite the elevator bank. There are pay phones there as well. Once you sign in, you may pass freely out of and into the room, as long as you are not carrying any papers with you. Papers must be

National Archives

examined going either in or out.

Copy credit regenerators are located behind the central desk.

Workstations consist of quadruplex tables. Each rectangular table is divided into quarters by glass partitions. Each workstation is equipped with a lamp and a duplex electrical outlet. Some of the tables are located beneath an eight-foot ceiling that is brightly illuminated with fluorescent fixtures. Where the low ceiling ends, the upper ceiling rises to a height of fifty feet. The entire front wall of this room consists of glass that rises to the full height of the ceiling, and that extends more than one hundred feet in width. Researchers have a wonderful view of the sky above a hardwood forest.

For convenience, research assistants and finding aids are located in offices on the inside facing of the room. The document retrieval station is situated adjacent to these offices. After a research assistant identifies your records, and you fill out your call slips, you can select a workstation and wait for your records to be pulled. Attendants do not announce the delivery of records because the room is so huge. You have to check periodically at the reference desk.

The same rules for viewing and photocopying documents at Archives One apply to Archives Two. Attendants at a central station will examine documents prior to photocopying on the four copiers that are available to researchers. The bulk copiers are located in the same room. The desk attendants at Archives Two are more friendly than the desk attendants at Archives One.

Although they are quite knowledgeable, occasionally the research assistants in the office will determine that you require more expertise than they can provide, and will suggest the name of an archivist who can assist you better. A research assistant will give you a special visitor's badge and escort you to a locked door at the end of the room. The research assistant's badge will unlock this door, but yours will not. The research assistant will accompany you to a lobby and leave you in the care of a receptionist. Sign the sign-in book, and wait for the archivist whom the research assistant requested.

The archivist may be working with another researcher at the time, or he or she may be in the stacks identifying documents. Generally you won't have to wait more than a few minutes. When he arrives, he will escort you to a room that houses more finding aids than are available in the outer office. You and he will sit down at a table and discuss the nature of your research. He may have to leave the room temporarily to look in the stacks, or to access a database on his computer terminal. Sometimes he will take you to his cubicle so you can work together on locating records.

After the call slips are filled out, the archivist will either escort you back to the locked door that separates the archivists' office area from the Textual Research Room, or he will send you on your way by yourself. Your badge will open the door in this direction.

If you need to review research materials that you left in your locker, or if you want to retrieve your lunch, you have to walk down the fire escape or take the elevator down from Level 2 to Level 1, check out through the guard station, then walk down the stairs to Level B. The researchers' elevators do not go to Level B.

Multi-Level Research

Other archival holdings are located on other levels. Level 3 has the Cartographic and Architectural Research Room, and a Library. Level 4 has the Microfilm Research Room, and the Motion Picture, Sound, and Video Research Room. Level 5 has the Still Picture Research Room. Level 6 has the Classified Research Room and the Electronic Records Research Room.

In order to make efficient use of my time while waiting for the delivery of records in the Textual Research Room, I run up (literally – I rarely wait for the elevator because it is so slow) to the Still Picture Research Room on Level 5. I do photographic research and turn in call slips, then go down to Level 2 to review records that were pulled during my absence. Meanwhile, the photos

National Archives

are being pulled on Level 5.

The pull system applies in Archives Two the same as it does in Archives One, except that there is no coordination between textual research and still picture research. Pictures are organized in categories, but a researcher may ask for the retrieval of pictures in any number and from any category. I will discuss picture research in a dedicated chapter called Picture Sources.

Cartographic and Architectural Research

A dedicated research room on Level 3 in Archives Two holds plans of Navy vessels: deck arrangements, cross sections, outboard profiles, inboard profiles, rigging plans, and so on. You can view plans in the room.

In the 1970's, when I started diving heavily on the *San Diego*, I purchased all the construction plans of this fascinating armored cruiser. These plans were of invaluable help to me in making penetrations through the collapsing wreck, in ascertaining entrances and escape routes beforehand, and in knowing the functions of the compartments that I was exploring.

Some of these plans measured seven feet in length. Special equipment is required to copy them in full scale. They were also available at half scale. Copies are quite expensive.

In *U.S.S. San Diego: the Last Armored Cruiser*, I provided a list of the available plans. When some of my readers attempted to buy the plans, they found that one of them was missing. (I forget which one.) Archives staff members had no explanation for its disappearance. All the *San Diego* plans were rolled together. Researchers are permitted to view only one set of plans at a time. My guess is that the missing plan got rolled up with a set of plans of a different vessel, when a research assistant was replacing it after it had been pulled for copying. This plan will remain misfiled until someone pulls the plans for that other vessel, and notices a plan that doesn't belong there.

Microfilm

Microfilm reels can be pulled at any time by the researcher. A research assistant is always in the room to help in deciphering the finding aids, explaining the filing system, loading the reel on the spindle, and threading the leader onto the take-up spool. I generally squeeze my microfilm research into the dead time when I am waiting for the delivery of textual records.

Microfilms that may be of interest to shipwreck researchers are split between the two buildings.

Level 4 in Archives Two holds U-boat deck logs from both world wars. The deck logs were captured when the Allies invaded Berlin in 1945. Germany maintains the original deck logs, but British intelligence personnel microfilmed them and made copies for archival purposes.

The last time I accessed them, the microfilms of old Coast Guard records were housed in Archives One. There is a slow flow of records from One to Two. I have never known of records that were transferred to Archives Two to be returned to Archives One. Check with the Navy/Maritime Team before going there.

Those microfilms that may be of interest to shipwreck researchers are:

T-720 – U.S. Coast Guard Reports of Assistance to Individuals and Vessels 1916-1940 (247 rolls).

T-919 – Index by District to U.S. Coast Guard Reports of Assistance 1917-1938 (19 rolls).

T-920 – Index by Station to U.S. Coast Guard Reports of Assistance 1924-1938 (7 rolls).

T-921 – Index by Floating Unit to U.S. Coast Guard Reports of Assistance 1917-1935 (5 rolls).

T-925 – U.S. Coast Guard Casualty and Wreck Reports 1913-1939 (21 rolls).

T-926 – Index to U.S. Coast Guard Casualty and Wreck Reports 1913-1939 (7 rolls).

M-1052 – Secretary of the Navy/Adjutant General Board of Inquiries and Courts-Martial.

M-1160 – Maury Abstract of Logs 1796-1861.

National Archives

In both facilities, microfilm readers and copiers are available on a first come, first served basis. Rules and procedures differ between facilities.

In Archives Two, if you know in advance that you will want to make copies, inform the research assistant and you will be permitted to view the microfilm on a combination reader/copier. Otherwise, use a dedicated reader.

In Archives One, you must first view the microfilm on a reader. After finding a microfilm page that you would like to copy, you remove the primary reel and the take-up reel from their spindles, carry the two reels (with the draped microfilm between them) to a microfilm copier, load the reels on the spindles, adjust the frames and the focus, and make your copy. If you want copies of consecutive pages, you may advance the film and make additional copies. If you need to search for more frames to copy, you must return the reels to your reader until you identify additional pages.

The microfilm copiers accept your research card for payment. Copies made from microfilm presently cost fifty cents per page. The copier can usually copy two consecutive pages at a time on a large sheet of paper.

The Movies

Level 4 in Archives Two also has a room for the storage of motion pictures. The holdings include, for example, old newsreel footage of burning tankers during World War Two, Coast Guard aerial footage of the sinking of the *Andrea Doria*, and official documentary footage of the destruction of the *Ostfriesland* and *Frankfurt* by Billy Mitchell's bombers.

The finding aids are difficult to use. Staff members are helpful and will point you in the right direction, but you have to sift through the finding aids yourself.

These movies were shot on 16-millimeter film, but the ones that I have watched have been transferred onto videocassettes. There is no pull time system, as the videocassettes are stored in drawers in filing cabinets that are located right in the room.

Videocassette viewers are available on a first come, first served basis. If you want to make dupes, you may bring your own duplicating equipment subject to approval, or you may rent an on-site duplicator by the hour. You can also hire a vendor make duplicates for you.

Regional Archives

On one trip to the National Archives, my list of research topics included the World War Two records of the Fourth Naval District. This district was headquartered in Philadelphia. Its area of responsibility spanned from southern New Jersey through Delaware to the *Winter Quarter Shoal* Light Vessel. When I described my research objectives to the research assistant, he informed me that any such records – if they existed – would be found at the Regional Archives for the Mid-Atlantic Region, which was located in Philadelphia.

I said, "Do you mean to tell me that I drove three hours this morning to get here from Philadelphia, only to have you tell me that the records I want are less than ten miles from my house?"

He said, "Yes." He gave me the contact information.

After several days of research at various DC facilities, I went home and called the Philadelphia branch to get directions and their hours of operation, and to schedule an appointment. I visited the Regional Archives the following week. When I explained the nature of my research to the research assistant, he was dumbstruck. No one had ever asked for Fourth Naval District records before.

I thought that was odd. I indicated the half a dozen researchers who were examining records in the small reading room. "What are *they* researching?"

"Genealogy." He told me that practically all research at the Philadelphia branch was genealogical research. I was the rare exception. And since that was the branch's specialty, he had no idea if the branch's holdings included Fourth Naval District records. The finding aids showed no such listings.

National Archives

Serendipity

The research assistant invited me to walk with him through the stacks. We checked a few areas without finding anything relevant. Then, as we passed one aisle, the white labels on one of the file boxes caught my eye. There were three boxes of World War Two records that related to U-boat casualties: precisely what I was looking for. Or so I thought.

These three file boxes were not listed in the finding aid because they had never been catalogued. We never found anything relating to the Fourth Naval District, but when I asked if I could see the contents of these three files boxes, he said, "Sure." We grabbed them and carried them to the reading room.

What I discovered was a virtual goldmine: data sheets and black and white glossy prints of vessels that had been attacked by German U-boats off the U.S. eastern seaboard. Some of the photos showed the vessels in flames; some were stock photos of the vessels prior to attack. Many of the photos I had never seen before, either in the DC facilities or in any museum.

I had not come prepared for this bonanza. I returned two days later with my camera and copy stand. It took me a day and a half to photograph the prints and photocopy the data sheets.

After I was done with the records, the research assistant returned the boxes to their original location. He did not catalogue them. There are no negative numbers for these pictures. I am the only researcher who ever saw them. I am the only researcher with copies of the pictures and data sheets.

Back to the Regional Archives

I was making a point before my diversion into serendipity. Not all the records that are held by the National Archives are stored in the DC or College Park facilities. The National Archives maintains regional branches to house records that are likely to be of interest to people who live in the area. Thus the Philadelphia branch holds local genealogical records, so that people who are researching their ancestors do not have to travel to DC to do so.

The thirteen Regional Archives are located in or near major cities: Anchorage, Alaska; Atlanta, Georgia; Boston, Massachusetts; Chicago, Illinois; Denver, Colorado; Fort Worth, Texas; Kansas City, Missouri; Laguna Niguel, California; New York, New York; Philadelphia, Pennsylvania; Pittsfield, Massachusetts; San Francisco, California; and Seattle, Washington.

Don't overlook them when doing local research.

Serendipitous Research

Many are the times that I was looking for one thing and found another. The incident that I recounted two sections previous is a prime case in point. I suppose that if you are researching hundreds of shipwrecks instead of just one, this is eventually bound to happen. But it never ceases to amaze me how I discover information about a wreck in a file which, had I been looking for it intentionally, I probably would not have located it.

Whenever this happens, I stop what I am doing and photocopy the fortuitously found documents. Then I proceed with my original quest.

I call this coincidental happenstance "serendipitous research."

Archives Anecdotes

Some of my experiences in the National Archives are not only interesting, but informative and instructional.

For example, once when I requested Custom House records, I learned that some of the documents were not available to researchers. Angie Spicer, the research assistant, helped me to fill out call slips for those documents that *were* available. In the Central Research Room, I received several king-size horizontal boxes in which the sheets of paper were laid flat. Each sheet was separately sealed in a clear plastic sheet protector, much like slices of sandwich cheese in individual wrap-

National Archives

pers. I was able to see both sides of each sheet.

The curious thing about these sheets is that they were badly burned around the edges. The sheets had originally been rectangular pages of a large ledger. Each disbound page was now misshapen, and some of the text near the edges was missing.

Afterward, out of curiosity, I asked Spicer about the singed condition of the pages. She informed me that the ledgers had been burned in a Customs House fire, and that they were in the process of being conserved. When I asked for the date of the fire, she told me that it had taken place in 1932!

I conducted this research in the early 1990's. The Archives had been working on the conservation of these ledgers for sixty years! The other ledgers were not available to researchers because they had not yet been conserved due to staff and time limitations. For all I know, they are still working to conserve those ledgers.

On another occasion, in the downtown facility I found an annotation which stated that the Archives held the cargo manifest of the *John Morgan*. This freighter sank off the mouth of the Chesapeake Bay in 1943 after a collision with the tanker *Montana*. John Vandereedt, the research assistant, took me into the stacks in order to confirm the existence of the manifest. The so-called stacks consisted of massive, dimly lit rooms whose ceilings arched more than 20 feet overhead. Steel shelving units reached nearly to the ceiling, and stretched for hundreds of feet along claustrophobically narrow corridors. Each shelf was filled with file boxes that were stored three deep.

Vandereedt pulled the appropriate box and found the manifest in question. When I asked if the Archives held manifests for every voyage of every American vessel, he explained that only certain manifests from World War Two were in the holdings. The *John Morgan* was headed for Bandar Shahpour, an Iranian port on the Persian Sea, with a lend-lease cargo of war materiel that was consigned to Russia.

The reason the manifest had been kept for all these

years was that Russia had never paid for the cargo! The manifest was proof of the unpaid bill. In light of Cold War hostility and communist aggression, I thought that the possibility of Russia anteing up after all these years was slim to none – and Slim left town. Vandereedt chuckled in agreement.

In the early 1980's, I called for a group of photographs of the *Sumner*. What I got was a package that was wrapped in brown shopping-bag paper and tied with string like a doughnut box. I considered the likelihood that this package had probably never been opened since the pictures had been archived after the *Sumner* stranded in 1916. When I saw these pictures again after the Still Picture Branch was moved to College Park, they were boxed like all the other pictures. Changes such as this are ongoing.

In the 1970's, one day's objective was to go through my list of wrecks for which I wanted to obtain pictures. I was working intently when Jim Trimble, the sole research assistant in the Still Picture Branch, said that I had only fifteen minutes left. I didn't wear a watch, but I realized that I was getting pretty hungry. Although Trimble sometimes let me stay in the stacks when he went to lunch, he wasn't supposed to let me. I figured on eating the sandwich that was in my briefcase. When I mentioned this to Trimble, he told me that it was not fifteen minutes till lunchtime, but fifteen minutes till closing!

I had been so enraptured by the pictures I was finding that I had worked straight through lunch without knowing it.

Research *can* be exciting.

Naval Historical Center

The Washington Navy Yard is the repository for U.S. Navy archival records. The Yard is an active Navy base that is located on the shore of the Anacostia River, a few miles upstream from its confluence with the Potomac River. Entry to the base is determined by the degree of terrorist threat. I am happy to report that after years of denied or restricted access, visitors may again drive onto the base by simply showing a valid photo ID such as a driver's license.

Getting There is Half the Battle

Until the terrorist attacks on the Pentagon and the World Trade Centers – on September 11, 2001 – the initial difficulty for researchers entering the base was finding a place to park. Parking has always been woefully inadequate, although the recent construction of a multi-level parking garage for assigned personnel has somewhat alleviated the problem. There were times when researchers had to park off base in unattended dirt lots.

Whether driving or walking, visitors are allowed to use only certain entrances (or perhaps only one entrance) to the Yard. The allowable gate has changed throughout the years, so I suggest that you call for instructions prior to your planned visit. The Shore Patrol guards all gates.

The easiest way to get to the Yard is to drive. Find your way onto Interstate 295, on the east side of the Anacostia River. Exit at the 11th Street Bridge (an overhead sign also says Navy Yard). Get in the right lane. As soon as you cross the river, exit right, then follow the signs to whichever gate is open.

There are ways to get there by going through DC, but they are difficult to describe and are always laden with traffic. The most viable through-town route is Interstate 395, which becomes the Southwest-Southeast Freeway. Exit the freeway onto 6th Street, and follow a complicated set of twists and turns that even an

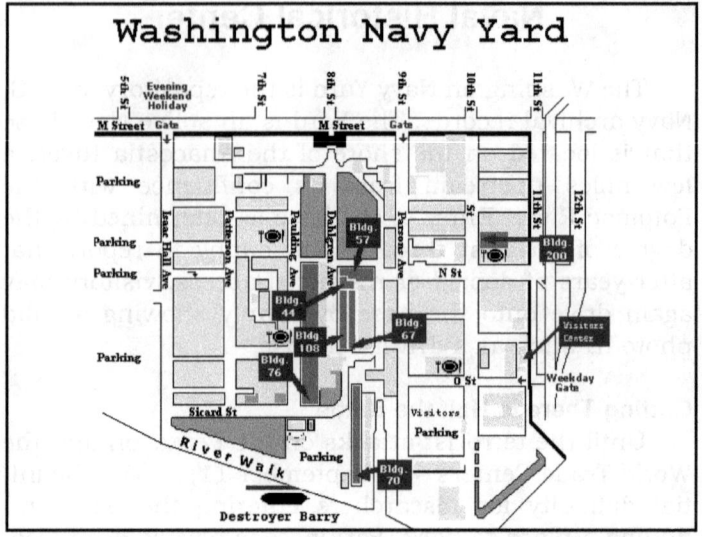

Layout of the Washington Navy Yard. The Operational Archives is located in Building 57. The Navy Department Library is located in Building 44. The Naval Photographic Center is located in Building 108. Ships History Branch is located in Building 200. (Courtesy of the Naval Historical Center.) Although this map is a recent download, when I visited the Yard several months ago, the so-called weekday gate on O Street was barricaded; this gate is conveniently located at the bottom of the exit ramp from the bridge over the Anacostia River. The gate that was open for visitors at that time was the one on N Street. Visitors are no longer allowed to park in the so-called Visitors Parking lot. The visitor's gate is subject to change, so call and ask. Then ask the guard at the gate where visitors are allowed to park.

onboard GPS unit has difficulty in tracking: at the bottom of the ramp proceed straight, turn right onto 8th Street SE, turn right onto M Street SE, turn left onto 6th Street SE, and enter the M Street gate (if that is the visitor's gate at the time of your visit). Otherwise, try the 9th Street gate, or turn right onto 11th Street and try the N Street gate or the O Street gate.

It is important to remember that DC is a ten-mile square that is divided into four quadrants: Northeast, Southeast, Southwest, and Northwest. If you find yourself on 6th Street NE instead of 6th Street SE, you are in the wrong quadrant. Read the street signs carefully.

Ask the guard at the gate about visitor parking. Visitors are permitted to park only in specified lots and spots. You will need a parking permit. The last time I

Naval Historical Center

visited the Yard, the lot on the map that is designated for Visitors Parking was closed to visitors, and was reserved for assigned personnel, as well as nearly all the other parking lots. Parking for visitors of all kinds rarely exceeds a dozen. Your vehicle will be ticketed or towed if it is parked in a non-visitor lot or spot. The Shore Patrol patrols constantly for violators.

The most convenient place for researchers to park is in one of the handful of spots that are designated for visitors in front of Building 57. Enter the building and go to the second floor to obtain a parking permit. Go back outside and place the permit on your dashboard.

Mass transit access is difficult at best. The closest approach of the Metro subway is a twenty-five minute hike from the yard: pleasant in spring and autumn, but frigid in winter and insufferably hot and humid in summer.

Touching All Four Bases

Most historians, librarians, and research assistants are civilians. The staff is overseen by officers, but you won't see them because they are engaged in administrative work. You may encounter some sailors working as clerks in the Operational Archives.

There are four facilities in the Yard in which to conduct research. All four of them used to be housed under the same roof – although, technically speaking, they were located in three different buildings. Let me explain.

The Ships History Branch and the Operational Archives were located in Building 57: Ships History Branch on the first floor, and Operational Archives on the third floor. By walking straight ahead and down a flight of steps, what appears to be a hallway is actually a roofed-over connecting corridor to Building 44, which houses the Library. You reach the Naval Photographic Center by climbing up a flight of steps from the Library, and proceeding along a narrow covered passageway to Building 108. You will never know that you went from one building to another.

I will cover the Naval Photographic Center in the chapter on Picture Sources.

Navy Department Library

The Library is an awesome collection of naval and maritime books that is the best that I have ever seen: more than 150,000 volumes. Browsing is heartily suggested. To locate a specific title, the card catalogue has now been replaced by a computer database that is user friendly. One or two librarians are always on hand to lend friendly assistance.

The Library contains primary publications such as the *Annual Report to the Secretary of the Navy*. Inform a librarian of the nature of your research, and he or she will be glad to help you locate volumes that you might not think to look for among such extensive holdings.

This is not a lending library so you cannot borrow books (unless you are assigned to the Yard in an official capacity). The outer door to the Library in Building 44 may be locked. I always enter through Building 57. The Library is open only on weekdays. No research assistance is available on Wednesday, although the Library is open for browsing.

Ships History Branch

This Branch has been plucked from the tree and re-rooted a couple of blocks away in Building 200, next to the Subway: a convenient and reliable eatery. You can enter the vestibule but the inner door is locked. Press the buzzer for assistance. A staff member will unlock the door, instruct you to leave your outerwear and personal belongings in a locker in the vestibule, and escort you to the specialty of your choice: ships or aviation. You can bring notepapers with you. Sign the sign-in book.

The Ships History Branch keeps a folder on almost every major Navy vessel that was ever commissioned. Folders on eighteenth-century and early nineteenth-century vessels may be slim. Folders on small auxiliary craft may be non-existent. This latter category includes

Naval Historical Center

unarmed tugs, oilers, and yard craft, plus small warships such as patrol boats, minesweepers, and sub chasers.

The *Dictionary of American Naval Fighting Ships* was written from the records in the Ships History Branch. More detailed information will be found in the file folders than was published in DANF. Furthermore, because DANF is rife with errors and omissions, you can obtain a more accurate and complete history of a Navy vessel by accessing the primary source materials.

This Branch also holds the Deck Log Section. However, as the section holds deck logs for only the previous thirty years, it is not much use to shipwreck researchers. Older deck logs are archived at the National Archives.

The staff members at the Ships History Branch are friendly and accommodating. They even let me use the photocopier without charge. I do not abuse the privilege.

The Ships History Branch is open on weekdays except for Wednesday.

Operational Archives

In the 1970's and 1980's, the room that was designated as the Research Room of the Operational Archives faced south, and was not air-conditioned. It was a sweatbox in summer even with the windows open. I learned to plan my visits for seasons when the climate was more tolerable.

In those days, though, when Bernard Cavalcante and Mike Walker ran the show, the Operational Archives was a virtuous and valuable institution that was devoted to the dissemination of historical information to researchers of all denominations. I gathered a massive amount of material not only on Navy ships and Naval operations, but on merchant vessel losses during both world wars.

Archival holdings included the Tenth Fleet Assessments, Anti-Submarine Warfare records, the War Diary of the Eastern Sea Frontier, comprehensive reports of the Fifth Naval District, U-boat post mortems, records of U-boat operations during World War One, and other choice documents that are too many to mention.

Cavalcante handled most of the mail order queries, while Walker took charge of identifying and pulling records for visiting researchers. I explained to Walker what I was looking for, and he located the file boxes and brought them to the Research Room.

Security was fairly light in those days. There were no lockers. After signing in, I simply left my coat and briefcase on the floor in the outer office, and took my notebook with me into the Research Room. There were never more than a handful of researchers throughout the day, and usually only two or three. The waiting time for records was not long.

There was a copy machine in the room, but researchers were not allowed to operate it. I had to tab documents for Walker to copy. If he spent too much time on pulling records for researchers, and did not have enough time to make photocopies, I totaled my tab, paid ten cents a copy in advance, and he would mail the copies to me within a few days.

I needed plenty of copies because I was doing bulk research on ships that were sunk all along the East Coast, not just on one or two isolated shipwrecks. Toward the end of the 1980's, I stepped up the quantity of my research because I signed a contract to write *Track of the Gray Wolf*.

Around this time, the Operational Archives started tightening the reins on the productivity of researchers by allowing them to make only fifty photocopies *per year*. They kept count. The staff was hampered by regulations that were made higher up.

Gina Akers, the new kid on the block, was assigned to work with me on my book project (although Cavalcante and Walker were there to lend their able assistance and long-time expertise). She had to obtain special dispensation to enable me to make more than my allowable fifty copies, and to her I owe a great debt of gratitude.

Naval Historical Center

In retrospect, it eventually came to light that another newby, Kathy Lloyd, had a hand in my research. But more on that later.

The *Gentian* Report – Turnabout is Fair Play

One of the most heartwarming aspects of shipwreck research is meeting kindly people in the pursuit of historical documentation. One such person was Denny Breese. In 1990, when I was researching *Shipwrecks of North Carolina*, someone in Wilmington gave me his phone number and suggested that I contact him. I called him, told him who I was, and what I was doing. Breese was a treasure salvor who was living on a salvage vessel that was moored off Wilmington.

He invited me to come out for a chat. One of his employees picked me up at the dock in a motorboat, and drove me to the site that Breese was working. He and I hit it off well. Obviously we shared an interest in submerged maritime history, but more than that, because we both knew so much about the subject, we were able to converse intelligibly in a way that neither of us had much opportunity to do with other people. There aren't many shipwreck scholars in the world. We had so much to talk about that I ended up staying overnight.

Breese had information on a number of local wrecks that he was happy to share with me. He didn't have a photocopy machine onboard, so he gave me his original files and told me to mail them back to him after I made copies ashore. This was extremely gracious and trusting of him; he didn't know me from Adam. The only other person to ever trust me with original documents was Clive Cussler – on more than one occasion.

In addition to documents about specific local shipwrecks, Breese loaned me a large report about the *Gentian* survey of 1944. The *Gentian* was a Coast Guard cutter that served as a platform for a group of scientists from the Lamont-Doherty Geological Observatory. These scientists were testing their state-of-the-art underwater camera and flash system on shipwrecks off the coast of North Carolina. The *Gentian* located many of the ships that were torpedoed by German U-boats in the first half of 1942. The scientists took photographs of wreckage with a drop camera.

The report was more than one hundred pages in length. It was replete with information about wrecks that I was covering in my book. The report referenced a report about an earlier cruise aboard the *Gentian*: one that occurred in 1943. On my next visit to the Naval Historical Center, I asked Mike Walker for the 1943 report. Throughout the day, he kept telling me that he was still looking for the report. Finally, late in the afternoon, he admitted that he was unable to locate it. Bernard Cavalcante joined in the search, but to no avail. In exasperation, Walker asked me where I found the citation for the report.

Fortunately, I had brought with me the photocopy that I had made from Breese's copy. (By then I had mailed all of Breese's documents back to him.) I took the report from my briefcase in the outer office, showed it to Walker, and indicated where it referred to the earlier report. Armed with the citation information that was given in the 1944 report, both he and Cavalcante delved deep into the stacks. Just before closing time, Walker returned to the Research Room with two three-by-five file cards that referenced the *Gentian* reports. According to the notations, both reports had "disappeared" about ten years earlier.

Cavalcante joined us. He asked to see my copy of the 1944 report. I showed it to him and explained how I had obtained it. As an historian, he was obviously excited about the reappearance of a report that had been lost for so long. He asked me if I would let him make a copy for their files.

Now here was a decided turn of events: I was there to obtain documents, not to furnish them. I couldn't help but mention the irony of the situation. They both snickered.

I said, "Of course you can copy it." Then I added casually, "But you're only allowed fifty photocopies per

Naval Historical Center

year."

They were nonplussed for a moment, until my grin told them that I was only joking.

They wasted no time in copying the report in its entirety. The 1943 *Gentian* report is still missing.

Gone are the Good Old Days

Long gone are those halcyon days when the staff at the Naval Historical Center was dedicated to providing historical records to researchers – going out of their way, even, to track down records that were difficult to locate. The new guard is just that: a guard against unwanted intrusion into what they consider to be their private domain.

The depravity of the current attitude was brought to my attention in October 2000. For reasons that will soon become apparent, I did not act upon the situation until six years later. What follows is a complete verbatim transcript of a letter that I sent to Admiral Paul Tobin, the Director of the Naval Historical Center, on January 1, 2007:

> I am presently writing a book about U-boat warfare off the American eastern seaboard during World War One.
>
> On December 19, 2006, I visited the Washington Navy Yard for the express purpose of accessing a manuscript entitled "U-boat Operations in the Western Atlantic During World War I," written by Richard A. von Doenhoff and Harry E. Rilley. I have accessed this manuscript often over the past twenty years, as my research dictated, for other book projects. Originally I asked to have the manuscript photocopied for future reference, but my request was denied because – as I was told – there was a limitation on photocopies of 50 pages per calendar year. The ongoing nature of my research demanded that I "save" my meager photocopy privileges for different relevant work.
>
> I have always relied on reference assistants to

locate the manuscript in the stacks, and to pull it from the stacks for viewing. On this occasion, no one was able to locate the manuscript – or even to confirm its existence. The "best guess" was that the manuscript (which, to the best of my recollection, was stored in two or three blue cardboard file boxes) had been transferred to the library downstairs.

The librarians were unable to locate the boxes that contained the manuscript. Nor were they able to find a transfer order. They called upstairs to obtain the number of the transfer order from Kathy Lloyd. She was unable to provide such a number, but stated that she had personally transferred the manuscript to the library. The reference assistants then stopped searching for the manuscript in the Operational Archives.

The matter ended in limbo. My trip from Philadelphia was wasted.

This brings to mind another and more serious matter that occurred in October 2000. On that occasion I visited the Operational Archives in order to obtain additional information for a revised edition of *Track of the Gray Wolf*, a book about U-boat warfare off the American eastern seaboard during World War Two. I researched and wrote *Track of the Gray Wolf* in the 1980's. I conducted much of my research at the Naval Historical Center. The book was published in 1989.

Kathy Lloyd assigned a recently hired research assistant to help me. After hearing the nature of my research, this assistant went into the stacks to obtain documents that were relevant to my research. Upon his return, he asked me to accompany him to his office so that we could talk in private. Behind closed doors, he told me that Kathy Lloyd had given him specific instructions to withhold certain documents from me. These documents were not classified; nor was there any valid reason why they should have been withheld.

He explained that he did not think that it was

right for public documents to be withheld from a member of the public; that these documents were being held in trust for the American people; that he disagreed strongly with Lloyd's instructions; but that he could not bring out the documents that I asked for because he could lose his job if she caught him disobeying her specific instructions. He also asked me to protect his anonymity should I choose to lodge a complaint with her superiors.

At that time, I felt that any complaint that I lodged must implicate him directly and jeopardize his job. Now, after the passage of six years, and after not seeing him in the Operational Archives during my recent visit, the time is ripe to bring this matter to the attention of people in authority – to people who may not be aware of Lloyd's dictatorial policy regarding the release of documents to researchers; or, perhaps, to people who are part of the conspiracy to withhold public documents from the public.

The documents that were withheld from me six years ago were also withheld from me twenty years ago, when I was researching and writing *Track of the Gray Wolf*. This information should have been disseminated to the public through the publication of my book. Instead, the public was cheated out of some of its heritage.

This situation constitutes a serious breach of ethics. By withholding public documents, Lloyd abused the authority that is vested in her. This is not merely a matter of inefficiency, or lack of dedication in the performance of her duties, but a conscious decision on her part to dictate who should have access to public documents, and who should not have access.

This is not her decision to make. Nor is it the Navy's decision to make. These documents are merely held in trust by the Navy for the public. This is a Congressional decision to make. Congress has long since deemed it proper that researchers, historians, and the public at large have access to public documents.

Furthermore, mine are not isolated incidents. On more than one occasion, when I telephoned Lloyd months after submitting a written request for information, she told me that there was no record of receipt; my mailed requests were mysteriously "lost." I have heard complaints from others who have had difficulties in dealing with the Operational Archives in general and with Lloyd in particular: difficulties that have now reached epidemic proportions.

Fortunately for my continued research, many of the World War Two documents which the Naval Historical Center controlled when I wrote *Track of the Gray Wolf* were transferred to the National Archives in 1996. These documents are more accessible to the public at their new premises, not only due to the policies of the National Archives and to the able help provided by research assistants who are honest and sincere in their endeavors to aid researchers, but because there is no limitation on the number of photocopies that a researcher may make. The new custodians of these documents are simply that: custodians, not self-appointed despots.

I want these matters investigated at once. I want to be kept apprised of any action – or inaction – that is taken to rectify the extremely important matter of willfully withholding public documents from the public. Of secondary importance, I also want to be notified of the "discovery" of the location of the von Doenhoff and Rilley manuscript.

Perhaps the Naval Historical Center is not a suitable agency for archiving national historical documents that pertain to the American heritage.

So that co-conspirators at the Naval Historical Center do not sweep this complaint under the rug, I am sending copies to my representatives.

Copied to: Captain Peter Wheeler, Deputy Director,

Naval Historical Center 131

Naval Historical Center
Representative Mark Cohen
Representative Allyson Schwartz
Senator Arlen Specter
Senator Robert Casey

Lame Excuse

As you can see, I don't pull any punches. I call 'em as I see 'em.

One purpose of my letter was to determine how far the conspiracy went in the hierarchy of the Naval Historical Center. Here is Tobin's reply in its entirety:

> We apologize for our inability to provide you with access to the Richard A. von Doenhoff and Harry E. Rilley manuscript, "U-boat Operations in the Western Atlantic During World War I," which as you correctly indicated has been in the custody of the Operational Archives for many years. The five boxes of material have not been moved from their location in the archives but we did fail to list the title in our TRIM database that is the primary reference tool of our archivists. That oversight has been corrected.
>
> With regard to your visit to the Operational Archives in October 2000, we regret that your experience was not a positive one and that you were unable to gain access to materials related to your research on U-boats in World War II. Please be assured that our policy is to withhold no unclassified archival documents from the public. Mrs. Lloyd, Head of the Operational Archives, is a dedicated and professional civil servant who would only withhold documents bearing a security classification or covered under Privacy Act restrictions. If you can identify those documents you require for your research, we will do all we can to locate them and once assured they are releasable to the public offer them to you. Moreover, we no longer have a policy of limiting 50 photocopied pages per researcher in a

given year.

We regret your unfortunate experience in the Operational Archives and welcome your future research visits to the Naval Historical Center.

Conspirators Unite

In my opinion, Tobin was either totally ignorant of how Lloyd operated under his command, or he was part of the conspiracy. It will soon become apparent why I suspect the latter.

Tobin was being either facetious or absurd when he suggested the I "identify those documents you require for your research." This is a classic catch-22. A researcher cannot know when documents are being withheld from him if he has no knowledge of their existence, and if the research assistant goes out of her way to hide that knowledge from him.

As for the records that had been maliciously withheld from me on two occasions – first in the late 1980's after Lloyd started exerting her authority, and second in 2000 at her direct intervention – I no longer needed them. A few weeks after my October 2000 visit, I received a one-inch-thick packet of photocopied documents in the mail. The package was from the research assistant whose anonymity I promised to protect.

That day in his office, my anonymous benefactor said that Lloyd told him not to give me anything with wreck locations. She kept a close watch on the records that he pulled for me, and examined them before she let him show them to me. In *Track of the Gray Wolf*, I appended a chronological list of every U-boat attack in the Eastern Sea Frontier, along with attack positions in latitude and longitude. The packet that I received contained hundreds of attack locations that I could have used in compiling my appendix. None of these documents was classified.

U.S.S. San Diego: the Last Armored Cruiser

The morning of November 31, 1995 found me doing microfilm research on the 4th Floor of the National

Naval Historical Center

Archives in DC. Because of the self-retrieval process, I squirreled my microfilm research into odd moments when I was waiting for the delivery of records to the Central Research Room. I studied the finding aids, then went into the stack area to locate the aisle, cabinet, and drawer in which the reel that I wanted was stored.

Just as I wrapped my fingers around the drawer handle, another hand grabbed the same handle from the opposite side. We looked up at each other in surprise. What are the chances that two researchers wanted reels out of the same drawer at the same time, when there are thousands of drawers? But that was only the beginning of the coincidence.

No, we did not both want the same reel. But we were working in the same microfilm group: T-925 – U.S. Coast Guard Casualty and Wreck Reports, 1913-1939.

In accented English, he introduced himself as Patrick Lize, a freelance researcher from Paris, France, who had been hired by a French treasure salvage outfit to conduct research in American archives.

When I told him my name, he looked stunned for a moment. Then he told me that he had just seen my name on the cover of a book in the Central Research Room. Since he too was doing shipwreck research, he spent some time talking with the gal who was using my *San Diego* book as a reference guide. She told him that she was a private researcher from California, and that the Navy had hired her to confirm the facts in my 1989 publication.

This was a bizarre twist of events. Lize and I chatted for a while about our research projects, exchanged contact information, then proceeded with our research.

Reverse Research

Later that morning, in the Central Research Room, I surreptitiously sauntered past the workstations until I saw my book on the desktop in front of a woman who had a cart full of file boxes that related to Naval activities during World War One. She was going through the book, and checking my facts with archival documents.

She was doing "reverse research." This is much like the reverse engineering that is conducted by a company that purchases a product from a competing company with the idea of duplicating the product. She was locating the originating sources of the facts that were in my book.

I knew what she was looking for, and I could have told her where to find it. The Navy could have saved the taxpayers a great deal of money by hiring *me* to provide the document whose existence she was trying to confirm.

I had done extensive research on the *San Diego* prior to writing the book on the warship's history, and I had photocopied every relevant document that I had found. I knew from current Navy scuttlebutt which individual document she was hoping *not* to find; or, if she found it, was hoping that I had misread, misinterpreted, or intentionally misconstrued the information that the document contained.

For years, minions at the Naval Historical Center had been trying to make all sunken Navy vessels off-limits to divers – not to protect or to preserve the collapsing hulks, for mankind is powerless against the inevitable forces of nature and the corrosive undersea environment – but to exercise their control.

Control Freaks

The commonly accepted belief is that the Navy wants to prevent divers from seeing that part of their cultural history that exists in the form of sunken Navy vessels. Nothing could be further from the truth.

Consider this. In the 1990's, I wrote to the Navy Sea Systems Command in an attempt to obtain historical information that I was unable to obtain from the Naval Historical Center. The commander who replied was blunt when he wrote that the purpose of the Navy is national defense, not the preservation of history. He was right.

The "Navy" has little or no interest in its submerged fleet of yesteryear. The faction that is hell-bent on the

Naval Historical Center

shipwreck power play is a handful of *civilians* who work in the Operational Archives. This handful – literally five people – continually abuse the authority of their association by utilizing Navy funding and resources to promote their collective personal agenda. These people do not represent the Navy, nor do they represent the *wishes* the Navy. They are employees of the Navy who have taken it upon themselves to control useless resources for which the Navy has no need.

The leader and chief conniver of this group was Bill Dudley, then Director of the Naval Historical Center. Next in command was Dean Allard. Dudley is now retired, but his unethical legacy lives on in the minds of brainwashed underlings who carry the torch to burn present and future generations of divers. This civilian but uncivilized cancer within the Navy is solely responsible for the ongoing efforts to oppress freedom under the guise of historic preservation.

The Witch Hunters

Dudley worked hard to brainwash his compatriots about the harm that divers were doing to Navy shipwrecks. In effect, he created a witch hunting fleet whose sole aim was to maintain control over all shipwrecks of Naval origin. Ostensibly, the individuals in this radical fleet are equivalent to privateers who signed letters of marque that legitimized their confiscation of enemy vessels. In actuality, they act more like pirates.

The witch hunters delighted in prosecuting salvors for alleged illegal underwater activities. They were extending their authority far beyond the pale of ethics.

The prime target on their hit list of shipwrecks was the *San Diego*: perhaps the most often dived U.S. Navy shipwreck in the world. It irked the witch hunters to no end that divers visited this wreck nearly every weekend.

Unfortunately for Dudley and his malicious cronies, the Navy had sold the *San Diego* to Maxter Metals for its scrap value. The purchase price was $1,221.00. The sale was consummated on October 27, 1957. I duly noted these facts in my *San Diego* book. If the wreck had been sold to a private salvage outfit, then the Navy – and by extension, the Dudley group – could not claim dominion over it.

For Dudley and his group to have exclusive control over the *San Diego*, they had to disprove my claim that Maxter Metals bought the wreck legally. Unfortunately for the powermongers, I did not invent or imagine the Maxter Metals ownership. In my files I had a copy of the document that qualified as a bill of sale.

Idly, I wondered if she would try to steal or destroy the document, so as to enable the Navy's legal team to contradict my statement of ownership in a court of law. If that happened, I opined, I could produce my copy to bolster the truth of the situation. I knew that if she looked as hard as I did, she would find the incriminating evidence.

The Naval Hysterical Center

Back to the Archives on November 31, 1995. After seeing the gal with my *San Diego* book, I checked out of the room temporarily so I could read the names on the sign-in sheet. You can't do this today with the card swipe system, but in those days everyone had to print and sign his or her name upon entry to the Central Research Room.

Several women were in the room that day, so I didn't know which one was the gal in question. The next day I went to the Naval Historical Center. I got there only minutes after they opened, but already there was one name on the sign-in sheet, and it was one of the names that was printed on the Archives sign-in sheet the day before. The woman was doing research at the Operational Archives, but I never saw her because she had special dispensation to do her research in private. Her connection with the Navy explained how she managed to carry my book into the Central Research Room.

Kathy Lloyd was on duty that day. She was in her typical abrasive mood. Nonetheless, I managed to obtain some materials for my ongoing research for my Popular Dive Guide Series. Someone circulated word

Naval Historical Center

that I was in the building. I had barely started looking through documents when an individual entered the Research Room and said that he had heard that I was there, and that he wanted to meet me. He introduced himself as Otto Orzech.

Orzech was ex-Navy. He now did consulting work for the Navy. He was the leader of a team of researchers from California, all of whom were doing archival research on the *San Diego*. He knew of me through my book on the subject. The woman I saw in the Archives was his associate. He cheerfully tuned me in to the big picture.

The Naval Historical Center had hired him and several others to work on the *San Diego* project. Because Orzech was ex-Navy, and a diver, he was also in charge of the Navy divers who were examining the wreck and the munitions that it contained, endeavoring to ascertain if the munitions were dangerous, so as to use that as an excuse to prohibit divers from visiting the site. He and his associates had been working on the project since July. I shook my head at the monumental waste of taxpayers' dollars that were being spent to gratify the whims of a few sanctimonious civil servants who were serving themselves instead of their country.

Orzech had no axe to grind. He did not know that the witch hunters held me in contempt. It was through his forthright conversation that I learned so much about the *San Diego* project.

The Lion's Den

Orzech returned at noon with an invitation for lunch from Bill Dudley. I could have declined, of course. I had brought my own lunch with me. I was not naïve enough to believe that Dudley was offering me an olive branch. He and I were implacable enemies, and would remain so until the end of time. He wanted control; I believed in freedom. There was no middle ground between us.

Did he want me to share his lunch, or did he want to *have* me for lunch: to chew me up and spit me out in little pieces? All these thoughts raced through my mind in the second before I hesitantly uttered, "Okay." I knew what I was getting myself into.

I had never eaten in the cafeteria because it was operated only for Yard personnel. Orzech led the way. He introduced me to Dudley and three of his henchmen who would be sharing the table with us. Then we went through the self-service line and chose our food. Dudley's invitation did not include buying my lunch. I had to pay for my own meal.

Dudley and his minions fired questions about my many explorations into the hull of the *San Diego*. I was cautious with my replies, looking for innuendoes and implications that were not implicit in the wording or phrasing of the questions. Yet I have to admit that, although they were not overly friendly, they were neither aggressive nor accusatory. I expected to be crucified, but they were never less than civil. That didn't mean that their attitude toward me (or toward wreck-divers) had moderated, only that they had more oligarchic ways of achieving their goals. Or perhaps they thought that they could kill more bees with honey.

I would like to say that I bearded the lion in his own den, but in all honesty I can't. Our conversation was almost innocuous.

Poor Losers

Ultimately, Navy lawyers must have advised the witch hunters that their case would never hold up in court. The Navy had indeed sold the *San Diego* to Maxter Metals. The Navy could not reclaim it.

Orzech's diving team determined that the munitions on the wreck were neither unstable nor particularly dangerous.

Instead of letting the matter drop, however, the witch hunters spearheaded efforts to take the wreck away from divers by claiming that the inverted hull was an important marine habitat, and having the wreck designated as an underwater preserve. That stopgap status did not prevent divers from diving on the wreck,

Naval Historical Center

but it did prevent them from legally taking souvenirs of their dive.

With all these secret machinations going on behind the backs of American citizens, you can understand why the Naval Historical Center is not a healthy climate for researchers who are known to the witch hunters as wreck-divers. The witch hunters now spend prodigious amounts of time in surfing the Internet to find potentially incriminating evidence that can be used to prosecute wreck-divers.

All too often, they achieve their nefarious aims by making threats of prosecution, despite the lack of merit in a case. They know that most people are easily intimidated, and will fold a winning hand because of the cost of litigation. Time and again, using the unending font of taxpayers' money, these witch hunters have tracked down divers who have made claims on the Internet – either in forums, in discussion groups, or on personal websites – that they possess items that the witch hunters can construe might possibly have been recovered from so-called Navy wrecks.

The witch hunters have gone as far as to dispatch Navy investigators and agents of the Federal Bureau of Investigation – who have better things to do in the fight against *real* crime – to people's private residences or places of business, in order to confiscate alleged Navy property, or to make arrests and haul people to prison in handcuffs. It *has* been done, and the process is ongoing and getting worse.

Afterward, the accused individuals must prove their innocence beyond a shadow of a doubt, and at their own expense. Constitutional rights notwithstanding, in these cases a person is guilty until he establishes his innocence.

These aggrandizing political maneuvers have nothing to do with the preservation of historical documentation, and the dissemination of information to the public: a fact that the Naval Historical Center has apparently chosen to ignore is its sole rationale for existence.

The Castrated Operational Archives

You may recall from the Introduction that I stated emphatically that under no circumstances should you ever admit to a librarian or research assistant that you are a wreck-diver. That statement goes double or even triple when dealing with the Operational Archives.

According to the spurious Vision Statement of the Naval Historical Center, "We envision the Naval Historical Center as the indispensable resource for the U.S. naval history and heritage." What this Vision Statement neglects to mention is that they hold that resource for only selected individuals, not for the public at large. Wreck-divers are definitely not among the chosen. The Center has underhandedly reserved for itself the right to decide which historic documents its research assistants shall dispense, and to whom.

The significance of these double-dealings to shipwreck researchers is obvious. The good news is that, for the most part, the present generation of researchers doesn't have to deal very much with the Operational Archives. In April 1996, practically all the records of value to shipwreck researchers were transferred to the National Archives in College Park.

This transfer included Navy records from World War Two: action reports, operational reports, war diaries, plans, orders and related documents, locational charts and maps for Allied and Axis naval units, immediate office files of the Chief of Naval Operations, Tenth Fleet records, Ultra decrypts, convoy and routing instructions, antisubmarine warfare documents, measures division, strategic plans, war plans (division), and selected reference materials from the World War Two command file.

The Operational Archives was left primarily with early history records, and operational records from 1946 onward. Thus little of interest remains in the Operational Archives for shipwreck researchers to research. The incestuous handful of people who dictate Navy archival policy now possess only a vestigial fiefdom.

Judge Advocate General

Although JAG is closely associated with the Navy, JAG records are not. JAG headquarters is located in Alexandria, Virginia: immediately outside of DC proper, across the Potomac River.

Among other records, JAG archives courts-martial and courts of inquiry. A court-martial is a military trial against an individual for offenses that fall under military law and jurisdiction. A court of inquiry is a formal, fact-finding investigation concerning any matter of grave military importance.

The kind of court proceeding that is helpful to shipwreck researchers is one that investigates the loss of a Navy vessel, or one that investigates an incident in which a Navy vessel was involved (such as collision with a merchant vessel). Unlike a civil trial – in which lawyers create mayhem by raising objections and by trying to obfuscate the truth – a Navy tribunal generally makes an honest attempt to ascertain the facts to the fullest extent possible.

In its purest form, the court of inquiry is conducted like a scientific research project: one that is not biased or prejudiced by preconceived notions. Witnesses are permitted not only to answer questions freely and without qualification, they are encouraged to offer additional information that they believe may be pertinent to the case. After court appointed legal council and investigating officers ask their questions, the judges may either ask for clarification or put questions of their own to the witnesses. It is this forthright testimony that is so valuable to shipwreck researchers.

I used to visit the JAG offices regularly in the 1980's. In those days, the courts-martial and courts of inquiry were indexed on a card file system. The three-by-five cards were stored in full-width drawers in a metal cabinet that measured three feet square and that stood four feet high. Thousands of cards were arranged alphabetically by name of vessel or individual.

After checking into the JAG office without making

an appointment, an officer or secretary would accompany me to the basement of the multistory building, point to the cabinet, and leave me on my own. I found the cards of the vessels that I wanted to research, read the typed summary of the file, and jotted down the locator information on a sheet of paper. I then returned to the office upstairs, filled out forms that were equivalent to Archives' call slips, and handed them to the officer in charge.

The actual courts of inquiry were not kept in the JAG building. They were archived at the Washington National Records Center in Suitland, Maryland: about twelve miles away. It took two to three days for the paperwork to be filed and the records to be pulled. I planned my JAG visits for the beginning of the week, so I could access the records by the end of the week.

Washington National Records Center

This one-floor archival facility is spread out like a mammoth multifamily ranch house. It is difficult to reach by public transportation because it lies so far away from the last Metro station; wear roller skates. Nor is there any shuttle service. Prince George County operates a bus that connects the last station on the Green line with the Suitland Federal Complex, but because it is a different system, you have to pay an additional fare. It is easier to drive. There is ample parking because the number of researchers is generally so few. I won't give directions for reasons that will soon become apparent.

I would always call the JAG office first to confirm that the records had been pulled. The sign-in procedure was simple: I entered my name and the date in a book. I did not need to show identification. I did not need a research card, nor did I need to wear a badge. There were no armed guards. I simply entered the Research Room and provided my name to an aide. Within minutes an aide brought the file boxes to me.

One time I was fortunate enough to be taken into the stacks in order to help search for a file box whose locator information had been transcribed incorrectly. The mammoth warehouse consisted of aisles, rows, shelves, and tiers. The aisles were incredibly long: closing in perspective in the distance, and seeming to come together like train tracks. Each aisle was lined with interlocking shelving units that extended from floor to ceiling. Each vertical row was numbered, and each shelf on the row was numbered. The boxes that were stored on the shelves were stacked three boxes deep.

Let's say that the locator information placed a file box on Aisle 24, Row 12, Shelf 4, Tier 3. You would walk along Aisle 24 to Row 12 (which was a vertical stack). The file box in question would be found on the fourth shelf behind two other file boxes: the third one back. Inside that box there would be several folders, one of which was the one that I wanted. The other folders in the box had nothing to do with the vessel, nor were they arranged in any systematized manner. There was no continuity of name or subject matter. Folders were filed haphazardly until no more folders fit in the box.

Under this system, several folders could have the same locator information. The key to finding a particular folder was in knowing in which box on which shelf in which row in which aisle the folder was filed. Pay attention, because this information will soon assume considerable importance.

Standard research rules applied for reading documents. Only one file box was permitted on the table; only one folder at a time could be removed from the box.

Self-service photocopiers were available in the room. Documents did not need to be examined prior to copying. For ten cents per page, I could make as many photocopies as I wanted. I spent lots of money, because most courts of inquiry are several hundred pages in length. The longest court of inquiry that I ever found was the one on the *Murphy*: a destroyer escort that was cut in two by the *Bulkoil* off the coast of New Jersey. (For details, including the sad saga of how dives on the wreck provided the Naval Historical Center with the ammunition that it needed to pass restrictive shipwreck legislation, see *Shipwreck Heresies* by this author.) The file included more than one *thousand* pages of testimony, and included photographs, charts, and diagrams.

The tribunal or panel of judges summarized their findings and made recommendations, but the foremost value of a court of inquiry is in its eyewitness accounts of a maritime disaster. There is nothing more primary than the actual words of the survivors, faithfully transcribed by a court reporter – instead of being misquoted, paraphrased, or hyperbolized by sensationalistic correspondents whose cardinal goal is to sell newspapers.

Accuracy is so paramount in a court of inquiry that, after a witness's testimony is transcribed, the witness is asked to review the written record and to make corrections or additions. This *never* happens in a civil court case, in which the primary goal is to obscure the truth, not to reveal or elucidate it.

For reasons that are given in the following section, I haven't visited the Suitland facility in many years. Should you need to do research there in record groups other than courts-martial or courts of inquiry, be advised that you must now go through a security check and present photo identification at the guard station in the entrance lobby.

The JAGuar

In the 1990's, JAG tightened its control over courts-martial and courts of inquiry. No longer was I allowed to see the original records at the Washington National Records Center. Instead, JAG had the file folders pulled and shipped to the headquarters building in Alexandria. The entire file was photocopied. A JAG officer then redacted the photocopies before permitting me to see them.

Redacting means editing text and deleting information. A JAG officer, or redactor, did this by applying

Judge Advocate General

indelible ink onto passages that JAG no longer wanted the public to see. The process is somewhat capricious and arbitrary, and is a time consuming process to implement. In essence, the redactor has to read the entire transcript word for word, and redact every passage that JAG, in its wisdom, has decided to hide from prying civilian eyes.

In some places, isolated words, partial sentences, or disunited lines were redacted. In other places, complete paragraphs or half a page of text were redacted.

I now had to make two trips to JAG: one to submit my requests, and another to review the heavily redacted documents. When I arrived at the JAG office on the second occasion, an officer gave me the redacted version for which JAG had no further use: it had been photocopied and redacted specifically for me. Even if I found only a few pages relevant to my research, I was given the photocopy of the entire transcript.

The JAGged Edge of Stupidity

Later in the 1990's, JAG computerized its index card filing system. The text that was typed on each index card was input into a database for quick and easy retrieval. Unfortunately, it appears that the data input personnel who were employed by JAG to do the job were either careless or incompetent.

Since then, of the courts of inquiry that I have requested, JAG has been able to retrieve only one out of two. The other half cannot be found. The enormity of this loss to present and future generations is incalculable. Imagine: fifty percent of the transcripts of all the courts of inquiry that were ever convened, are missing – and likely forever.

When the boxes are pulled from the Washington National Records Center, the file folder that is the object of the search is *not* found in the box. One might presume that the folder was misfiled – perhaps the last time that it was pulled. But that is not the case. Or, if it is the case, it is only in a few instances. The reality of the matter is far more insidious.

I asked a JAG officer, who was one of those in charge of these materials, how such a dire situation could occur. They concluded that the most likely explanation was that a typographical error was made during the transfer of data from the file cards to the database. If only a single digit was mistyped, the box could not be located.

Referring to the hypothetical locator information given above – Aisle 24, Row 12, Shelf 4, Tier 3 – any mistake or reversal could designate the wrong aisle, row, shelf, or tier. The typist could have typed Aisle 23 instead of Aisle 24; or Row 13 instead of Row 12; or Shelf 5 instead of Shelf 4; or Tier 2 instead of Tier 3. A dyslexic typist might have reversed the numbers, and typed Aisle 42 instead of Aisle 24; or Row 21 instead of Row 12. Perhaps an entry contained more than one mismatch. There is no way of knowing. And trying all the possible permutations would be an exercise in futility.

After hearing this, I asked the officer why, when a transcript wasn't found where its locator information stated that it belonged, they didn't just go down to the basement and refer to the original file cards. Not only could they then obtain the correct locator information, but they could revise and correct the database.

Any rational human being is going to find his answer difficult to accept. After adopting the database system, the Navy – and this time I mean Naval officers and not a group of misguided civilian dictators – discarded the file card cabinet along with its contents.

What monumental stupidity!

In a multistory building that occupies nearly one square block, the amount of space taken by one small cabinet in an out-of-the-way basement storage room is inconsequential. Yet they threw away the cabinet and file cards instead of keeping them as a backup in case of an unforeseeable computer malfunction, or a glitch in the retrieval program, or a viral attack. Such lack of forethought is inexcusable, and inexplicable in this age of computer savvy Naval officers.

Judge Advocate General

The Modern Capitalistic JAG

Once again, the good old days of independent and uncomplicated research are gone. Researchers are no longer allowed in JAG headquarters. All requests are handled by snail mail or e-mail. You can't send a simple request for the transcript of a court of inquiry; you must now submit a formal application pursuant to the Freedom of Information Act.

Upon receipt of a FOIA request, JAG will approximate the cost of conducting a "search" and "review" of the requested materials, and the "direct cost" of photocopying the documents. A first-time requester must pay in advance; requesters with a good payment history will be billed at a later date, but payment is due within thirty days. A number of charges are involved, and they are cumulative.

"Search" means a computer search for the records in question, then the time that is spent on pulling them. This search may include a page-by-page or line-by-line identification of materials to determine if they are responsive to the request. The requester is charged at an hourly rate that may be as high as $45 per hour.

"Direct cost" is the actual cost of making photocopies. This is not a standard charge per page, but an hourly rate that is charged for the amount of time that it takes someone to make the copies, plus the cost of operating the duplicating machinery. Again, the charge may be as high as $45 per hour.

"Review" means redacting the text. The requester may have to pay as much as $45 per hour for someone to read the entire transcript, and redact the very information that is relevant to his research.

A transcript that is several hundred pages in length may easily cost a requester hundreds of dollars. If JAG predetermines that the cost is likely to exceed $250, the requester is notified to pay in advance.

You have to pay a search fee even if JAG cannot locate the requested documents.

U.S. Coast Guard Historian's Office

Although the majority of Coast Guard records are held at the National Archives, one should not overlook the Coast Guard Historian's Office as an additional source of information pertaining to Coast Guard activities – primarily search, rescue, and renders of assistance.

In this case the office is literally that: a one-room office in the multi-story Coast Guard headquarters building. Don't go there without first making an appointment, else you won't get any farther than the lobby due to tight security.

The easiest way to get there is to drive. Until recently, parking has always been a problem. I've had to park in the street more than a half a mile away – if I was lucky enough to find a spot. Now there is a parking lot right across the street; the fee is nominal.

You can get close by public transportation, but be prepared for a circuitous walk in weather that may not always be clement. The nearest Metro subway station is at least fifteen minutes away at a fast pace, longer if you are not used to hiking.

Upon arrival, an armed guard will direct you to the receptionist's desk. The receptionist will ask if you have an appointment. If your answer is yes, you will be asked to produce a photo ID. I don't know what happens if you don't have an appointment. You might learn that the Historian's Office is closed, or that no historians are in that day. Be sure to make an appointment.

The receptionist will telephone the historian. There are generally three to four people who hold this position, but only one might be in the Office at any one time. The historians are civil servants, not active service members. The historian will walk to the lobby to act as your escort. If you have a briefcase, someone will examine it while the historian is on the way. You will then be issued a badge. After the historian arrives, you and your briefcase and other personal belongings will pass through a metal detector. The historian will then escort you to the Office, which is on the ground floor.

Once you have passed through the security hoops, you basically have free reign of the building. This means that you can go to the restroom unescorted. The visitor's badge does not entitle you to roam the corridors, enter other offices, or go to other floors. If you stray from the straight and narrow hallway between the Historian's Office and the restroom, Coast Guard personnel will take note of your badge and politely ask your business. If you are lost and are looking for the restroom, someone will pleasantly indicate the way. Generally speaking, unless you do something seriously inappropriate, the security pomp ends once you meet your escort.

The historian will show you how the files are arranged: alphabetically by vessel in folders on tiered shelves, with one vessel per folder. The folders may contain wreck reports, Coast Guard investigations, newspaper clippings, photographs, and so on. A photocopier and a copy stand are sequestered in the crowded room. You can photograph anything you want, and make a reasonable number of photocopies without charge. The historian will leave you to your own devices, but will be at his desk should you have a question or require assistance that does not require helicopter evacuation.

I have often found gems of information at the Historian's Office. It is well worth a visit if you are doing global shipwreck research. If you are researching only a single wreck, call or write and ask if they have a folder on that particular vessel.

Library of Congress

The Library of Congress is the largest library in the world. Among an incredibly large number of other items, its holdings include some 30 million catalogued books, 61 million manuscripts, 12 million photographs, 5 million maps, and 15 million microforms.

The Library of Congress is a vast complex of buildings and collections that is awesome to behold. The primary facilities are located on Capitol Hill east of the Capitol. These consist of three monumental edifices: the Thomas Jefferson Building (which opened in 1897), the John Adams Building (1938), and the James Madison Building (1981). The three premises are grouped together between Independence Avenue SE and East Capitol Street, and between 1st Street and 3rd Streets. Second Street separates the Jefferson Building from the other two structures.

Two remote buildings are located in Maryland, at Landover and Fort Meade. These storage facilities are not open to the public. If you require items that are stored offsite, you may have to wait a day or so while they are retrieved and delivered to one of the downtown buildings.

Transportation and Parking

As always in Washington, DC, the best way to get anywhere is by public transportation. Both the blue line and the orange line of the Metro subway system stop at the Capitol South station, which is located at 1st and D Streets, two blocks south of the Jefferson Building. Bus routes also serve Capitol Hill.

The Library of Congress does not have public parking facilities. No commercial parking lots are located in the immediate vicinity. Those that exist in the distance are expensive. Street parking may be available east of downtown proper, but may be restricted by parking meters with time limitations.

My advice is to park in Maryland or Virginia, and take the Metro.

Books Galore

Most people think of books when they think of a library. The Library of Congress started as just that: a reference library for members of Congress. Originally, the Congressional library was housed in the Capitol. The books were lost when British troops burned the

Library of Congress

building in the War of 1812. Thomas Jefferson then sold to the government his personal library of more than 6,000 volumes.

The Library continued to accumulate books and other historic documents until they exceeded the storage space that was available in the Capitol. In 1897, the Library was moved into its own dedicated facility: the aptly named Jefferson Building. Since then, the Library has been expanded to four additional buildings.

I was brought up to believe that every book that was ever published, and submitted to the Copyright Office for registration, was kept in the Library of Congress. My rude awakening occurred when, out of curiosity, I looked for my own books during a research visit to the Library. It was then that I learned that not every book that I had written – and that I had submitted for copyright registration – had been archived.

A selection committee determines which books to keep and which to trash. This arbitrary selection process means that a vast portion of the American heritage is disposed by government fiat.

Notwithstanding the above, the Library is still an awesome source of reference materials that shipwreck researchers should not overlook. If you can't find a book in your local library, chances are that you can find it in the Library of Congress.

Even if the Library does not have the book that you want, it is worth visiting the Jefferson Building just to see the cathedral grandiloquence of the Main Reading Room. The ornate dome ceiling of this incredible enclosure stands 160 feet above the floor. Some 70,000 books are stored on shelves in multi-tired alcoves for ready reference. The rest of the books and bound periodicals are stored in closed stacks.

After submitting a call slip, the average retrieval time is a couple of hours – unless, as noted above, the book is stored offsite.

The Library of Congress is not a lending library. You may read books in the Main Reading Room, but you may not borrow them.

Initial Checkpoint

The security program is much like that at the National Archives. Since I have already described this process, there is no need to go into excruciating detail. Go to the Madison Building for your first visit. There you must pass a guard station, go through a metal detector, and send your belongings through an x-ray machine. Go directly to the Reader Registration Room on the first floor. Fill out an application form and have your photograph taken. You will need a driver's license or passport to verify your identity. The attendant will issue you a Reader Identification Card.

This card is valid in all three buildings. However, you must follow standard security protocol whenever you enter (or re-enter) one of the buildings. Library Police are authorized to examine all property in a person's possession, including but not limited to suitcases, briefcases, attaché cases, handbags, large envelopes, packages, and office equipment. Personal possessions will also be inspected upon departure. Facilitate matters: the less you take with you, the quicker you can pass inspection.

Each reading room has its own rules, regulations, and restrictions with regard to personal belongings. Although these policies differ, work on the presumption that overcoats and briefcases are disallowed. Place these items in a locker in a cloakroom. Then inquire at each reading room for which items may be taken into the room. Restrictions change all the time – generally in the direction of more restrictive.

There are cloakrooms in the Jefferson Building and Madison Building, but not in the Adams Building. There is a cafeteria on the sixth floor of the Madison Building. All buildings have public restrooms.

The Madison building is connected via tunnel to the House of Representatives across the street. A tunnel connects the Madison Building to the Jefferson Building, and another tunnel connects the Jefferson Building to the Adams Building. You can easily go from building to building without encountering traffic or

Library of Congress

inclement weather. You still have to go through security checks.

The Jefferson Building

I don't want to give short shrift to the book collection, but there is not much more that I can write about it. If you want to refer to old and out-of-print volumes, the Jefferson Building is certainly a central location that will probably have every book on your list. Let me remind you, however, that most books do not constitute primary source materials. Generally speaking, a book contains information that someone else has already researched.

Books that *do* constitute primary sources are those that were written by people who were actually involved in a shipwreck. For example, *In the Wake of the Andrea Doria* was written by Eugene Gladstone, a survivor who penned a personal narrative of his rescue. *The Maine: an Account of her Destruction in Havana Harbor*, was written by the vessel's captain, Charles Sigsbee.

In addition to the Main Reading Room on the first floor, you should not overlook the Rare Book and Special Collections Reading Room on the second floor. Here

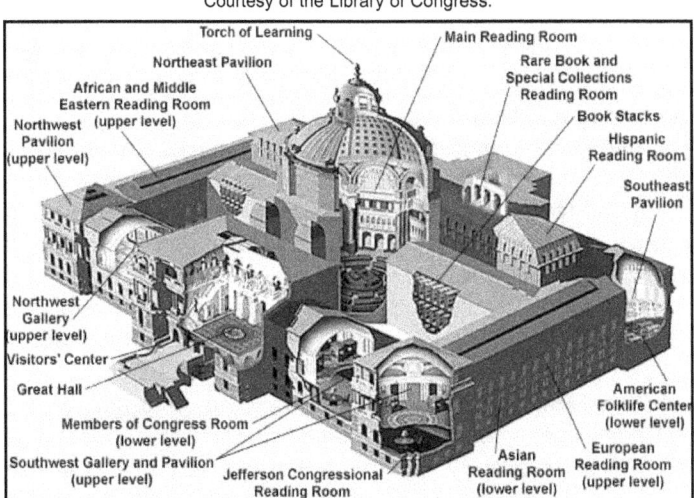

Courtesy of the Library of Congress.

you may find books from the 1800's – books that, while they may not constitute primary sources, were written closer to the time at which a shipwreck occurred. The value in this case is that the primary sources on which the books were based may no longer exist. These books may be your *only* source.

The Library of Congress has no such thing as a self-defeating "pull time." Call slips are turned in immediately. The advertised two-hour delay is purely a function that relates the number of patrons to the number of librarians. The Library is a busy place – far busier than the National Archives.

In Chapter One I discussed at length the newspaper holdings of the Library of Congress. The Microfilm Reading Room is located on the first floor. Included in this collection are current serials and periodicals (magazines).

The Madison Building

The basement floor has the Geography and Map Reading Room. For what it is worth, this includes a huge number of treasure maps. Why anyone would publish a map to a trove of fabulous wealth, instead of going there himself to recover the loot, is beyond the bounds of reason (or, at least, beyond the bounds of *my* reason). Nonetheless, these maps may possess historical value and putative locations that might be of interest to shipwreck researchers, should you be so inclined as to pursue this avenue of research.

Over the years, the Library of Congress received so many requests for treasure maps that, in order to make it easier to respond to requesters, two of its librarians compiled lists of such maps that exist in the Library's holdings: "An Annotated List of Treasure Maps in the Library of Congress" (1955), and "A Descriptive List of Treasure Maps and Charts" (1973). As my Latin teacher used to say, caveat emptor (let the buyer beware).

The Library has also prepared what is called "Wreck Charts and Information Lists." Before you hasten to spend your money on this item, be advised that the wrecks on the charts and lists are identical, and that the locations on both are either erroneous or approximate (with 3 to 5 mile position accuracy). The information was compiled during World War Two, and refers mostly to U-boat casualties.

The charts were originally printed as transparent overlays that could be placed on top of standard nautical charts. They were accompanied by legends that named the charted wrecks. The same information was then printed in text form as the Wreck Information List of 1945, and, with some modifications, the Navy Wreck List of 1957. As noted in Published Sources, the locations were incorporated into the AWOIS list, along with the annotations. The AWOIS is freely available online, and can be downloaded onto your computer in geographical sections.

Perhaps of greater value, the cartographic section contains old nautical charts that show how the coast line has changed throughout the years. This could be helpful if you are trying to locate a vessel that stranded on a shoal that is no longer shown on modern charts, or that ran aground on a beach whose contours have moved.

The first floor has the Manuscript Reading Room. This is where I read and photocopied, for example, Billy Mitchell's typewritten manuscript concerning the 1921 aerial bombardment of the *Ostfriesland*, the *Frankfurt*, three destroyers, and three U-boats off the coast of Virginia. This and millions of other manuscripts were never published.

The second floor has the Law Library Reading Room. Legal issues can be of particular interest to shipwreck researchers because many shipwrecks, especially those involving collision, resulted in lawsuits. If a case went to trial, the judge's rendered opinion would be published in the law reviews. In writing an opinion, a judge typically summarized the facts that were presented as evidence in court. This evidence constitutes the sworn testimony of witnesses: valuable first-person accounts that were distilled by direct examination and cross-examination. This is about as primary a source as you can get. The only source better would be a transcript of the proceedings.

The Congressional Record can be a valuable source of information, particularly in the 1800's, when Congress made resolutions and passed bills that related to the safety of life at sea, and to the particular shipwrecks that brought the issue of safety to public attention.

The third floor has the Prints and Photographs Reading Room. This is where you can view and copy photographs. The rules for copying are different from those at the National Archives and the Naval Photographic Center. Artificial light is *not* permitted. This means that you may not use a strobe, a flash, or floodlights on a copy stand. You must take your pictures with whatever light is available in the room from the overhead fluorescent tubes. You *are* permitted to use a tripod.

You may not scan or photocopy prints, either. Most of these photographic prints are originals, and are not backed up with negatives (as they are at the National Archives). Archivists are afraid that continued exposure to bright light might cause the photographs to fade over time.

In contradiction to this concern, if you utilize Library of Congress services to photograph the prints for you, the paid photographers will employ additional illumination in order to produce a properly exposed image.

If you decide to shoot your own images, use high-speed film or a digital camera on a high ISO setting. Shoot next to a window.

The Adams Building

The holdings here are not of particular interest to shipwreck researchers. Records relate mostly to science and business.

Library of Congress

Copying Services

Most of the reading rooms have self-service copiers for textual records and/or microfilm. The charge per copy is inflationary, and varies according to the type of material to be copied and the kind of machine that copies it. A copy card is used in the same manner in which it is used at the National Archives.

Unlike the National Archives, the Library of Congress does not employ outsourced vendors to copy materials. The Library continues to provide a full range of copying services in-house. This includes color photography, black and white photography, digital photography, slides, prints, negatives, microfilm and microfiche scanning, cartographic scanning, and so on. Scanned images can be stored on compact disks in different file formats. Duplication services can be ordered by mail.

Duplicated records are subject to copyright law.

Librarians

Library of Congress staff members are professional, courteous, helpful, but perhaps not insightful. I don't mean this latter comment to be derogatory. At the National Archives, research assistants need to have a profound grasp of the materials that relate to their area of expertise, and must know where to search for specific records and documents. That comprehension is what makes them archivists instead of librarians.

A librarian is a person who is versed in library science: the cataloguing, systematic arrangement, and retrieval of books, periodicals, newspapers, and other reference materials. A librarian is not an archivist. A librarian can help you to find a book or reference material, but *you* need to know what you are looking for.

Smithsonian Institution

I would be remiss if I did not mention the Smithsonian Institution in this chapter on research facilities that are located in the Washington, DC area, even if this is not a prime source for shipwreck researchers.

The Smithsonian complex occupies approximately one mile of frontage between Independence Avenue and Constitution Avenue: from 3rd Street to 14th Street. Ten megalithic buildings are located west of the Capitol, both north and south of the National Mall that spans between the Capitol and the Washington Monument. The Mall also serves as the dividing line between northwest and southwest addresses.

Previously stated DC parking advices apply. Take the Metro subway to the Smithsonian station.

The Smithsonian has in its possession some 13 million images. These images are distributed throughout numerous collections and buildings. The building that concerns shipwreck researchers is the Arts and Industries Building, located at 900 Jefferson Drive, SW.

Shipwreck related items may be found in the Division of Naval History records and the Division of Transportation records. These records relate mostly to very early maritime history.

I have never found applicable textual records at the Smithsonian, because generally I do not research shipwrecks of antiquity, but I *have* found photographs of vessels that were not available anywhere else. See the chapter on Picture Sources for details.

Part Three
Maritime Museum Libraries

After waxing long and discoursing at length about the vast amount of primary information that is available from government sources, one might conclude that there is no reason to conduct shipwreck research elsewhere. Nothing could be farther from the truth.

While it is true that I never could have written *The Fuhrer's U-boats in American Waters* from information obtained only from maritime museum libraries, it is also true that there are many chapters in my Popular Dive Guide Series that I could not have written *without* information obtained from maritime museum libraries. Indeed, some chapters relied on information obtained *only* from maritime museum libraries. Government archives are severely lacking in many areas.

These two sources compliment each other, and sometimes one takes up the slack for the other.

First let me define some terms. According to the dictionary, a public library is "a place in which literary and artistic materials, such as books, periodicals, newspapers, pamphlets, prints, records, and tapes, are kept for reading, reference, or lending." I would update this definition by adding that many public libraries now keep videotapes and digital videodisks, and well as audio media.

A museum is "a building, place, or institution devoted to the acquisition, conservation, study, exhibition, and educational interpretation of objects having scientific, historical, or artistic value."

A maritime museum specializes in maritime objects. A maritime museum library specializes in all forms of written and photographic records that relate to the sea, to shipping, to navigation, and to all things naval and nautical. This seafaring specialization distinguishes a maritime museum library from a general public library, which is global in the scope of its holdings, and which is likely to be less inclusive in its maritime holdings.

Depending upon the depth of research that is necessary for you to achieve your goals, you may find everything you need to know in a maritime museum library, and never have to visit a government archival facility.

Hundreds if not thousands of maritime museums are scattered across the country. Most of these museums only display maritime memorabilia; they have no associated library. Some have small libraries, or perhaps only a single filing cabinet containing materials that relate to local maritime history. A very few have major maritime libraries that cater to researchers, and perhaps encourage research.

Like government archival facilities, most maritime museum libraries are open only during business hours on weekdays – even if the museum itself is open on Saturday or Sunday. Because most shipwreck researchers have full-time employment, these limited hours and days of operation make it costly to take advantage of the resources – and that is to say nothing of the distance that one must travel.

Note, too, that museums are private institutions, and not necessarily nonprofit institutions. This means that they can establish their own rules, charge admission fees, and set their own prices for their services.

They may be supported by grants, donations, and membership dues. These revenues may not be enough to cover expenses and overhead, so some museum libraries charge a fee just to respond to mail queries. This additional income helps to defray the cost of staff salaries, utilities, building maintenance, new acquisitions, and so on.

One is not Enough

All too often, it is necessary to query or visit more than one maritime museum library in order to obtain a variety of information about a particular subject. This

Maritime Museum Libraries

is because the holdings of each one are different.

As examples, the records of the Thomas A. Scott Wrecking Company were donated to the Mystic Seaport Museum, while the records of the New York Ship Building Company were donated to the Independence Seaport Museum, and the records of the Newport News Ship Building and Dry Dock Company were donated to The Mariners Museum. These company records are unique to each collection.

On the other hand, most maritime museum libraries have the *Lloyd's Register* and the *Record* of the American Bureau of Ships. *But*, not all have complete sets. Certain years may be missing from one collection, and different years may be missing from another collection. In short, there is no single maritime museum library that has everything. This poses additional complications for the researcher.

A researcher can never be certain of obtaining all the information that a maritime museum library has on a subject if he relies solely on correspondence to conduct his research. There are a number of reasons for this.

Some libraries are not adequately staffed to handle the number of queries that are received. Indeed, some of the smaller libraries have a solitary librarian to handle all the duties of the library. If your query letter arrives at a time when the librarian is overwhelmed with research requests in addition to a flood of other work, your request may be given short shrift.

Some of the smaller maritime museum libraries that I have visited did not even have a photocopy machine.

Attitude is Important

Then there are those maritime museum libraries whose librarian doesn't care about doing work of any kind if he can get out of doing it. I will cite a couple of examples.

I have always had trouble with Nathan Lipfert at the Maine Maritime Museum. Throughout the 1980's, my mail order requests for information or photographs were not answered for many months, sometimes as long as half a year. In 1990, at Lipfert's suggestion, I visited the museum in person. When I arrived and announced the purpose of my visit, the museum receptionist placed a call to the library. Lipfert claimed that he was too busy to see me or to allow me to use the library.

In the early 2000's, I sent a check to the museum in payment for a copy of a photograph in the library's collection. After the passage of six months, during which time my check was not cashed, I called Lipfert to ask about the status of my order. He told me that he was too busy to send out the photograph for reproduction, and that until he did so he would not cash my check. Now, more than five years later, he still has not cashed my check or sent the photograph.

Another facility that is controlled by an obnoxious librarian is the Submarine Force Library and Museum. The library consists of a large room whose shelves are filled with file boxes. I could easily have pulled relevant file boxes off the shelves, but the librarian – whose name I never learned – enforced compliance to a strict policy that made it mandatory for me to ask her to take each box off the shelf – one at a time. I went along with the program.

I hauled my copy stand from the parking lot to the second floor, and prepared to photograph prints of the submarines that were on my list of subjects. The librarian's office was on the other side of a glass partition. Because she was staring at a computer screen, she did not see me waiting for service.

I entered the office, and said, "Excuse me."

She looked up, obviously annoyed at the interruption, and said, "You're not allowed back here."

I nodded in acquiescence, then told her which submarine I wished to research first.

She pulled the box for me without further comment.

I shot my pictures. Each time I wanted another file box, I had to enter her office in order to get her attention. She got gruffer as the day progressed. Finally, I got close enough to her desk to see why she was staring so intently at the computer screen. She wasn't working; she was playing games!

Fortunately these examples are far from the norm. The point that I am making is that, while the rules of most maritime museum libraries are established by policy, the librarian may dictate the actual conduct of the library. And sometimes those rules are of his or her invention.

Now let me relate some of my experiences with various maritime museum libraries, so you can see that, more often than not, you can expect to receive informed and professional service. I will also expose a few quirks that will serve to warn you about aberrant tactics and behavior with which you might have to deal in order to achieve your research objectives.

Philadelphia Maritime Museum

Because I live in Philly, I have spent a great deal of time conducting initial shipwreck research at the Philadelphia Maritime Museum. I joined the museum in the mid 1970's. Annual dues entitled me to unlimited access to the museum and library, as well as a discount on photocopy charges.

The PMM possesses a complete set of *Lloyd's Registers* from the early 1800's to the present; the *Record* of the American Bureau of Ships from 1872 to the present (although some eighteenth-century years are missing); the *List of Merchant Vessels of the United States* from 1869 to present; the *Annual Report of the United States Life-Saving Service* from 1868 to 1908 (for 1909 to 1915, I have to go to the National Archives in College Park); hard copy and microfilm of the *New York Maritime Register* from 1869 to 1941 (except for a six-month holiday in the latter half of 1939); some hardcopies of the *Lloyd's Weekly Shipping Index* from the early 1900's; 12,000 thousand books on open shelves; 9,000 vessel construction plans, and numerous miscellaneous materials. In short, a research trove of maritime information that is conveniently located less than ten miles from my home.

When I commenced my life-long shipwreck research ambition, the museum and library were located at 321 Chestnut Street. The librarian was Dottie Mueller. After compiling my initial list of vessels that were lost off the New Jersey coast (and off the adjacent coasts of New York and Delaware), I tasked myself with obtaining copies of the Lloyd's listing for each and every vessel in which I was interested. Hundreds of vessels meant hundreds of photocopies.

Mueller showed me where the photocopier was located – in a small room that was more accessible to staff members than to library patrons, of whom I was always the only one. Because construction was slow in 1973, I was unemployed for days or weeks at a time. This afforded the perfect opportunity to conduct research. Every day I showed up at the PMM library to pour through aged texts. That was when I began to create my *Lloyd's Register* collection on shipwrecks of the eastern seaboard. Each day I made a stack of photocopies, and paid the requisite charge per page.

The second week, Mueller handed me a hastily typewritten memo which, although it did not mention me by name, was targeted precisely at my recent usage. It seemed as if Mueller thought that I was absconding with too much of her information. She intended to reduce my productivity by limiting the number of photocopies that a library patron was allowed to make to ten copies per day. I could do all the research I wanted, but I couldn't photocopy the results of my efforts.

This was my initiation to the junkyard dog complex that I defined in the Introduction. I looked Mueller straight in the eye and asked if this memo was directed specifically at me. She glanced away and mumbled that it was just a routine policy change.

Mueller resigned a few years later. When Anne Wilcox took the helm, she said nothing about any photocopy limitations, and this serious damper to my research output was removed; my work proceeded efficiently. That was when I learned that Mueller's copier restriction did not reflect official museum policy, but was something that she thought up and implemented on her own.

Independence Seaport Museum

In July 1995, the Philadelphia Maritime Museum moved to new premises on the Delaware River waterfront. The museum also changed its name to Independence Seaport Museum. Compared to the dark, cramped, and crowded quarters that the library occupied on Chestnut Street, the new facility was bright, spacious, and modern.

I was sufficiently familiar with the collection to require very little attention. I simply needed to learn where the books and microfilms were located in the new library. Rarely did I have to ask Wilcox for help. Usually, that was when I needed a volume that was stored in the stacks in the basement, and she had to retrieve it for me by sending it upstairs on the dumbwaiter. Only once was I stumped by not knowing where to look for a particular item of information.

I handed Wilcox a sheet of paper on which I had written the objective of my research, and asked, "What would you do if someone asked about this?"

She looked at the paper and, without batting an eye, replied, "I would give them your phone number."

She had done that on previous occasions. I appreciated her vote of confidence, but being the avowed expert did not allow me to consult a more knowledgeable specialist.

As curiosities, I would also like to relate some incidents that fall between the sublime and the absurd. The library had a strict policy against items leaving the premises. Wilcox reminded me of this when I asked about the possibility of taking a large-size blueprint to a nearby copy shop for reproduction. She wouldn't allow it, so I had to photocopy the blueprint in sections, and tape the sheets together at home.

A couple of weeks later, a Navy officer from the

nearby base asked how to obtain copies of a thick sheaf of papers, drawings, and photographs for a research project which the commandant had assigned to him. She immediately told him that he could take the entire folder with him and return it when he was done! She didn't even ask for a receipt. I was shocked by her flagrant discrimination. Wilcox had known me for more than a decade. This was the officer's first visit; he was a complete unknown to her.

According to another library policy, patrons were not allowed to be in the library unless the librarian or an aide was there to watch him. This meant that I had to leave the room any time that Wilcox left the room. When she went to lunch, I had to leave whether I was hungry or not. There was no lunchroom for patrons, so I ate my lunch while sitting on the floor outside the locked door until she returned.

In the late 1990's and early 2000's, the library took on a number of volunteers to respond to mail queries. These volunteers were ex-Navy officers who had served during World War Two. It was fascinating to listen to them talk among themselves about their wartime experiences while they looked up references and copied information for Wilcox to dispatch. If they were in the room when she went to lunch, I was permitted to stay – as long as someone, anyone, was there to watch me.

The ultimate irony occurred one day when only one volunteer showed up. It was his first day of service, yet he was authorized to watch me when Wilcox went to lunch. By this time, I had been a faithful dues paying museum member for a quarter of a century. As we sat at the table, each involved in his own work, I pondered the incongruity of the situation: a person who had only two hours of volunteer service under his belt was more trusted than a person who had been supporting the library for twenty-five years, and who was known to and respected by the librarian. It was ludicrous!

After Wilcox resigned unexpectedly, the new kid on the block was Michael Angelo. For real! I joked with him about how he must have had a tough time defending

Maritime Museum Libraries

his name in school. Anyway, when he assumed the role of librarian, he knew nothing about the collection, had never worked in a maritime library, and had not had the benefit of tutelage from Wilcox. He had to learn the collection cold turkey.

In an ironic turn of the tables, I gave him a tour of the collection and showed him where many of the books and microfilms were located. He had a mind that absorbed information the way a sponge soaks up water. By the time of my next visit, he knew the collection better than I did. When I asked for the files of a shipyard whose name I couldn't remember, he knew from my description of the file boxes which shipyard I meant, and showed me where they were stored.

Angelo was more lenient and trusting than Wilcox. He let me continue to work whenever he left the room. If any museum staff members came looking for him during his absence, he left it to me to tell them that he would return shortly. He even let me eat my lunch in a cubicle in the library.

I was sad to see him go to a job at another library. His replacement, Megan Fraser, learned the collection nearly as quickly as Angelo had learned it, and without any help from me. She is a stickler for the rules, but otherwise friendly and helpful. She is hard-pressed to answer the many queries that the library receives. If I could only convince her to call me Gary instead of Mr. Gentile . . .

The point of this memoir is that the conduct of a private library is somewhat subservient to its librarian. If there is no system of checks and balances, and a librarian is allowed to operate autonomously, you may find that policy takes a back seat to personal agenda.

You might have a wonderful experience at a library on one occasion, and find yourself completely stymied the next time. Earth abides, but librarians come and go.

The Mariners' Museum

If I were asked to suggest the pre-eminent maritime museum library at which to conduct shipwreck research, I would have to say unequivocally The Mariners' Museum (complete with The with a capital T, and an apostrophe after Mariners).

They may not have it all, but they have most of it: a complete set of *Lloyd's Registers* from the early 1800's to the present; the *Record* of the American Bureau of Ships from 1872 to the present; the *List of Merchant Vessels of the United States* from 1869 to present; microfilm version of the *New York Maritime Register* from 1869 to 1941 (except for a six-month holiday in the latter half of 1939); *Lloyd's Wreck Returns* from 1940 to present (under several different names); 78,000 thousand books (unfortunately in closed stacks); 600,000 photographic images; 20,000 post cards; 5,000 charts and maps; the Eldredge notebooks; and hundreds of thousands of miscellaneous items.

This maritime cornucopia is the most extensive collection in the country. The museum and library complex is located in Newport News, Virginia, on a 550-acre wooded park that boasts a large lake and a scenic 6-mile walking and jogging trail. Because the library is a 6-hour drive from Philadelphia, I conducted my initial research via mail. Not until the 1980's, when I started diving out of Virginia Beach, did I begin to visit the library personally. Since then I have worked library visits into my diving schedule. I stop there on my way to points south, or on my return trip home.

The turnover in librarians throughout the years has never affected the exceptional service. Librarians and their aides are the most professional people in the business. They are happy to see researchers utilize the facilities, they are helpful beyond belief, they are courteous to a fault, and their knowledge of the collection is consummate. What more can I say?

My only grievance pertains to the closed stacks. The official ship registers stand on open shelves for ready access, but the rest of the books are kept from public

Maritime Museum Libraries

pawing behind closed doors. This does not affect me personally because I seldom rely on secondary sources, but to the bulk of shipwreck researchers it is a decided inconvenience.

The books are listed in card file cabinets that are alphabetically arranged by title and author. If you know either the title or author of a book, you can look it up, jot down the location number on a slip of paper, hand to slip to a librarian, and have the book in your hands within a minute or two. It is that simple. If you're not sure how to find books about your area of interest, a librarian will cheerfully assist you by making informed suggestions.

But you can't browse through file cards. At the Independence Seaport Museum, for example, once you find a book on sailing vessels, you can browse through a slew of nearby books in the same category because they are shelved together in accordance with the Dewey decimal system. You can pull each one off the shelf, and refer to the index or table of contents to determine if other books have information on your subject matter. Okay, enough said on my pet peeve.

Visiting patrons are few – seldom more than one or two people beside myself. This doesn't mean that the library staff is idle. The library handles voluminous snail mail and e-mail requests that keep them more than busy. It is amazing to me how they can break away in the middle of writing a letter, in order to pull files or photos whenever I need them.

Be sure to ask a librarian to check the Eldredge collection for the name of the vessels you are researching. Elwin Eldredge was a meticulous and impeccable collector of obscure tidbits about vessels of all kinds – thousands of them. He typed these tidbits into small loose-leaf notebooks, each page of which was dedicated to a particular vessel. The Mariners' Museum inherited these notebooks. I often find tiny gems of information that help to flesh out a vessel's history.

As this book goes to press, The Mariners' Museum library is closed and is in the process of being moved to the campus of Christopher Newport University. The museum library and the university library are to be housed under one roof, although the collections are to be separated. A new street address has not yet been assigned. The librarians are hoping to keep the same phone and fax numbers. The new premises will be only a mile away from the present location.

I will discuss the extensive photographic collection in the chapter on Picture Sources.

Mystic Seaport Museum

The expansive and well-stocked G. W. Blunt White Library is tucked into a building that is located inside the fence on the museum grounds. The incredible holdings consist of more than 1,000 ships registers that run the gamut of the 1800's and 1900's (Lloyd's and the American Bureau of Ships, among others). Better yet, many nineteenth-century registers are available online at the Seaport's website. These registers are searchable by year, and printable. This virtual font of information may save you a trip to a maritime library!

The library has hardcopies of the *New York Maritime Register* from June 10, 1869 through 1948, including the latter half of 1939 that is missing from the collections at the Independence Seaport Museum and The Mariners' Museum.

You could get involved for days, if not weeks, in perusing the historical papers collection. Holdings include hundreds of boxes of manuscripts and other original records from individuals who were shipbuilders, ship owners, shipmasters, marine engineers, naval architects, and so on. As one prime example, the library holds the company records of Thomas A. Scott: a commercial salvor who later merged his expanding business with two other outfits to form Merritt-Chapman & Scott.

You will need much more time to read 1,300 ships logbooks, plus journals, ledgers, diaries, and miscellaneous documents from various maritime industries. These go back as far as 1720.

Maritime Museum Libraries

The periodical collection includes more than 700 titles. Other holdings boast more than 100,000 naval and architectural drawings, 9,000 nautical charts and maps, 70,000 books, 2,000 microfilms, and 1.3 million photographic images.

The library's reading room may not be large, but it is comfortable and warmly lit. Staff members are friendly and helpful. As you gaze at the books that line the shelves around you, keep in mind that what you see is only the tip of an incredibly large iceberg of primary research materials.

The library will respond to mail queries, but charges an hourly fee to conduct research for you.

Steamship Historical Society of America

In many respects, the Society's library is similar in size and breadth of holdings to that of the Independence Seaport Museum, except that it is not associated with a museum – although its collection includes a few steamship artifacts from yesteryear. The Society is a tax-exempt educational organization.

The library contains more than 5,000 books, thousands of vessel construction plans, and several thousand periodicals such as *Marine Engineering* (from the early part of the 1900's). Among the volumes are incomplete sets of the *Lloyd's Register*, the *Record* of the American Bureau of Ships, and the *List of Merchant Vessels of the United States*. Since these registers are available to me in Philadelphia, I seldom refer to them, or to secondary sources such as books.

My main interest in the Society has largely been photographic. The library contains several hundred thousand images. I shouldn't need to point out that the Society specializes in steamships. You won't find photos of sailing vessels in the collection; for those, visit The Mariners' Museum. More on this in the chapter on Picture Sources.

Despite extensive holdings, the library has consistently been a one-person operation: Laura Brown in the 1970's and 1980's, Anne House in the 1990's after

Brown retired, and Tom Hollowak in the 2000's after House resigned for health reasons. In various capacities, the present custodians are Bill and Sue Ewen, and Matt Schulte. Throughout my association with the Society, the librarians have always been helpful, knowledgeable, and a pleasure to work with. Handling correspondence constitutes the majority of their occupation. Usually, I was the only researcher on the premises.

Until 2006, the Steamship Historical Society library was located in Baltimore, Maryland, on the fifth floor of the library building of the University of Maryland. The massive room with its 20-foot ceiling occupied half the floor. The library has since been moved to a temporary location in East Providence, Rhode Island. Until permanent quarters are found, the only part of the collection that is accessible is the photographic archives. Everything else is packed away in boxes. Hopefully, the mothballed book and magazine fleet will soon be sailing the research seas again.

Peabody Essex Museum

The associated Phillips Library is stricter than the National Archives. It is the most mercenary library in the country, perhaps in the world, and is the least user friendly. The library charges an exorbitant daily fee just to enter the room. Librarians charge a fee to answer questions. The charges for photocopy services are at least twice as much as those of the National Archives.

In order to be granted research status, visiting researchers must first submit an application. The application is reviewed by a committee, which will decide whether or not to grant research status. Submit your application far in advance of your visit, because the committee will take two weeks or longer to approve it – *if* it is approved. The committee has the authority to deny research status. Don't mention that you are a wreck-diver.

You can submit research questions by snail mail or e-mail. As of this writing, the initial fee per question is $25, plus an hourly rate plus photocopy charges plus shipping cost. Results are sent to the correspondent in under two months. For picture requests, the initial charge is $50 per hour with a one-hour minimum. This is just to determine if the library *possesses* a particular picture in its collection. The fee for a copy of a picture, if found, is additional, and is the highest fee charged in the country; shipping charges are extra.

No admission was charged when I last visited the library in the early 1990's. Kathy Flynn, head librarian at the time, was curt and just shy of abusive – and this after two decades of correspondence. The rest of the staff was less than helpful.

Although the museum and library boast millions of items in their collections, only a minute portion relates to maritime history. For shipwreck researchers, the main attractions are the ship registers and photographic archives. Most of the 400,000 books are on non-maritime subjects.

If you want to feel like a convict doing research in a maximum-security prison that is supervised by hostile guards, visit the Phillips Library.

National Maritime Museum (San Francisco)

This spacious library is located in the San Francisco Maritime National Historical Park in San Francisco, California, in the Fisherman's Wharf neighborhood on the shore of San Francisco Bay. The National Park Service operates this huge government facility, which includes the J. Porter Shaw Library: the largest maritime library on the west coast.

Library holdings include 37,000 bound volumes (both books and periodicals) and 300,000 photographic images. The emphasis is global rather than maritime specific. Local maritime history is present in the collection of vessel construction plans of the Union Iron Works. There is also a collection of scrapbooks that contain clippings and correspondence.

The museum website includes links to the databases of the National Park Service: an online catalogue that accesses *all* of the Park's collections, not just those that are available at the Shaw Library.

Librarian Irene Stachura was always helpful to me. Today's reference staff readily responds to questions that are posed in person, and to queries that are submitted by phone, fax, snail mail, and e-mail. The photographic collection includes many vessel images.

South Street Seaport Museum

Located on the East River in Manhattan, New York, the one-room library is small and cozy. The books are primarily of interest to local researchers who are satisfied with secondary source materials.

The library answers queries from researchers. More often than not, librarian Marie Lore used to forward tough research inquiries to me. Researchers should not overlook the library's small picture archives, as I have found ship photos there that were not available elsewhere.

In addition to the library's own picture archives, in 1991 the picture archives of the Joseph Conrad Library of the Seamen's Church Institute in New York City were placed on permanent loan to the South Street Seaport Museum.

The open door policy has been closed, so that researchers who wish to visit the library now need to submit a request in writing, and pay a usage fee if permission is granted.

Hart Nautical Collections

One might not think of finding maritime related research material in a university that caters to engineering studies. The collection is small but unique. I have found vessel photographs here on occasion. The museum also has some books, construction plans, models, marine art, and technical records. Most of the collection originated from the New England area, and date from the late nineteenth century into the twentieth century.

Researchers are required to make an appointment. They may conduct research on site, or pay a staff mem-

Maritime Museum Libraries

ber an hourly fee to conduct research. The museum invites inquires by phone, snail mail, or e-mail.

Maine Maritime Museum (formerly Bath Marine Museum)

The collections relate almost entirely to the maritime history of Maine: 14,000 books, 53,000 issues of nautical periodicals, 40,000 photographic images, 2,000 linear feet of manuscripts (hand-written or typed papers from Maine mariners and maritime businesses), 1,000 maps and charts, 42,000 sheets of vessel construction plans (mostly from the Bath Iron Works), 620 reels of local and New York shipping newspapers, and miscellaneous ephemera (timetables, menus, broadsides, calendars, tickets, and handbills).

The museum charges an admission fee. The small desk in the cramped library can accommodate only one or two researchers. Staff members will reply to brief questions that can be answered in fifteen minutes or less. Otherwise an hourly rate applies.

The library is generally open on most weekdays, but an appointment is recommended in order to ensure that a staff member will be on duty at the time of a researcher's visit.

The library replies to queries that are submitted by snail mail or e-mail. The hourly rate applies if the fifteen-minute maximum response time is exceeded.

Penobscot Marine Museum

Holdings concentrate on the maritime history of mid-coast Maine with, despite the middle word in the name, little or no emphasis on the marine environment. The Stephen Phillips Memorial Library is the museum's research center. The library has books, manuscripts, nautical charts, maps, boat plans, and 30,000 photographic images relating to New England between 1880 and 1940. Some of these images are of vessels: either those that were constructed locally, or those that plied local waters.

Research hours are by appointment. A fee is levied for research that is initiated via snail mail and e-mail.

Maritime Museum Libraries

Outer Banks History Center

This regional archives and research library is operated by the North Carolina State Archives. The Center welcomes researchers, and will handle research projects that are submitted via phone, fax, snail mail, and e-mail.

Emphasis is placed on local coastal history, including ships, shipwrecks, lighthouses, and lightships. Holdings include a near-complete run of Geodetic and Coast Survey maps to the mid-1980's, more than 100,000 manuscript items, and an extensive collection of material on shipwrecks and the U.S. Life Saving Service and its successor (after 1915), the U.S. Coast Guard. One collection consists of several thousand original wreck reports, payroll records, telegrams, and other documents that date between 1883 and 1933.

When I visited the Center in the early 1990's, the curator was Wynne Dough. I joked with him about the razzing he must have taken in his school days. He and his assistant, Hellen Shore, were friendly and helpful, going out of their way to retrieve records, photocopy documents, and let me take photographs of prints.

Underwater Archaeology Branch of the North Carolina Office of State Archaeology

This archival center and conservation laboratory is located in Fort Fisher State Park. The office maintains file folders on hundreds of local shipwrecks. In the early 1990's, chief underwater archaeologist Richard Lawrence allowed me unrestricted access to these voluminous records. I had free use of the photocopy machine. I brought my camera and copy stand in order to photograph prints.

The Branch responds to queries that are made by phone, fax, snail mail, and e-mail. Call ahead if you plan to appear in person, in order to ascertain the hours of operation and to ensure that the office will be open to researchers on the chosen day of your visit.

Maritime Museum Libraries

North Carolina State Department of Cultural Resources

This North Carolina department is located in downtown Raleigh. Holdings are global, but it should not be overlooked if you are researching shipwrecks that occurred off the State. They have photographic images that are unavailable anywhere else in my experience. They also have some textual records that might be of interest.

The staff will respond to queries that are made by phone, fax, snail mail, and e-mail, although it is better to appear in person and browse through the files. You never know what items of interest you might find.

South Carolina Institute of Archaeology and Anthropology

Although the Institute's emphasis is not on maritime history, it maintains shipwreck files and photographic images that may not be found in other archives. Chris Amer, head of the underwater division, welcomes researchers who visit the facility. Call ahead to ensure that someone will be on hand to offer assistance.

The Institute maintains records on local shipwrecks, and may have pictures of them.

U.S. Naval Institute

The Institute has published the monthly magazine *Proceedings* since 1874. Each issue contains articles and essays on naval topics. Back issues are available at the Institute library. The Institute also publishes the monthly magazine *Naval History*, and numerous books on naval history (primarily those that were written by U.S. Navy personnel).

Holdings also include oral histories, but the collection that is of greatest interest to shipwreck researchers is the photographic archive, which consists of nearly half a million naval and maritime images, many of which are not available anywhere else.

The library is located on the spacious grounds of the United States Naval Academy: the well-known training center for U.S. Navy officers. I used to be able to drive unannounced to the library, but with security measures tightened as a result of terrorist activity, this is no longer permitted.

Researchers who do not possess current military identification and Department of Defense decals on their vehicle will not be allowed on the grounds without prior authorization from an Institute representative. This authorization must be obtained at least 24 hours prior to any proposed visit. You cannot pass the guard station without this authorization. After your identity and authorization are established at the guard station, you must obtain a visitor's pass at the Pass and ID office. Take your driver's license, proof of insurance, and vehicle registration with you into the office.

You can call the Naval Academy Security Department for updated information.

Some of the Institute's images are available online from the website. You can learn which other images are in the Institute's holdings by phoning, faxing, snail-mailing, or e-mailing queries.

Submarine Force Library and Museum Association

The library is located on the second floor of the museum complex at the Groton submarine base. As the name implies, the collection focuses exclusively on the history of U.S. Navy submarines. The library is not, as one might expect, the last word on submarines. Nonetheless, there are files on every submarine that was ever constructed for the U.S. Navy.

Some files are slender while others are voluminous. The collection includes photographic images that may not exist at other archival facilities, including the National Archives and the Naval Photographic Center.

Historical Collections of the Great Lakes (formerly Institute for Great Lakes Research)

What I found interesting about this research facility is that an escort is required to get from the ground floor of the museum to the sixth floor, where the library is located. Despite this auspicious beginning, once you

Maritime Museum Libraries

are over that hurdle there is clear sailing ahead. The archivists are friendly and accommodating, notwithstanding the large volume of correspondence which is their daily bread and butter, as an hourly service fee has been recently instituted. Bob Graham has been especially helpful to me throughout the years.

As one must imagine, the library holdings deal almost entirely with the Great Lakes region, from the nineteenth century to the present. Of particular interest to shipwreck researchers is the collection of vessel data sheets for more than 10,000 vessels whose careers were spent – in part or in whole – on the Great Lakes. The website has a link to an online database which, while not yet complete, continues to grow.

The database includes not only statistical information on a vessel, but generally a selected photograph of that vessel from the photographic archive of more than 130,000 images. Many ships that gasped their last on the eastern seaboard originated at one of the Great Lakes shipbuilding yards. If a vessel spent even a small part of its career in plying the fresh water shipping lanes, the library is likely to have a photograph of it.

The collection also contains more than 9,000 books, 4,500 pamphlets, 250 linear feet of periodicals (consisting of more than 350 titles), several hundred thousand drawings from several shipbuilders, 2,000 linear feet of manuscripts, and 550 volumes of news clippings. Not to be left out are ship registers: *Lloyd's, List of Merchant Vessels of the United States, Lake Underwriters, Canadian List of Shipping, Great Lakes Red Book,* and *Greenwood's Guide.*

Great Lakes Historical Society

As the name implies, the Clarence S. Metcalf Great Lakes Maritime Research Library collection deals exclusively with maritime history of the Great Lakes: vessels, lighthouses, and important events. Holdings include 20,000 vessel construction plans, 488 deck logs, *Beeson's Maritime Directory, List of Merchant Vessels of the United States* between 1884 and 1965, *Marine Review* between 1884 and 1931, some issues of the *Great Lakes Red Book*, thousands of photographs and scale line drawings of Great Lakes vessels, thousands of books about Great Lakes topics, and thousands of miscellaneous items (newspaper articles, personal histories, ticket stubs, postcards, technical information, and so on).

Some of the collection has been digitized and is accessible on the Society's website. Appointments are required to do research in person; they should be made at least one week in advance of your proposed visit. Staff members handle queries that are made via phone, snail mail, and e-mail. An hourly fee is charged.

Wisconsin Marine Historical Society

This adjunct to the Milwaukee Public Library houses data on more than 7,600 vessels that plied the Great Lakes between 1679 and the present. The index to this voluminous collection is available online on the Society's website.

The collection includes microfilm vessel enrollments for 24,000 vessels that were registered between 1815 and 1915, *Blue Book of American Shipping* (spotty between 1896 and 1913), *Great Lakes Red Book* (spotty between 1904 and 1994), *Shipmasters Association Directory* (spotty between 1898 and 1967), *Beeson's (Sailors) Marine Hand Book* (sic) (spotty between 1890 and 1922), *Marine Review* (spotty between 1894 and 1923), newspaper clippings that date from 1884 to 1907, a number of biographies of vessel owners and skippers, and 21,000 photographic images.

Local newspaper *Milwaukee Sentinel* has been indexed with a searchable database, between 1837 and 1890.

Researchers may conduct their own research at the library. Staff members charge a fee to conduct research by request.

Wisconsin Maritime Museum

In addition to 8,000 books and 40,000 photographic images, the collection of this non-profit organization includes a wealth of information relating to Great Lakes shipbuilding in general and the Manitowoc Shipbuilding Company in particular (specifically, submarine construction during World War Two). Holdings also include construction blueprints, deck logs, manuscripts, and local miscellany.

The library is available to researchers by prior appointment. For remote research, you can download a Research Request form, fill it out, and submit it to the Registrar/Collections manager. This system applies to photographic research as well as textual research.

Library and Archives Canada

This is the Canadian equivalent of the U.S. National Archives. The present name resulted from the 2004 merger of the Public Archives of Canada and the National Library of Canada. Rules and collections are similar to those of the National Archives, with emphasis on Canadian history.

Researchers are welcome to visit the facility, and will be assisted by archivists in identifying and retrieving pertinent materials.

Research assistants will answer questions over the phone, and will respond to queries that are submitted via fax, snail mail, and e-mail.

National Maritime Museum (London)

Not to be confused with the museum of the same name in San Francisco, this facility is the British equivalent of the U.S. National Archives.

The Museum will *not* – I repeat, *not* – answer research inquiries of any kind. Museum literature claims that the staff is *unable* to answer such inquiries. This implies that the staff consists solely of librarians, and not archivists, and that they do not have the ability or know-how to answer inquiries.

If you cannot visit in person, the Museum can suggest a number of paid private researchers who can be hired to do research in your stead.

Part Four
Embarking on Research

Now that you know from the previous chapters *where* to conduct shipwreck research, in this chapter I will instruct you on how to begin, and which shipping lanes to take in order to expand your knowledge – and which pitfalls to avoid.

Once again I must caution you against reliance upon secondary sources, unless you know and trust the source. Most people nowadays conduct research of any sort strictly on the Internet. This can be good and useful, but unless you are circumspect it is likely to prove fatuous and worthless – often worse than worthless because it might lead you down the wrong path to perdition.

According to ancient wisdom, you shouldn't believe half of what you read, and you should be suspicious of the other half. The written word is not gospel, and this goes double or triple for the Internet. This is because what is written on the Internet seldom goes through any kind of peer review, editing process, or academic challenge. It is often written by individuals who themselves relied upon secondary sources, or who possess no expertise in the subject matter, or who intentionally altered the facts in order to achieve some nefarious purpose.

The Internet Fallacy

Consider this miscegenation of gross misinformation. Two websites currently espouse the notorious history of a ship called the *General Sherman*, which supposedly began her career as the *Princess Royale*. The "American schooner" purportedly raided Chinese coastal villages in 1865. Chinese warships captured and confiscated the *General Sherman*, then sold her to a British company in Tientsin. In 1866, Korean natives

Embarking on Research 183

destroyed the *General Sherman* on the Ping-Yang River, and murdered the entire crew.

This story may or may not be true. I don't know. Great detail is provided, making it appear that there is some factual basis to the incidents that are described. But the websites also furnish the *General Sherman's* background and subsequent career. They claim that she was the *Princess Royal* (no final "e") that was commissioned into the Union Navy as the USS *Princess Royal*, then sold into merchant service after the Civil War, in 1865, at which time her name was changed to *General Sherman*. They then jump to the *General Sherman's* putative loss off the coast of South Carolina, in 1874.

U.S. archival records substantiate the domestic history of the *Princess Royal*, which did in fact become the USS *Princess Royal*. But when the Union Navy sold her, the new owner changed her name to *Sherman*, not to *General Sherman*. The *Sherman* was a steamship, not a schooner. She was indeed lost off the South Carolina coast in 1874. But there is no mention in the records of her career that she ever went to China. Quite the contrary, she transported freight and passengers between New York and New Orleans.

In order to fit the facts of her ultimate demise, both websites claim that the *General Sherman* must have been raised, repaired, and returned to service – although they were not able to substantiate this claim with documentation. They simply jumped to this conclusion by way of explanation of a documented loss in the Atlantic Ocean.

Thus the story of the *General Sherman* in China is sandwiched between the *Princess Royal* and the *Sherman* in the United States. One website hinted that the U.S. Navy covered up the vessel's Oriental escapades. Each website appears to have borrowed information from the other. This back and forth dissemination further confuses the issue. The result is a hodgepodge of urban legend based upon a kernel – or perhaps two kernels – of truth.

As I have written elsewhere, if the only information you want is that which is free, you are likely to get what you pay for. It is not too farfetched to dub the Internet as "the misinformation superhighway."

Encyclopedia Sales on the Internet

While I am on the subject of the dubious value of Internet data . . .

It seems that an alarming number of Internet surfers rely upon Wikipedia for general information. This website purports to be a comprehensive reference source, touting itself as a web-based encyclopedia. This gives the impression that it holds to the same standards of quality and authenticity as published, multi-volume encyclopedias. Nothing could be farther from the truth.

If you follow the link About Wikipedia, you will learn that its topics are written by volunteers. Some of the articles were obviously written by scholars who knew their subject matter, but many articles were just as obviously written by people whose so-called knowledge was based on hearsay, not research. Anyone can add input to an existing article, or create an article from whole cloth. I have found numerous errors in articles whose subjects I consider to lie within my area of expertise. And not just minor errors, but gross errors.

When I have written articles for encyclopedia entries, other experts checked my work. By the same token, I have been asked to edit and annotate encyclopedia entries that other experts wrote. This system of examination and cross-examination ensures the best possible accuracy. Facts in question are addressed and rectified before the encyclopedia goes to press.

Not so with Wikipedia. Wikipedia articles are not subjected to scrutiny or peer review in the manner of paper-and-ink encyclopedias. Some articles may be edited by other volunteers, but that still does not guarantee authentication of facts, because those other volunteers may not have the necessary expertise either. Each volunteer is an individual, not a member of a

Embarking on Research

review committee.

Wikipedia promotes itself as a free encyclopedia. As I noted in the previous section, if you get something for free, you are likely to get what you paid for. If you are looking for convenience, subscribe to an online encyclopedia that is based upon a long history of paper-and-ink encyclopedias.

Dive Websites

I have also seen dive-related websites on which shipwreck histories or discoveries contained erroneous or misleading information. This generally occurs because the writer based his report on unreliable secondary sources: magazine pieces, newspaper fillers, hearsay, or other Internet sites.

These perversions of the facts can have deleterious secondary effects. If a reader accepts the write-up as gospel, he might pass along the misinformation as factual. Then someone else – or a number of others – pass it along farther, perhaps perverting it more in the process.

Misinformation tends to have a snowball effect. You might remember the grade school amusement in which one child whispers a phrase or sentence to an adjacent child, who then whispers it into the ear of the next child in line, and so on until the final child hears nothing but gibberish.

Some website contributors have fudged the facts intentionally by claiming discoveries that they didn't make, or by rewriting history the way they wished it could have been, or by extolling nonexistent personal achievements in order to present themselves to the public the way they wish to be perceived.

Dave Bright did this by creating a fictitious organization of which he was the so-called president: the Nautical Research Group. In fact, the "group" consisted of only a single individual: himself, and no one else. His website gave the "group" the appearance of substance and validity, when in fact it existed only in his fertile imagination. Among his exaggerated claims were more than 120 dives on the *Andrea Doria*, when he actually made fewer than 30. He scammed a lot of people – including newspapers and wire services – into believing that he was someone he was not.

Nonetheless, people read his guff and believed it. It never occurred to them to ask for a membership list. Bright successfully created a fictitious persona that bore no resemblance to his real self.

Here Today, Gone Tomorrow

Keep in mind that websites are ephemeral and subject to change. If the owner doesn't pay his rent on time, the website vanishes from the Internet, perhaps never to return. The webmaster may alter the content without notice. And sometimes, for any number of reasons, websites are temporarily unavailable. This latter condition is usually the fault of the Internet service provider, which may be experiencing technical difficulties; or it could be a web host issue; or it could be a connection problem . . .

Books and printed documents are absolutely stable. They never disappear; their content never changes. Their pages experience none of the troubles that plague Internet screens.

Bookmark useful websites for future reference, but print those screens that contain pertinent information, and keep the printed documents in accessible file folders.

When all is said and done, ink and toner are more reliable than recycled electrons.

Reading is Believing – Not!

As I noted above, there is an age-old belief that anything that is printed in ink must be absolutely factual. This belief is so far from the truth of the matter that it boggles the mind to wonder how people can be so gullible. It appears that gullibility must be an inborn facet of human nature, and that some people take advantage of it in order to deceive the public.

This irrational acceptance of the infallibility of the

Embarking on Research

written word may have started in prehistory with the credence lent to cave paintings. It was then extended to include hieroglyphics that were chiseled in stone. Next came the credibility of papyrus and Guttenberg. After ink came toner. Now there is reverence of the Internet.

When all is said and done, electrons are no more plausible than chemical compounds. Alchemy cannot turn base metals to gold, and the Internet cannot convert fiction to fact.

Some people find comfort in unfounded beliefs. They ignore bland facts because dramatic stories that are laced with embellishment are more entertaining. They prefer histrionics to history. The *General Sherman* quackery is right down their alley.

But for a shipwreck researcher – a true maritime historian – fables, fairy tales, and cock-and-bull stories won't suffice.

In most cases, the Internet is just another secondary source. Perhaps it is even a tertiary source, or worse. Yet people are inclined to believe what they read on it, often without question.

My advice is to utilize the Internet for the primary sources that it offers, and to reject its secondary sources as suspect. Do not heed what you read in chat groups or blogs (web logs). Be wary, or you will join the ranks of the great misinformed.

It is better to be *un*informed than to be *mis*informed.

You can't even trust all government websites. When George Orwell wrote about the Ministry of Truth in *1984*, he described a government agency that continually rewrote history the way the government wanted the masses to perceive it. This is a common practice today in, for example, the National Marine Sanctuary Program of the National Oceanic and Atmospheric Administration. If you visit the NOAA website on the Civil War ironclad *Monitor*, you won't see a word about my successful lawsuit against the Administration with regard to diver access to the wreck site, or how the present permitting system came about. NOAA has conveniently deleted this part of the *Monitor's* history in order to present a misperception to the public: as if the permitting process always existed as a voluntary endeavor on the part of NOAA. In truth, the permitting process was forced upon NOAA by a federal judge, and held to account by Congressional intervention.

This "uninformation" is as insidious as disinformation, perhaps more so.

Last but not least, do not believe something simply because you read it first. Another human fallibility is the illogical acceptance of primaries. Many people reject all new information that repudiates something that they heard or read beforehand. To these people, there is no such thing as follow-up or correction: first is not just foremost, it is indefectible.

Avoid this pitfall by examining each new fact in relation to its validity, not by the order in which it was beheld. Facts are not sequential; they are cumulative. If a newly uncovered fact belies previous information, perhaps the previous information was incorrect. Invalidation of information is at least as important as validation.

Because of its importance, I reiterate: pay heed to the old saying that goes, "Don't believe everything you read in the newspapers." Again, this goes for triple for the Internet.

Valid Internet Sources

Not to pooh-pooh the Internet in its entirety, under certain circumstances it is quickly becoming an invaluable primary source, and a good place to begin your shipwreck research, if only as a starting point before embarking on in-depth archival research.

The more information that you have in hand before visiting a maritime library or an archival facility, the better prepared you will be to cut to the chase and obtain the valid information that you want. Much of this preparatory work can now be done on your computer in the comfort of your own home – with a cup of coffee in your hand and your feet propped up on a

Embarking on Research

stool.

By way of example, in 1993 the U.S. Coast Guard Historian's Office published *A History of U.S. Lightships*, by Willard Flint. This is the quintessential source of statistical information on lightships. The published volume is available in hardcopy in most maritime libraries, and even in many public libraries. The book is an accurate source whose facts were gleaned from official Coast Guard records.

Because the Coast Guard sanctioned the book by publishing it under the auspices of its Historian's Office, it can be considered a primary source. The Historian's Office has now scanned the book and made it available on the Coast Guard website. The appearance and format are the same as they are in the book.

Like the plane geometry theorem of transitive equivalence, online information that mirrors paper information from primary source documents is the same as primary information.

Let me cite a few more examples. The Mystic Seaport Museum has posted thousands of pages of eighteenth-century ship registers on its website (mostly the *Record* of American and Foreign Shipping). These are scans of the actual pages from the annual registers, indexed first by year and then by the letters of the alphabet. If you find the vessel that is the object of your research, you can print the page and save yourself a trip to a maritime library.

At http://ul.bgsu.edu/cgi-bin/xvsl2.cgi, you will find an index of Great Lakes vessels courtesy of the Bowling Green State University library, under the title of Historical Collections of the Great Lakes. When you enter a vessel's name in the appropriate box, the search engine will produce an item number that links to a page that provides construction statistics (tonnage, dimensions, when and where built, and so on), a list of owners, name changes, historical notes of interest, and final disposition. Library historians assembled these data from original vessel registers and other primary sources.

I could cite other examples, but the list is growing faster than I can write. My advice is to check periodically for primary Internet sources, gather as much information as possible, then head for the brick-and-mortar archives and libraries to complete your research.

The Future of the Internet

All government archival facilities and most major museums now have an Internet presence. Information that is obtained from these websites is just as accurate as information obtained from the brick-and-mortar archives and museums.

Government facilities are in the process of scanning gobs of documents in order to make them available on the Internet. Museums scan teasers, but are likely not to make all their information available because they are private institutions, and as such want to exercise control over their resources in order to make money from them. Keep in mind that public archives and libraries are funded by the government (federal, State, city, and so on), whereas private museums and libraries must obtain money from grants, donations, admission fees, and so on.

I suppose if you look far enough into the future, you can prognosticate a time when *all* primary documents will be available online. This may be a boon or a nightmare.

First, let me state that there are billions – perhaps trillions – of documents that are tucked away in file boxes in various federal archives. Scanning all these pages will take an enormous amount of time: decades, perhaps centuries.

Consider the anecdote that I related about the burned Customs House records that National Archives conservationists have yet to preserve after more than 70 years. In my lifetime, and in the lifetime of the present generation of readers, researchers will still have to obtain primary documents by making physical appearances at the facilities that hold them.

Consider, too, my comments about Internet search

engines. Unless refinements are made in the way that Internet searches are conducted, perhaps in coordination with some kind of indexing system that can intelligently separate relevant data from irrelevant data, locating specific items online will be a near impossible task that could take longer to perform than it would take to visit the hardcopy holding facilities that house the original documents.

Snail Mail

Most modern day researchers have no idea what it was like to conduct research before the existence of the Internet. At my high point in 1996, I had 83 unanswered query letters in circulation. I sent every one by mail, and paid first-class postage for the privilege.

Letters that I sent overseas were in transit for weeks. Depending upon the size and dedication of the recipient's staff, months might pass before someone got around to answering my query. Return mail required more weeks in transit.

Some sources never bothered to reply. Some replied six months or more after I posted my query letter. Some replied that they did not have the information that I sought, but suggested other possibilities. This in turn induced me to generate additional query letters.

Keeping track of the volume of queries, replies, and follow-ups was nearly a fulltime occupation. In this new age of instant gratification, many people would find themselves frustrated by the delay. If it took six months to get an answer to a query, it might take another six months to get a second answer to a question that was raised by the reply to my original query. Sometimes years passed before I achieved a final resolution – or ascertained that the avenue was a dead end.

E-mail

Electronic mail has succeeded admirably in significantly reducing the amount of time that passes between the posing of a question and the receipt of an answer. E-mail queriers need to understand, however, that the time that a recipient must spend in researching a question remains unchanged. The time that is saved is transit time, and the time that used to be spent on typing letters, addressing envelopes, licking stamps, and so on.

Nowadays, the typing is done on a computer, after which the reply is transmitted by the simple expedient of clicking on the Send tab. Not only does this method save actual time, it saves the mental energy that the recipient used to expend on purely clerical and secretarial work.

Even high-salaried executives now type their own business letters. The days of dictation and shorthand are over.

Today I have far fewer queries in circulation. I seldom write letters, and my queries to archives, libraries, and museums receive prompter attention.

Alternative Internet Sources

The Internet makes it possible for a researcher to locate potential sources of information that he might never find without the ability to conduct global searches. Consider this 15-year saga.

In 1992, Bob Meimbresse, skipper of the *Down Deep*, took an Atlantic Divers charter to an offshore site that had never been dived. Gene Peterson owned Atlantic Divers. Peterson and I went down first. We discovered a wreck whose vintage we estimated lay between the two world wars.

Two years later, I found the remains of the wheelhouse off the port side of the wreck. In the debris lay the helm and brass stand. The next day, four of us worked to cut the stand out of fishing net and send the stand to the surface under a couple of liftbags. The four were Lynn DelCorio, John Moyer, Gene Peterson, and this author. Peterson wanted to clean the helm and display it in his shop, which was okay with me. I hoped that there was writing on the stand that would identify the wreck.

Stamped on the cover of the stand was "John Hastie

Embarking on Research

Co. Ltd, Patented Greenock," and a serial number: "2705." Unfortunately, the stamping did not refer to any British vessel that was known to have been lost in the area. And so matters stood for thirteen years.

In 2007, Peterson initiated an Internet search for the John Hastie Company. A series of e-mails took him on a circuitous path that eventually led to the Glasgow University Archives. The Archives had inherited the records of the John Hastie Company. Peterson learned that the company furnished steering gear to local shipbuilders. Extant company records contained the serial number of every steering gear that the company had manufactured, and the name of the shipbuilder to which the gear had been consigned.

Swan Hunter & Wigham had contracted for the steering gear in question. The shipbuilder had two vessels under construction at that time. The *St. Mary* burned and sank in the Mississippi River in the 1950's, and was subsequently scrapped. The *Miraflores* disappeared without a trace on a passage to New York, after departing Haiti on February 14, 1942.

The *Miraflores* is not mentioned in the war diary of the Eastern Sea Frontier. Secondary German sources credited the *U-432* with the tonnage. For some reason, post-war Allied assessors did not confirm this credit, so the *Miraflores* was not listed in the statistics of merchant vessel war losses. Nonetheless, the wreck lay in the grid square in which the *U-432* torpedoed an unidentified vessel on February 19, 1942.

Admittedly, it was possible to undertake this kind of detective work before the existence of the Internet. But the job would have been onerous in the extreme. Snail mail communication between the United States and Scotland would have taken months for each and every query. Peterson did in a couple of months what would have taken years in pre-Internet days.

As more archival facilities come online, this kind of research will become quicker and easier. It is in this manner in which the Internet will achieve its greatest potential in the conduct of shipwreck research.

Back to Basics

Not all research can be done on the Internet. In fact, as of this writing, very little of a research project can be done on the Internet; or, if it can be *started* on the Internet, it can't be completed there. There are not enough primary sources on the Internet. Reliance upon secondary Internet sources will result in the collection of partial information at best, and misinformation at worst.

Initial research still relies upon the tried and true methods that have proven so effective in the past.

In order to begin research on a shipwreck, the two most important items of information that are essential to possess are the name of the vessel and the date of the casualty. It is possible to start with only the name, but the lack of the date will increase the difficulty of the search, and may cause confusion with other vessels of the same name. The location may help in lieu of the date.

The first thing I would do is look up the name in the *Encyclopedia of American Shipwrecks*. If the wreck is listed, most of my problems are solved right off the bat. Berman provides the date and location of the loss. This information distinguishes the wreck in question from every other wreck.

Next, by way of confirmation, I would look up the date in the *New York Maritime Register* or *Lloyd's Weekly Shipping Index*. I should find the vessel listed alphabetically in the Disaster column. This will verify that Berman's information is correct, and will add some explanatory material about the location and nature of the loss. At this point I am certain that the wreck actually exists, and that the facts in my possession are essentially correct. I make a copy of the page.

Next I would look up the vessel's name in the *Lloyd's Register* or the *Record* of the American Bureau of Ships (or, failing to find it, in the *List of Merchant Vessels of the United States* if the vessel had American registry). I photocopy the page on which the vessel is listed. Now I have the vessel's official number and her

Embarking on Research

vital statistics.

Uncertainty might arise if there are multiple listings for the same name. In that case I must determine which listing is my subject vessel. If the construction dates are different, and only one corresponds to the date given by Berman, I need look no farther. Alternatively, because NYMR and LWSI provide the vessel's rig and nationality, that information can be used to distinguish one vessel from the others.

Generally, I would look in the last register in which the vessel's name appeared. To ensure that I have gotten the right vessel, I might refer to the subsequent edition. The vessel's name should be absent. A vessel may also be absent if her name was changed. If I have any suspicions, I look in the back of the book for the list of name changes.

Sometimes I might backtrack and look in previous registers, perhaps as far back as the vessel's first appearance. I might do this in order to have a copy of each listing under the vessel's prior names. Remember, though, that the official number will always be the same.

If the vessel is not listed in any of the registers, and if the vessel's homeport is in the United States, you can obtain the Certificate of Enrollment from the National Archives.

To flesh out details, I would then look in newspapers: the *New York Times* first, because it is indexed, then in local newspapers.

Step one (Berman) I can do at home. Step two (NYMR or LWSI, and register) would require a trip to a maritime museum library. Step three (newspaper) would require a visit to a public library. If I wanted to pursue additional research, step four would necessitate a tour of the federal archival facilities in Washington, DC.

For example, if the loss occurred in the nineteenth century and involved a steamship, I would look through the records of the Steamboat Inspection Service at the National Archives. If the wreck ran aground, I would look at the appropriate *Annual Report of the United States Life Saving Service*. If the wreck occurred during one of the world wars, I would peruse the massive record groups at the National Archives. If the wreck were that of a U.S. Navy vessel, I would check the Ships History Branch at the Washington Navy Yard.

I would also consult various maritime museum libraries.

If I wanted additional in-depth detail, I could try more exotic sources: local historical societies, the ship owner if it was still in business, the insurance company that underwrote the loss, and so on. There is no end to the possibilities. Shipwreck information may be found in the most unlikely places.

Insurance and Reinsurance

Ship insurance is big business. Underwriters distinguish two kinds of policies: one for the hull and one for cargo. Hull insurance covers a vessel and all its appurtenances against damage or loss. Cargo insurance covers the cargo or portions thereof against damage or loss.

No individual insurance company ever underwrites all the coverage for hull and cargo. Instead, insurance is spread among several, often many different companies both domestic and foreign. This system is based on the old but true adage that it doesn't pay to carry all your eggs in one basket, because if you drop the basket all your eggs may break; carry your eggs in several baskets.

After a shipping line chooses a company to insure a hull, the underwriter than sells portions of the coverage to other underwriters. This is called reinsurance. The primary company will also purchase portions of coverage on vessels from other underwriters. Thus the underwriters provide partial coverage for scores or hundreds of vessels. This way, if a vessel becomes a total loss, no single insurance company is liable for the entire amount of coverage. I've often wondered why homeowner's insurance doesn't operate the same way.

Embarking on Research

Generally, a merchant obtains shipping insurance for his cargo. A freighter may transport merchandise for dozens of consigners, each of which has his own insurance carrier. Again, in the event of damage or loss, this system saves an individual underwriter from assuming the liability for an entire cargo.

Any number of companies will provide reinsurance for a particular vessel's voyage. All these insurance companies keep records of every voyage in which they held an interest. At the very least, these records include the cargo manifest. A file on a loss might also include newspaper clippings, testimonies of survivors, trial documents, and so on. You just never know.

In the 1970's, when Drew Maser worked for the Insurance Company of North America, he had access to the company archives. Because he was a wreck-diver, and was interested in shipwreck history, he spent his lunchtime researching East Coast shipwrecks from as long ago as World War One. He found information that was not available anywhere else – information that he shared with me.

Insurance companies are not benevolent historical societies. They are private businesses that keep their records for in-house use. In the 1990's, I had a meeting with the INA archivist on another matter (the salvage of the *Lady Elgin*, which sank in Lake Michigan in 1860, and in which INA had an interest because the company had insured the hull and had paid the claim for the vessel's loss). She told me that access to company archives was now restricted, and that even INA employees no longer had the privileges that Maser had had twenty years earlier.

This does not necessarily imply that other insurance companies are as strict as INA, or that INA might not respond to a query from a private researcher. All avenues must be explored in the quest for shipwreck information. A letter or e-mail might meet with rejection, or open a trove of documentation.

Bumps in the System

Shipwreck research does not always go as smoothly as I described in the ideal scenario above. Permutations are legion. It is frustrating when the well-ordered system breaks down for no apparent reason, and you cannot find information that should be readily available.

Not all shipwrecks were recorded. If they *were* recorded, they might have been recorded in one place but not in another. Sometimes erroneous or contradictory information was recorded. Some records were misfiled. Other records were trashed.

In a utopian society and a computerized world, one should be able to simply follow the steps to an inevitable outcome. But we live in the real world and not in a perfectly organized Utopia.

Some information is difficult to locate. Some information is *impossible* to locate, unless you are willing to devote your life to the pursuit of a particular bit of arcane knowledge that no one else really cares about. And some information does not exist. You can't find what isn't extant on paper.

I could give you countless examples of problems that I have encountered throughout the decades, but it would be pointless.

Learn to accept the limitations of shipwreck research.

Work with dedication, but be willing to admit defeat when you encounter a dead end and there is nowhere else to look.

Mistaken Documentation

Archivists and librarians are people like everyone else, and therefore they occasionally make mistakes. I have uncovered a few.

Two years ago, I browsed through the online disaster/event files of the U.S. Coast Guard Historian's Office. I noticed that the *Marine Merchant* was listed as having been lost in the Gulf of Mexico in 1961. In fact, the vessel broke in two and sank in the Gulf of Maine.

When I visited the office a few months later, I informed the historian on duty of the error. He acknowledged receipt of the information and said that he would look into it. As of this writing, the error has not been corrected on the website.

I have found misfiled documents at the National Archives. The Archives has neither the expertise nor a mechanism to rectify mistakes. Remember that an archivist is an expert at locating files, and not necessarily an historian with exacting knowledge about the information that is contained in those files. Researchers are not permitted to reorganize misfiled documents, even though they can prove conclusively that the documents are misfiled.

The Archive collection is static. If a document was misfiled in historical times through a common clerical error, the mission of the Archives is to preserve that error as if the error itself has significance.

I have bought pictures of vessels from museums, only to learn later that the picture was miscaptioned: it represented a different vessel of the same name. I have also found misfiled or incorrect documents in museums. In most cases, because a museum staff is small and because staff members are knowledgeable about maritime subjects, they can confirm mistakes and are willing to correct them.

The worst botch that I ever encountered was an article that I found at the Submarine Force Library and Museum. The librarian knows nothing about submarines. All she knows is how to pull boxes off of shelves. In the file on the American submarine *L-8*, I found a magazine piece about a cruise across the Mediterranean Sea, through the Suez Canal, and across the Indian Ocean, stopping at such places as Aden, Colombo, Ceylon, China, Sumatra, Singapore, and Penang. This voyage supposedly occurred in 1919.

The account appeared to be authentic because it was written by a crewmember. Yet from previous research I knew – or thought I knew – that the *L-8* never left the United States. The article made me suspect that the *Dictionary of American Naval Fighting Ships* omitted the cruise. This was not completely out of bounds, for I have found many instances in which DANF sanitized a warship's history by neglecting to mention such discreditable tidbits as collisions and loss of life. But why would it leave out a seemingly innocuous circumnavigation of the Earth?

The only way that I could be certain of the facts was to refer to the *L-8*'s deck log. I called for the log at the National Archives. A year's worth of hand-written entries could not have been faked. During the time in question, the *L-8* was stationed exactly where the Navy records claimed she was stationed: at San Pedro, California.

This was a real conundrum. I finally solved the mystery by recollecting that the British navy also used alphanumeric designations for its early submarines. After more research, I ascertained that there were two submarines that were named *L-8*! One was American and one was British. The British *L-8* made the worldwide cruise while the American *L-8* stayed in port.

A librarian at the Submarine Force Library and Museum had stuck the article in the *L-8*'s file box in the mistaken belief that it referred to the American submarine.

The moral of the story is: it's okay to be suspicious of documented facts that don't seem to fit with other documented facts. Sometimes you may be embarking up the wrong tree.

Unexpected Sources

My purpose in writing this book was not to detail every source that I have utilized in more than thirty-five years of shipwreck research, but to provide an overview of the sources that are available, and to encourage you to make good and effective use of them.

I have done a lot of shipwreck research on college campuses. In addition to libraries that possess rare and out-of-print books, many universities have newspapers on microfilm. Some have primary documents.

Embarking on Research

Other sources may be so obscure that no one would ever think to look for them.

Case in point: after publication of *Shipwrecks of Rhode Island and Connecticut*, I received a letter from Massachusetts, from one Paul Johnson. He had just read the chapter on the loss of the *Myronus*, and took exception to an unreported fact that he found personally important.

The schooner *Myronus* sank in 1907 after a collision with the passenger steamer *Tennessee*. The schooner sank in two minutes, carrying down with her the four crewmembers who were asleep in their bunks. Only the captain and mate escaped; they were on deck at the time of the collision. Captain Belatty nearly drowned because he did not know how to swim.

According to the documents in my possession, the captain was drowning "when Joseph Kenny, a clerk of 320 Broadway, and Michael J. Coffin, an oiler on the United States battleship *New Jersey*, jumped overboard and supported him until the boat reached them." The boat was a lifeboat from the *Tennessee*, on which 350 passengers were taking passage. Kenny and Coffin were passengers.

Johnson disagreed with the quoted statement because he possessed documentation that contradicted it. He kindly sent me copies of records that he had gathered from a variety of sources: contemporary newspapers, a Navy magazine, sworn depositions, and the Treasury Department. The reason for Johnson's interest was his relation to the rescuer, who was his grandfather.

Johnson's documents contained their own inconsistencies. For example, the oiler was assigned variously to the USS *Virginia* and to the USS *New Jersey* (which were sister ships). The spelling of the name of the captain of the *Myronus* was given differently as Baratty and as Bellutty.

The bane of the ardent researcher is that he is beholden to original documents without being able to attest to their veracity.

Despite these nonconformities, official documents concurred on two important points: the correct spelling of the name of the oiler was Michael F. Crosson; and Crosson was awarded a medal in recognition of his gallantry. (To add confusion, one report boasted that the medal was struck from gold, while another claimed that it was struck from silver. Joseph Kenny was not mentioned in any of the supporting documentation.)

The tidbit about Johnson's grandfather receiving a medal for heroism was not just a family myth that had been handed down from generation to generation. Official documentation supported the claim. These documents were relegated to files that no shipwreck researcher was likely to discover.

You can never cross the last "t" or dot the final "i". And you can never be certain that your source documents are 100% correct.

Honesty in Reporting

One time I held two official Navy documents, each one of which by itself I would have accepted as gospel. Yet each differed in citing the number of fatalities that occurred. What to do?

My stern advice is this: report what you find, not what you suppose, interpret, or interpolate.

A true historian neither makes nor fudges the facts. He reports the facts as they were written in contemporary documents. There is no room in the realm of history for creativity. Creative writing is for fiction, where scenes are invented in such a way as to heighten dramatic appeal.

In the case of the contradictory Navy documents, I cited both figures without prejudice.

On occasion, when in my experience I cited a source that I considered to be less authentic than another, I cited both but humbly rendered my opinion on the comparative veracity.

In my nonfiction, I never put words into the mouths of real persons or thoughts into their heads. I don't describe a hull as rotten unless that fact was noted in an historic document. I don't imagine stormy weather when accounts neglected to mention the state of the sea. However, if I relied upon a local newspaper article for a description of a wreck in its area of coverage, I might look on a different page in order to see what the weather was like when the casualty occurred.

True history is not the same as historic fiction. True history is a record of actual events: objective, immutable, and unchangeable. Let's keep it that way.

A Final Word about Research Assistants

During one research trip to the National Archives, I collected as much information as I could on a wreck that I was diving. (I forget which wreck.) Several months later, Joe Milligan visited the Archives to research the same wreck plus several others. We were sharing information, so when we got together to compare notes, we discovered that he had documents that I did *not* have. Thorough as I am, how could I have missed them?

The truth is that I did *not* miss them. My research assistant missed them – by not pulling the box in which they were stored.

I've stated it before but I will state it again: a researcher is only as good as his research assistant.

The documents you need may actually exist in the facility in which you are conducting research, but you may never know it if the research assistant who is assigned to you is new to the job, is unfamiliar with the files, is overworked, is burdened with requests, has personal problems on his mind, or got up on the wrong side of the bed. Only rarely are they lazy. These conditions may be temporary, but if any of them apply on the day of your visit, they will work in your disfavor.

You may never know what documentation you missed.

Sometimes you can get better information by submitting a written request than by appearing in person. When a query letter sits on the desk of a research assistant, he has time to mull it over before conducting the research and responding to your request.

On the other hand, a research assistant may scoff at a query letter that is poorly written, or that makes it seem as if the writer is not a serious-minded researcher. In that case, the research assistant might think that in-depth research is uncalled for, or unworthy of much attention, and that the researcher will be satisfied with some superficial information that is nonetheless pursuant to the request. In other words, you might get short shrift so that the research assistant can devote more time to more serious requests.

You might write first in order to feel out the waters, so as to determine if a visit is worth your while. Don't ramble when writing a query letter. Be succinct. But be sure to give the impression that you are serious about your research – because you are.

Part Five
Picture Sources

A staunch adjunct to textual documentation is pictorial imagery. As the saying goes, "A picture is worth a thousand words." It is far easier to see what a vessel looks like in a photographic print than it is to imagine the vessel from a detailed written description.

Picture sources are as numerous as sources of printed and written records. Many archives, museums, and libraries have both. On the other hand, some excellent picture sources have little or nothing in the way of textual records. In this section I will discuss the many ways and means to obtain images of vessels: how they appeared on the ways, at sea, and after their ultimate demise.

Pictures come in many forms. By definition, a picture is "a visual representation or image painted, drawn, photographed, or otherwise rendered on a flat surface."

Most people think of vessel pictures as black and white photographs. This is the form that is most commonly found in the majority of published sources such as books, magazines, and newspapers. The quality of the original picture is compromised to different degrees by the type of paper on which the image is reproduced.

Newspaper images are the worst for two reasons: newsprint is made from cheap wood pulp whose surface is rough and uneven, and the images are formed by the application of dots of ink, not smooth strokes of black pigment as in a painting. This type of imagery looks like a dot matrix display, and is similar to stippling, an art form in which an image is created from individual dots of paint. Think of it as a child's connect-the-dots drawing with a lot more dots.

Photogravure is only slightly better: the image is carved smoothly in a lead plate, but the ink is still pressed against cheap wood pulp. These images appear dull or muted because of the lack of contrast.

Slick magazines are a distinct improvement because of their high-quality glossy paper. Black and white halftones and color separations are superior reproduction processes that are nearly indistinguishable from photographic prints – unless you enlarge or copy the image, in which case the ink overlays become apparent. Also, if the registration marks are not synchronized properly in the printing process, the image will look fuzzy – like a 3D picture that is viewed without correction lenses – because the inks are misaligned and are superimposed on adjacent elements.

Book images can be either bad or good: bad if the pictures are printed on low-quality rag paper on which text is normally printed, or good if they are printed on high-quality inserts of coated stock.

Low-resolution images that are downloaded from the Internet suffer from pixelation. This is a condition in which the pixels, or picture elements, are discernible to the naked eye. A pixel is equivalent to the dot that is part of a picture in a newspaper. If you look at a newspaper picture through a magnifying glass, you see groups of isolated dots. Likewise, when you look closely at a digital picture, or if you enlarge a digital picture, the array of square display elements becomes distractingly visible.

When all is said and done, there is nothing quite like a photographic print for high contrast and distinct detail.

Not everyone has to have high-resolution, publishable-quality pictures. If photocopies or low-res scans suit your needs, so be it. Many picture sources will make photocopies from pictures at a fraction of the cost of making photographic prints.

Brevity Counts

Unlike textual information, many pictures can be readily obtained through the mail. This is because of the way pictures are indexed: alphabetically by name.

Picture Sources

You still need to distinguish a vessel from others with the same name, but generally the facilities that hold and sell pictures have them organized for instant retrieval. The card file systems of yesteryear are gradually yielding to computer databases.

In 1973, I compiled a list of vessels for which I wanted to obtain pictures. I had either dived on these wrecks already, or I planned to dive on them when the opportunity presented itself. I did my homework first, so that for each vessel I could furnish the dates of construction and loss, tonnage and dimensions, and the names of the shipbuilder and owner. My completed typewritten list totaled 67 vessels.

In my introductory letter I stated that I wanted to buy every picture that was available. In other words, this was not just a pure research project that was designed only to ascertain picture availability, but a business proposition. I photocopied the list and submitted it to ten domestic maritime museum libraries and two overseas.

I thought that they would have been happy to make the money. I learned otherwise. Some librarians returned my list untouched, with a note that stated that the list was too long. Never have I gone to a store to be turned away at the checkout counter because I wanted to purchase too many items or too much merchandise. Other librarians put my list aside to deal with later. After several months, I sent reminders so that the librarians would know that I hadn't forgotten the matter.

When I finally began to receive replies, I sent payment right away for whatever pictures were in their holdings. Because I had to buy these pictures sight unseen, I received a number of duplicates, even a few triplicates. More than one facility held the identical picture in their collection. Yet each claimed that I had to have *their* permission to publish the picture. More on that later.

The most valuable lesson I learned, and which I am passing along to my readers, is that some librarians have limited attention spans. One librarian suggested that I resubmit my list in segments of five or six vessels: a suggestion that sadly failed in logic, as it takes the same amount of time to look up 67 vessels from twelve lists as it takes to look them up from one list. The only difference is in the amount of postage that is required for the submissions. In the end, the librarian had to do the same amount of work – actually, more work, because then he had to reply a dozen times instead of just once.

The lesson was not lost on me. Thereafter, I submitted lists of no more than five or six vessels. Years later, even this amount became too onerous for some librarians. I reduced my lists to two or three, and received quicker responses.

In the 1980's, some sources began to charge a service fee just to look up a vessel in their picture file – even if it developed that they didn't have a picture of the vessel in question. In other words, you had to pay for negative information. At first there was a threshold: if I submitted a list of three vessels or less, the search was free; four vessels or more incurred a service fee.

Nowadays, many picture sources ordinarily charge a service fee per vessel. For your money, they generally send photocopies of any pictures that they find, along with a cost sheet for ordering photographic prints of different kinds and sizes.

Glossy versus Matte

Glossy prints have a shiny finish; matte prints have a dull finish. Both finishes have advantages and disadvantages, depending upon your reason for wanting the picture.

A glossy print is sharp and clear. The high contrast intensifies colors, and accentuates shades of black and white. These features are instrumental if your purpose is to study the vessel's design and layout, for you can distinguish fine details of the hull and superstructure.

The downside of glossy prints is that they are, well, glossy. The shiny surface reflects light like a mirror. In order to see the picture without reflections obscuring the view, you have to cock the picture at an angle to the light; by doing so, the reflection is deflected away from your viewing point.

It is difficult to photograph a glossy print without getting your own reflection in the picture – and the reflection of everything that is behind you. When you cock the picture to keep out your own reflection, you will pick up the other reflections, not the least of which may be the light source. The best way to copy a glossy print is to scan it on a flatbed scanner. There the light source is spread evenly over the surface, and there is nothing to reflect on the bottom of the scanner lid.

A glossy print attracts dust, which adheres to the surface because of the difference in electrostatic potential between the dust motes and the chemical reagent that is used to stabilize the image on the photographic paper. The glossy surface is easily smudged, and the lightest touch of your finger will leave a nearly indelible print.

Glossy print paper is basically waterproof, so if a lint-free cloth doesn't remove the dust, smudges, or fingerprints, you can clean the surface with a damp cloth without harming the paper. Fingerprints are more difficult to remove because the oil in your fingers is impregnated on the glossy surface, to which it clings tenaciously. Try rubbing a tad of grease remover from your kitchen cleaning supplies over the fingerprint, then wiping it clean with liquid soap and warm water.

I store all my photographic prints in sheet protectors. This prevents the surface from getting smudged during handling, and from getting scratched inside the file folders (which is where I keep my pictures). Each sheet protector has an extended tab with three holes punched in it, so it can be kept in a three-ring binder if that is your preference.

Matte prints are ideal for pictures that you want for decoration, framed and hung on a wall or propped on a desk. The non-reflective surface ensures that you can look at the picture from any angle without seeing any annoying glare or ghost images. The matte surface attracts less dust than a glossy surface, and it does not smudge or collect fingerprints as readily.

The downside of matte prints is that the images do not stand out in stark contrast the way they do in glossy prints. Because the colors and halftones are dull and muted, they do not make good study pictures.

Size Matters

Small prints show better detail than oversized enlargements.

Prints that measure 11 inches by 14 inches, or 16 by 20, are suitable for framing. But the more a picture is enlarged, the more its imperfections are emphasized. Although it may be counterintuitive, there is less visible detail in a large picture than there is in a small picture. This is because when you make a picture larger, you also enlarge the grain of which the picture is composed. This tends to blur the image or make it appear soft or out of focus.

Grain is the photographic equivalent of computer pixelation (and digital camera picture noise).

Prints that measure 5 inches by 7 inches, or 8 by 10, are best for study purposes. Grain is reduced to a minimum. The contrast is more distinct. Oddly, you can see fine detail better by viewing a small picture through a magnifying glass than you can by viewing an enlargement with the naked eye. If you view an enlargement through a magnifying glass, instead of seeing greater detail you will see more grain, which obscures some of the detail.

The standard film size of both negatives and transparencies is 24 millimeters by 36 millimeters. These dimensions yield an aspect ratio of 2 to 3. To capture an entire image on an enlargement, the dimensions of a print should be a multiple of the numbers of the aspect ratio, else some of the image will be lost or cropped because it doesn't fit on the photographic paper.

Full mask enlargements are 4 inches by 6 inches, 5

Picture Sources

by 7.5, 6 by 9, 7 by 10.5, 8 by 12, 9 by 13.5, 10 by 15, 11 by 16.5, 12 by 18 . . . and 16 by 24.

For some reason, most standard print sizes do *not* coincide with the standard aspect ratio of film. I don't know why, but bear this in mind when you order prints to be made from negatives. You may have to specify cropping marks on a photocopy, or suffer a loss of imagery that is determined by the dark room technician.

Neither 5 by 7 nor 8 by 10 nor 16 by 20 are perfect fits. For full mask pictures, ask for nonstandard print sizes such as 8 by 12 and 16 by 24. A standard print size is 4 by 6, but this is too small for study purposes.

Picture Source Overview

Over the years, I eventually visited the major facilities that hold ship pictures: at least, those along the eastern seaboard and around the Great Lakes. These research trips enabled me to look up the pictures myself, or look them up in the catalogue system and ask for them to be retrieved from storage. Seeing the pictures before purchasing them was advantageous: it saved me from buying duplicates, and from buying different views whose quality was poor.

Instead of buying pictures during a research tour, I photocopied them. After the tour, I compared all the pictures and sent purchase orders by mail for those pictures that were unique; or, if more than one facility held the same image, I bought the one that was the clearest or from the earliest generation.

Gradually I came to learn that some facilities held pictures whose original negative was held by another facility. The secondary facility made a new negative from a print that it obtained from the primary facility. If a tertiary facility then bought a print from the secondary facility, and made another negative, there was a further degradation in quality. Unlike digital copies, every generation of a film reprint produces a more inferior image.

I also learned that some pictures were misnamed:

that is, the name of the vessel was correct, but the accompanying information, which distinguished one vessel of that name from another vessel of the same name, was *not* correct. Mistakes happen, so be wary.

Each facility has its own rules of engagement: rules that have changed over time, always becoming more restrictive and, as a consequence, more difficult and time-consuming for the researcher.

If you have read this book in the order of pagination, you should have noticed by now that the usage guidelines of archives, museums, and libraries are designed for the convenience of the research assistants, not for the facility of the researcher.

Be that as it may, the value that is inherent in vessel pictures makes it well worth the time and effort that must be expended in locating them. Whether you call, write, or visit in person, here are the picture sources that I have found the most useful, and why.

Great Lakes Vessel Picture Sources

Great Lakes shipwreck researchers are most fortunate. Maritime photographers have done an incredible job of photographing vessels that were constructed in the Great Lakes, and salt-water vessels that plied Great Lakes shipping lanes at any time during their career. Either that, or Great Lakes maritime museums have been more assiduous than other maritime museums in collecting vessel pictures.

If you are researching a vessel that wrecked in the Great Lakes, first look for pictures in the Great Lakes maritime museums that are given below.

Some vessels that were wrecked along the Eastern Seaboard were built at Great Lakes shipyards. If you are researching an ocean shipwreck, check the vessel's register listing for the place of construction, and conduct your picture search accordingly.

Other "salties" – as salt-water vessels are called in the local vernacular – which passed through the locks into the Great Lakes, may have been photographed during their inland voyage. If your historical research

Picture Sources

leads you to believe that a subject vessel traveled inland, it is possible that a Great Lakes maritime museum may have a picture of her underway, in a lock, or dockside.

The Great Lakes museums with the largest number of vessel pictures are the Historical Collections of the Great Lakes, the Great Lakes Historical Society, and the Canal Park Marine Museum. I first saw the impressive collection of the Canal Park Marine Museum in 1989, at which time it was housed in the top floor of C. Patrick Labadie's home in Duluth.

Smaller collections may be found at the Wisconsin Marine Historical Society and the Wisconsin Maritime Museum.

Global Vessel Picture Sources

Without a doubt, the largest collection of vessel pictures in the United States will be found at The Mariners Museum. That is the first place I would look for any merchant vessel picture, whether it be an aged sailing vessel, a foreign steamship, a Mississippi River boat, or a lowly barge. This is my first stop for all but Great Lakes vessels, although the collection includes a large number of those, too.

My second stop is the Steamship Historical Society of America. As the name implies, the Society's collection includes pictures only of vessels that were propelled by steam (and, by virtue of homology, by diesel). You won't find sailing vessels or barges (unless the barge was converted from a steamer by dint of the removal of its propulsion machinery).

The National Archives collection is somewhat eclectic. Its greatest concentration is on vessels that were owned and operated by the U.S. government: Navy, Coast Guard, Revenue Cutter Service, Light Ship Service, and Army. The collection in this regard is voluminous. Merchant vessels are represented by only a few hundred pictures, mostly from World War Two. But, you never know what you might find unless you look. I have found a few surprises at the Archives.

The Naval Photographic Center has pictures of nearly every warship ever commissioned into the U.S. Navy, except for very old ones and small or second-rate vessels such as PT boats, sub chasers, yard craft, and so on. This is not to say that they don't have pictures of some minor vessels, only that they don't have very many. The collection includes some foreign warships and a few merchant vessels. This should be your first stop for pictures of Navy vessels only because you can get professional assistance and quicker service in your search, whereas the National Archives is largely self-help.

Many pictures from the Naval Photographic Center collection are available on the website of the Naval Historical Center. If low resolution pictures are suitable for your purposes, look no farther than the Internet.

The Library of Congress also has a large assortment of pictures available online.

Secondary sources that are not as large are the Mystic Seaport Museum, the National Maritime Museum (in San Francisco), the National Maritime Museum (in London), and the Merseyside County Museum. The U.S. Naval Institute has pictures of Navy vessels that may not be found at the Naval Photographic Center or the National Archives.

Before you call attention to the fact that I noted previously that the Mystic Seaport Museum holds 1.3 million photographic images, let me explain the disparity: most of pictures are not images of vessels; or at least, not vessels of interest (those that sank). I base my secondary source rating upon my rate of success in finding relevant vessel pictures. Researchers with different interests may find the collection more rewarding.

Tertiary sources are those that have small collections, or whose collections are oriented geographically. The collection of the Seaman's Church Institute in New York City has been transferred to and merged with the collection of the South Street Seaport Museum. The Maine Maritime Museum and the Penobscot Marine Museum concentrate mostly on Maine in particular

Picture Sources

and somewhat on New England in general. The Hart Nautical Collections also concentrates mostly on New England.

For vessels that were lost off the coast of North Carolina, try the North Carolina Office of State Archaeology, the State Department of Cultural Resources, and the Outer Banks History Center. Try the South Carolina Institute of Archaeology and Anthropology for eponymous vessels.

As the name implies, the Submarine Force Library and Museum Association specializes in U.S. Navy submarines. There are submarine pictures here that you won't find at the Naval Photographic Center or the National Archives.

Don't overlook the Smithsonian Institution. Initially I sent requests by mail. I first visited the facility in the early 1990's. At that time, all the photographs in which I was interested were stored digitally on a laser disk: about the diameter of a long-playing record (if you remember LP's, or if you have heard of them). A printed list was arranged alphabetically by subject. Only a miniscule portion of the subjects were vessels. These were listed by name, followed by a negative number.

I inserted the disk in the player, sat back in a comfortable lounge chair, typed negative numbers on a remote selector, and viewed the images on a television screen. Research was never easier!

On a form I jotted down the negative numbers of the photographs that I wanted to order, and paid the reasonable reproduction fee. Black and white prints were mailed to my house a week or two later.

I place the Peabody Essex Museum in the tertiary category not because it doesn't have a good-sized collection, but because of its pronounced hostility toward shipwreck researchers. A couple of years ago I tried to obtain a picture that I had seen credited to the Museum. In an e-mail I provided all the descriptive information about the vessel and the picture. After a couple of months without a response, I wrote again to remind them that I was waiting for ordering instructions so I could purchase a print of the picture. I received an indifferent reply with the statement that they would look into the matter. Another reminder was not answered. I never got the picture.

Getting the Picture

After you've learned that a picture exists, you then will want to obtain a copy of it. Most facilities will furnish a photocopy for a nominal charge. If the quality of a photocopy floats your boat (or suits your purpose), go no farther. But if you want a high-quality image that will enable you to see the vessel's fine details, you will have to negotiate with the picture source for the kind of image you want.

The standard format is a photographic print, but some facilities now offer digital images, and a few offer transparencies. As these services and charges are always changing, you will have to obtain up-to-the-minute information at the time of your purchase.

Most museums will *not* let you copy pictures yourself. They compel you to utilize their copy services as a way to generate income. Some museums have their own darkroom for making photographic prints, but most have to outsource pictures to a photo lab. Since the photo lab also has to make a profit, the cost to the researcher may be exorbitant.

A museum might have a print but not a negative. In that case, the photo lab must first make a copy negative from the original print, then make a print from the negative. This process increases the fee that is charged to the buyer because the cost of the copy negative is not absorbed by the museum, but is passed along to the buyer. According to the policy of most museums, the buyer gets the print but not the negative; the museum keeps the copy negative that the buyer paid to have made. Subsequent buyers have to pay only for a print.

Copy Stand Work

On the other hand, some small museums exist solely as a service to the community, and have no mecha-

Picture Sources

nism for making copies; some don't even have a photocopy machine. For example, when I was researching *Shipwrecks of New York*, I visited the Long Island Maritime Museum, the Suffolk County Historical Society, and the Vanderbilt Museum, each of which had pictures that I wanted for the book. None had reproduction resources, so they were happy to let me bring my camera and copy stand, and photograph the pictures in their collection. This saved them the trouble of sending out the pictures to be copied – something that they had never done before – and then mailing the prints to me.

Some other public service facilities are historical and archaeological units. Among others, I did my own copy work at the Outer Banks History Center, the North Carolina Office of State Archaeology, the North Carolina State Department of Cultural Resources, the South Carolina Institute of Archaeology and Anthropology, and the Submarine Force Library and Museum Association.

I often carry my camera and copy stand on research trips. Copy stands are not designed to be mobile, but to sit permanently on a counter top in a photo lab. The two outstretched arms for the four bulbs do not allow the unit to fit through doorways. I modified my copy stand by drilling a series of holes through the mounting brackets for the arms, elongating the holes until they connected to create curved slots, and replacing the hexagonal nuts with a wing nuts. By loosening the wing nuts, I can slide the bolts along the slot, and stow the arms in a vertical position. Now the copy stand fits through doorways without having to disassemble the various components.

Use photoflood lamps for copy work. This high-intensity bulb simulates the color balance of sunlight (which is 5500° Kelvin). The bulb is extremely bright and hot – much more so than ordinary bulbs that are used for household illumination. Do not look directly at the bulb when it is lit, because doing so can damage your eyes – much like looking at the sun or a welding arc.

A photoflood lamp generates so much heat that it can curl a lightweight photographic print in a matter of seconds. I compose the picture and focus the lens before I switch on the lights. If the room is too dark to see the image well enough to bring it into focus, I get a rough focus first, then fine-tune the focus as soon as I switch on the lights. I switch off the lights as soon as the picture is taken.

Single-weight glossy prints curl the worst. I have seen the corners curl up more than an inch. This may not only damage the picture, but it places the raised portions of the image out of focus. To prevent curl and keep the picture flat, I carry a pane of non-reflective glass to place on top of lightweight prints.

Compose the picture first, then cover the print with the glass. Once in place, you will find that it is difficult to move the picture because you can touch only the glass. The glass will slide over the picture without moving it.

Double-weight glossy prints will not curl as readily as single-weight glossy prints. Matte prints generally don't curl.

Do not touch the bulb with your fingertips (or with any other body part). Obviously, a hot bulb will cause severe burns on the skin. Not so obviously, touching a cold bulb will damage the bulb. Natural oils on the skin will leave a smear on the glass. When the bulb gets hot, the smear of oil will be superheated and etched into the glass, creating a hot spot that turns black.

For one thing, the passage of light through the black spot is less than the passage of light through the clear glass or the outer coating (if the bulb is coated). This results in uneven illumination; parts of the subject may not be properly exposed. For another thing, etching weakens the glass and shortens the lifespan of the bulb. Microscopic pinholes will develop in the glass. The lifespan of the filament is extended by surrounding it in an atmosphere of inert gas. If the gas – or a minute portion of it – escapes, the filament will burn out quicker.

Picture Sources

The burn time of a photoflood lamp is short: generally in the range of a couple of hours. Photoflood lamps are expensive, so energize them only long enough to trip the shutter. When you handle or install a new bulb, keep it inside the corrugated cardboard packing protector. Press your fingers against the outside of the sleeve as you screw the bulb into the socket.

The filament can burn out at any time. I carry spare bulbs whenever I travel with my copy stand.

I also carry a couple of extension cords.

Strobe for Copy Work

A strobe or electronic flash doesn't usually work well for illuminating a picture. Whenever I've tried to photograph paintings in museums, the burst of light is reflected off the paint and into the lens. I get a picture with a bright spot of light in the middle. The same thing happens with glossy photographic prints, and a picture of any kind that is displayed behind glass.

For wall-mounted copy work, try bouncing the flash off the ceiling. You do this by changing the angle of the flash tube reflector head (although many strobes do not have an adjustable flash head that can be tilted separately in a different plane – the flash tube assembly and the electronics package are built into a single solid housing). If your strobe is equipped with a cord connector in addition to the hot shoe, you can handhold the strobe and then flash the tube in any desired direction.

The same may hold true for copy stand work, but I've never tried it. Obviously, a strobe that is connected to the camera's hot shoe cannot be tilted enough to illuminate the subject – an adjustable flash head won't turn more than 90°. And even if it could, the flash would be so bright that it would wash out the picture. If you could hold the strobe far enough away from the print, or bounce the flash off a sheet of cardboard, it might work.

Film Camera for Copy Work

Glossy prints create glare. If the light source is too

close to vertical – that is, in near alignment with the lens – the glare will be photographed and will obscure some of the image. As you may remember from high school physics, according to Snell's law, the angle of incidence equals the angle of reflection. Swing the light arms outward (or downward) until you no longer see the glare through the viewfinder. The annoying glare is reflected past the lens.

You may still have glare from overhead lighting. To avoid this problem, I hold a sheet of black artboard above the camera when I snap the shutter. This artboard sheet measures two feet by three feet: a standard size that can be purchased at any art supply store.

The viewfinder of a single lens reflex camera lets you see exactly what the film will see. When your eye is not pressed against the viewfinder, extraneous light may enter the camera through the prism, and appear on the photograph as a ghost image. To prevent this from happening, you can close the eyepiece shutter by actuating the lever (if your camera is equipped with this feature). This is not necessary if you are holding a sheet of artboard above the camera. Otherwise, simply place your hand an inch or so over the eyepiece of the viewfinder.

Rangefinder cameras are difficult to use for close-up photography because of parallax. What you see through the rangefinder is not what the film will see through the lens: the image will be offset. For all practical purposes, parallax eventually reaches a vanishing point. Even though by definition two parallel lines never meet, they *seem* to come together at some point before infinity: like railroad tracks that appear to touch in the distance.

But the closer the subject, the more noticeable parallax becomes. That's why nonprofessionals cut off people's heads when they use a rangefinder camera. The shutterbug sees the people's heads through the rangefinder, but the lens – which is positioned a couple of inches lower – sees only as high as their chins.

In copy work, the distance between the subject and

Picture Sources

the film plane is usually between one and two feet. If you must use a rangefinder camera, instead of trying to estimate the parallax – a difficult thing to do – stand to the side of the camera and draw an imaginary line down from the center of the lens to the center of the image. This will give you the vertical alignment. Look at the image through the rangefinder to ensure that the landscape aspect of the picture is wide enough for horizontal coverage.

Even when the camera is bolted firmly to the base plate of the copy stand, the act of pressing the shutter button induces slight shudder movement in the camera. These minute vibrations are called "shake." Shake can be eliminated by tripping the shutter with a cable release. Less cumbersome is the self-timer feature. I select the two-second delay, then press the shutter release button. All induced vibration has settled down by the time the shutter trips two seconds later.

Lens for Copy Work

Using the right lens for the job is important. The standard 50-millimeter lens is okay, but because it won't focus close, you have to hold the camera quite a distance from the subject. You may not be able to crank the camera's base plate high enough to cover the image.

A wide-angle lens focuses closer that a standard lens, but it also creates distortion around the edges. This distortion may not be noticeable in normal usage – say, for scenic outdoor pictures – but it is quite noticeable at a distance of less than one foot: the maximum distance at which you can position a wide angle lens above a photographic print without catching a large area of the copy stand bed. When you peer through the viewfinder and a wide-angle lens, you can clearly see that the borders of the print are bulged outward, as if the photograph had been inflated like a balloon.

The best bet is a macro lens. Mine focuses as close as 9 inches from the film plane, which is only 5 inches from the end of the lens. An extension tube enables me to get as close as 2 inches from the end of the lens, on an area that measures approximately 1-3/8 inches by 2 inches. This extreme close-up enables me to photograph incredibly fine details on the picture – assuming, of course, that the details exist on the picture and are not obscured by grain.

Focusing is critical because a macro lens has almost no depth of field. But it doesn't matter because you're shooting a flat subject that doesn't move, and the camera is bolted to a locked base plate.

Black and White Film for Copy Work

I take lots of film, too. The standard film for copy work is Kodak Tri-X Pan Professional (although this film may be discontinued in favor of equivalent films). This black and white negative film has an ASA/ISO of 400. ASA, the acronym for American Standards Association, is yielding to ISO, the acronym for International Standards Organization. The number is a measure of the light sensitivity of film. The higher the number, the more sensitive the film. Fast film has a high number, while slow film has a low number.

Fast film is used in low-light conditions because the faster the film, the smaller the aperture and the shorter the shutter speed are needed for proper exposure. A smaller aperture equates to greater depth of field. A shorter shutter speed equates to less blur from either movement of the camera or movement of the subject.

Fast film is not a priority for copy stand work: the camera is bolted solidly in place so it can't move. The print is placed flat on the bed of the copy stand, which is indoors and out of the wind. I suppose you might have a problem if ventilator ducts were blowing forced air across the bed of the copy stand, but I've never encountered such a situation.

Fast film is a prerequisite on those occasions when floodlights are not permitted, such as in the Library of Congress. Otherwise slow film is acceptable. Set the camera on aperture priority, or shoot manually with a

Picture Sources

small aperture. Remember that the smallest aperture has the highest number, while the largest aperture has the lowest number. In other words, an aperture of f16 is a very tiny opening, while an aperture of f4 is a very large opening. The smaller the opening, the greater the depth of field – not that it matters much in copy stand work because you are shooting a flat plane. But the more attention you pay to detail, the better will be your photographic results.

A smaller aperture requires a longer exposure. Since the camera and subject are stationary, long exposure time is irrelevant in this regard.

Filling the frame with subjects such as postcards and small prints require that the camera be held close to the bed of the copy stand, perhaps only a few inches away. In this case, the bulb arms must be depressed nearly all the way down to nearly a horizontal position, so that the body of the lens does not block the light. With a low angle of incidence, less light from the photoflood lamps illuminates the print, necessitating a longer exposure.

Close-up photos are often underexposed, especially when a long exposure time is required. This is partly due to reciprocity failure: the inability of a light meter to compensate adequately for film sensitivity in low-light conditions. Another reason may be the brightness range of the subject: some parts of the print are dark while other parts are bright. This latter condition can also result in a picture that is overexposed, although that is a rarity.

I use the three-shot technique in order to cover all eventualities. With the camera set to automatic exposure, I shoot one picture at the exposure that is suggested by the integral light meter. I then rotate the exposure compensation scale with which my camera is equipped: first to one stop of overexposure, then to one stop of underexposure. More often than not, the "overexposed" picture is the one that is properly exposed.

This may seem like a waste of film, as I get only 12 useful images out of a roll of 36 exposures, but compare this to the expense of having to return to a distant museum in order to reshoot an entire roll of dark pictures.

Once processed, high quality black and white prints can be made from the negatives. Store prints and negatives in clear plastic protective sleeves that are three-hole-punched for loose-leaf binders. You can keep them in binders if you want all your pictures together, or put the sleeves in your individual shipwreck file folders.

Color Film for Copy Work

I generally use color transparency film for copy work: Kodachrome 64. There are several reasons for this preference. I always have slide film in stock because I use it for outdoor photography. If a copy session terminates while there is still unexposed film in the camera, I wait until I shoot the rest of the roll before sending out the film for processing. Slides are smaller and easier to store than negatives and prints. I can enlarge an image by projecting it on a screen. And I can have prints made from slides if the need arises.

Kodachrome is a daylight film. Its color balance was designed for use in direct sunlight. It can also be used with an electronic flash, or strobe, without affecting the color balance. When used with tungsten filament incandescent bulbs, however, the film may show some color aberration: a yellowish or orange-reddish tint that is unwanted in the reproduction of pictures, whether they are color or black and white.

Special tungsten films are made for use with household bulbs, but I don't stock them. Instead, I achieve the neutral color tone of 3200° Kelvin by taking pictures through a corrective filter that is mounted on the front of the lens. The 80A filter corrects the yellowish or orange-reddish tint on daylight film. I use the filter whenever I shoot with artificial light.

Another color aberration that occurs with Kodachrome is caused by the light that emanates from fluorescent tubes. This cool light casts a bluish tint on the film. Most picture facilities are illuminated by fluorescent fixtures. In this situation, I either switch off the ceiling lights before I snap the shutter, or I get triple duty from my artboard, using it not only to prevent glare from overhead lights and as a shield to prevent extraneous light from entering the viewfinder, but to block fluorescent light from striking the print on the bed of the copy stand and discoloring the film.

Digital Camera for Copy Work

Digital photography does not suffer from all the quirks that plague film photography. Instead, it has quirks of its own.

Digital cameras work extremely well in low-light conditions. They can be used with virtually any kind of illumination. Color aberrations can be corrected by the use of software features after the image is downloaded onto your computer. A single click is all that is needed to convert a color photograph, or a color aberrant photograph, to a black and white image. This obviates the need for filters and artboard shields. Prints of any size can be readily made from digital images. And, of course, digital photography obviates the need to stock film.

On the other hand, low-end cameras may not have all the features of expensive professional cameras, such as close focusing capability and image storage capacity. The image recording quality is not the same for all cameras, because quality is a function of the number of pixels that the camera can record. The large file size that is required to create high-resolution images may strain the storage capacity of your memory card. After the images are transferred to your computer, they will take up space and may reduce the speed of the computer's operation.

For copy work, use the highest resolution and most stable file format that is available on your camera. The standard recording mode and file format is JPEG (Joint Photographic Experts Group). JPEG, or jpeg, is a compressed file format that takes less space on a memory card or hard drive than other file formats. The problem with compression is that some of the image quality is compromised.

Shoot in RAW mode if your camera supports the feature. RAW, or raw, is not an acronym, but a literal description of the image type. Whereas JPEG mode predetermines how to record an image with respect to color saturation, contrast, compression setting, and so on, RAW records everything and lets you manipulate the image by means of sophisticated software after you download it onto your computer.

The disadvantage of RAW is that the original file size is many times the size of a JPEG image: perhaps as much as six times the size. This limits the number of pictures that will fit on a memory card. If you plan to shoot in RAW, you should purchase a multi-gigabyte memory card.

Once you make adjustments to the settings, you can save the picture file on your computer as a JPEG or TIFF (Tagged Image File Format). A TIFF file is two to three times the size of a JPEG file, but it does not lose information in the compression process, so the image retains its original quality. Furthermore, because a TIFF file keeps the information that was captured in the RAW format, it can be copied – and the copy can be copied – without degradation of the image. A JPEG file loses tiny bits of information every time it is copied.

Digital cameras consume a lot of power. Battery life may be short – in some models, little more than a couple of hours. Keep extra batteries on hand. If your camera operates on a rechargeable battery, make sure the battery is fully charged before you begin your copy session.

Memory cards are not infallible; they can go bad. Keep a backup on hand.

National Archives Copy Work

Until the 1990's, the National Archives provided in-house copy services that were so efficient and so inexpensive that it did not pay to do my own copy work. I took my copy stand to the downtown facility only when

Picture Sources

I wanted to copy original prints that were stored in textual file boxes instead of in the Still Picture Branch; there were no negatives of these images. Otherwise, I let the Archives make copies for me. Black and white slides cost $2 each, while black and white prints cost $4 each. I couldn't go wrong for that price.

When the Still Picture Branch was moved to the College Park facility, the Archives terminated its in-house copy services and outsourced them to commercial photographers. The cost to the researcher increased tenfold. Photographers who applied for the job had to attend special training sessions in order to learn how to handle archival materials in accordance with archival standards.

At the same time, the Archives equipped the new and spacious Still Picture Research Room with brand new copy stands and photoflood lamps for free use by researchers. (Commercial photographers have their own room and equipment to which researchers do not have access.) This was a great boon for me because I was a professional photographer and full-time researcher who made regular visits to the Archives, but it did not help avocational researchers who lived far away and for whom taking a day off work and traveling to College Park was both costly and inconvenient. They had to pay big bucks for commercial photography work.

The Archives holds pictures in a number of different formats: photographic prints, film negatives of various sizes, glass plates, lantern slides, transparencies, microfiche, and so on. Certain fragile photographic materials are kept frozen in on-site freezers; if you request any of these, there is a two-hour delay in the retrieval process while the materials are slowly thawed.

Commercial photographers are charged a fee for every item that they must have pulled for their customers. At the time of this writing, this commercial pull fee is $5 per item. (Non-commercial researchers are not charged a fee.) This fee is added to the photographer's charges. This is another reason why it costs so much to hire a commercial photographer to copy pictures. The commercial photographer charges for his travel time to and from the Archives, as well as for the time that he spends in copying pictures, processing film, and making prints or slides.

Researchers are not allowed to handle or copy pictures that are indexed in the card file system for which the Still Picture Branch does not possess a negative. By the nature of their special training, only a authorized commercial photographers may handle and copy these pictures. The rationale is that an untrained researcher, even if he is a professional photographer, might damage the one and only copy of a picture.

I think this is a load of crap, but that's the way it is. After all, I've handled and copied scores of one-of-a-kind prints that I found in textual file boxes in the Central Research Room, and never damaged any of them. In fact, I did not even have to abide by the rules of the Still Picture Branch (such as wearing white linen gloves while handling pictures).

Other rules applied, however. For instance, when I wanted to photograph prints in the downtown facility, a reference desk attendant carried the file box to a room at the end of the hall, with me in tow. She sat at a desk and watched me while I set up my camera on the copy stand and took my pictures. After I returned the prints to the box, she carried it back to the Central Research Room. This formality ensured that the prints did not get separated from the box, and that the researcher did not abscond with any archival materials.

At College Park, a reference desk attendant carried the file box upstairs to the Still Picture Branch, again with me in tow. She explained the nature of my activity to the desk attendant, then left me in their care. After taking my pictures, a desk attendant called the Central Research Room to send a chaperone to accompany me back downstairs with the file box.

In both cases everyone was friendly and accommodating. We simply followed established procedure that was designed to safeguard archival materials.

Such strict protocol contradicted the state of affairs

Picture Sources

that existed in the 1970's. At that time the Still Picture Branch employed only one individual: Jim Trimble. He instructed me on how to use the card file system, showed me how the file boxes were numbered and organized on the shelves, then gave me free reign of the stacks. He told me to call on him if I needed help; otherwise I was on my own. He went about his business of processing mail orders.

Most days I worked alone; every once in a while, one or two other researchers passed through momentarily. This was long before research became a cultural imperative. I was among the few.

I pulled the pictures out of the boxes, noted the negative numbers of those for which I wanted copies, and submitted my photo order at the end of the day. The pictures were mailed to me a few weeks later from the Archives photo lab, along with an invoice. Everyone was so trusting . . .

Anyway, one day I couldn't find the picture I was looking for (the Revenue Cutter *Mohawk*). I double-checked the negative number in the card file. I had written the number correctly, but when I looked in the file box in which the picture should have been stored, I found several large gaps in the numbers.

Puzzled, I brought my consternation to Trimble's attention. He confirmed the negative number, ascertained that I was looking in the correct box, then told me that the missing pictures must have been purged, and that the file card should have been removed at the same time. In other words, I found a file card for a picture that had been trashed. He explained that pictures that someone deemed no longer worth keeping were periodically culled in order to make space available for incoming materials.

Who the culler was, and what basis was used to determine the comparative worthlessness of archived pictures, was unknown to Trimble. It was part of the process to which he was not privy.

The Archives card file system is well organized but massive. Finding aids that are printed on loose sheets of paper, and stored in filing cabinets, are difficult for the uninitiated to locate. Ask a research assistant in the Still Picture Research Room for help in wading through the complexities of arrangement. They will be happy to help you.

Every picture has a negative number. You must submit a call slip for each individual picture – unless a group of pictures is numbered consecutively and is stored in the same box. You must wear white linen gloves to handle pictures. These gloves make it difficult to manipulate the pictures, which are glued to oversized rectangles of stiffened cardboard on which captions are printed or written in ink. Nonetheless, if you remove them for greater dexterity you will be chastised for doing so.

Nearly every one of the prints was stored incorrectly, and continue to be stored incorrectly today. Nor is there any indication that the Archives is taking affirmative action to re-store the pictures correctly. As far as I can tell, the Archives is not even considering taking action. Let me explain.

Prints must be stored flat in order to remain flat. The prints in the Archives were pasted onto stiffened cardboard, then stored on edge. This vertical posture has caused the cardboard and the prints to curve – the same way a file folder curves when there aren't enough folders in the drawer to keep the folders pressed tightly against each other. And even then you still get some curvature.

So it is with the pictures in the Archives. Some pictures are only mildly curved, while others are so badly curved that you can't get the entire picture in focus because of the lack of depth of field; and even if you could get it in focus, the corners and edges of the image would be distorted.

Picture archivists recognized this problem after the collection was moved to College Park. To compensate for the curvature, they placed weighted wooden blocks at the copy stand station. Photographers could place these blocks on the edges of the cardboard backings in

Picture Sources

order to press the picture flat against the bed of the copy stand. A soft felt covering prevented the wood from scratching the pictures.

This stopgap solution to a serious problem was discontinued after a couple of years, when archivists adopted the belief that pressing the pictures flat was somehow damaging them. I don't understand how restoring a picture to its original condition can be construed as damage, but that's the way it is.

In my opinion, every picture should be reboxed in horizontal boxes instead of vertical boxes. To assist gravity in flattening the cardboard backings, a full-size heavy weight should be placed on top of the stack of pictures in every box. Alternatively, since negatives exist for every one of these pictures, archivists could make another print and store it correctly. I don't foresee this ever happening. The Archives appears to be content with the status quo.

Other Copy Work Protocols

As I've mentioned elsewhere, the Library of Congress does not permit researchers to use artificial lighting when photographing pictures. Archivists are afraid that continued exposure to bright lights might cause the pictures to fade. Yet Library lab personnel use artificial light when you pay the Library to make photocopies for you. What's good for the goose is obviously not good for the gander.

Other than the National Archives, the most accommodating picture copy facilities in the DC area are the U.S. Coast Guard Historian's Office and the Naval Photographic Center.

The Coast Guard has prints but no negatives. A copy stand is available for researchers to use. File boxes or folders are arranged on the shelves alphabetically by vessel name. Simply pull a box or folder off the shelf, look through the material, pull out the pictures that you want to photograph, shoot them, and put everything back the way you found it. No one looks over your shoulder while you work. Gloves are not supplied, but be careful not to touch the face of a print and leave fingerprints for the next researcher.

The Historian's Office has no mechanism for reproducing images other than by photocopying. Requests for photographic prints are outsourced to commercial photographers.

The historian on duty works in a cubicle that is out of sight behind shelving units in a corner of the room. Out of courtesy, I let him know when I am leaving.

At the Naval Photographic Center, Chuck Haberlein and Ed Finney bend over backwards to help you find what you want. Haberlein has been a fixture at the Center for as long as I can remember. Currently he is working on a long-term project to scan all – or nearly all – the images in the Center's collection and to upload them onto the Center's website. This keeps him pretty busy in the back room.

Finney has been there for fifteen years. He's a bundle of energy who can find any picture in the collection, suggest alternative ways of looking for pictures, and instruct you in the operation of the mechanized card file system so you can search or browse on your own. When you find an image that you want, jot down the negative number and he will pull the print for you.

The Center has an antique copy stand in a nearby room along the hall. It is equipped with ordinary household 100-watt bulbs that are barely adequate for the job. Either take long exposures (and use a color balance correction filter for color film), or unscrew the bulbs and place your own photoflood lamps in the sockets. Gloves are not available, so handle pictures carefully and hold them by the borders.

The bed of the copy stand is made of iron. Most of the prints are single-weight glossies that curl almost instantly under the heat of the lamps. To prevent this from happening while pictures are being shot, the Center provides heavy magnets that can be placed on the corners of the pictures to hold them down flat. These magnets are so strong that I have trouble picking them up off the iron bed. Watch that you don't crush your

Picture Sources

fingers when emplacing them!

The Center used to make reproductions in an on-site Navy photo lab. It was cheap, quick, and convenient – especially for remote researchers who requested pictures by mail or phone. Pictures could be ordered as large as 16 inches by 20 inches. This service has been discontinued. Reproductions are now outsourced to commercial photographers.

Picture Postcards

A valuable picture source that should not be overlooked is found in postcards.

In the late 1800's and the first half of the 1900's, before widespread use of the telephone, the primary means of communication were letters and postcards. Telegrams were fast but expensive – you paid by the word. Government sponsored postal service was cheap: three cents for a letter, a penny for a postcard.

Lengthy or private correspondence was conducted by epistles that were written on sheets of paper that were inserted and sealed in an envelope. For short notes and memoranda in which privacy was not an issue, you could jot a message on the back of a card and drop it off at any convenient post office or mailbox.

Any stiffened sheet of paper or piece of cardboard can be used as a postcard. I once sent messages home in the middle of a wilderness canoe trip to the outlands of northern Quebec by peeling bark off a birch tree and writing on the smooth inner facing. I mailed my birchbark postcards by giving them to the pilot of the floatplane that flew in fresh supplies after a week and a half on the river.

The U.S. Postal Service sold postcards on which the postage was pre-printed in the upper right corner. These postcards obviated the need to purchase stamps separately. The postcards were either divided by a vertical line in the middle of the obverse side, in which case the address was written on the right side of the line and the message was written on the left side, or they were undivided, in which case the address was written on the obverse side and the message was written on the reverse side. Buyers paid for postage but not for the card.

Although these postcards were free and convenient, they were formal, businesslike, and lacked artistic expression. Enterprising companies learned that they could *sell* postcards to people who could obtain them for free, as long as something of interest was either printed or pictured on the unused side of an undivided postcard. Proverbs, pithy poems, or airy doggerel sometimes graced the reverse sides, but what sold best were pictures: of cities, buildings, street scenes, natural wonders, and hundreds of other subjects, including ships and shipwrecks.

The picture postcard quickly became a mainstay in the industry. Photographers took pictures of everything under the sun for publication on postcards. When I used to visit maritime researchers Ken and Jean Haviland in Baltimore, Maryland, Ken would proudly escort me through his collection of picture postcards. He had tens of thousands of postcard pictures of vessels, all organized by shipping line. In order to locate a particular vessel, he had to look up the name in the *Lloyd's Register*, of which he and Jean had their own personal set.

It never ceases to amaze me how many obscure vessels have been pictured on postcards. Often I have seen the same image in a museum print collection. This has led me to suspect that practically all museum pictures originated from picture postcards. Either the museums somehow obtained the original negative, or they obtained the picture postcard and made a copy negative from it.

Be that as it may, there are many postcard pictures of vessels that are *not* to be found in museums. The negatives have long since been trashed or lost, so they exist only in the form in which they were published. Some of these pictures have been colorized. Some of them picture vessels that were wrecked on the beach: newsworthy events that attracted photographers and

Picture Sources

reporters alike.

I used to go to used book fairs and antique paper fairs on a regular basis. I kept my name on the mailing lists so I would know in advance whenever a fair was to be held in my neck of the woods. I attended most fairs that were held within a hundred-mile radius of my home.

Book fairs focused on the sale of used books, but sometimes they had booths for vendors whose stock in trade consisted of postcards. Paper fairs focused on paper products other than books, although they also had booths for used book vendors. Paper products included old magazines, pulps, comic books (before they became known as graphic novels), posters, labels, advertisements, brochures, trade cards, chewing gum cards (such as baseball cards and Hopalong Cassidy cards), drawings, paintings, lobby cards, gas station maps, bus schedules, calendars, and any other paper ephemera that people are wont to collect. There were also combination used book and paper fairs.

Among the collectibles at paper fairs were picture postcards. Lots of them. Tens of thousands of them. It normally took me the entire day to visit every booth at which postcards were sold. Fortunately, the vendors organized them into categories: States of the Union, foreign countries, trains, buildings, ships, naval vessels, and so on. By browsing only the categories that were relevant to my research, I had to handle only several thousand postcards.

Postcard pictures depicted vessels in various guises: on the ways, being launched, at sea, tied to a wharf, or stranded on a beach.

Picture postcards of vessels generally had the name of the vessel printed on one side or the other. I had two advantages over the typical shipwreck researcher who was looking for images of only one or a few vessels: my list numbered in the hundreds, and I had an encyclopedic familiarity with the names.

With the advent of the Internet, a number of postcard vendors began to sell their wares on their website.

As I have noted elsewhere, websites come and go depending on payment or nonpayment of the domain name and annual hosting fees, so I won't provide any names or addresses. Websites tend to be as ephemeral as the collectibles that they peddle.

A Google search for specific wrecks should eventually steer you to postcard vendors. Use the word "postcard" and the name of a vessel as search criteria. Bookmark worthwhile sites for future reference.

Many postcard vendors who don't have a website sell their merchandise on eBay. Use the same search criteria if you want to search for a picture postcard of a specific vessel. If you want to browse, search under the category for Collectibles: Postcards: Transportation: Boats, Ships. Then, if you want postcards of only shipwrecks, after the first screen appears type "wreck" or "shipwreck" in the search box, and check the box underneath it for "search title and description."

Woodcuts and Steelcuts

Before the invention of photography and photographic reproduction processes, there were woodcuts and steelcuts.

A woodcut is a picture that is carved into a block of wood which can then be inked and pressed against paper so that the picture is transferred from the block to a printed page. The engraving technique is the opposite of a line drawing, in which the artist draws a picture on paper using a graphite pencil or ink pen. Instead of drawing the lines that depict the image, the woodcut artist leaves the image lines on the surface of the flat block of wood, and carves away what would be the white space in a drawing. In other words, using a sharp chisel or knife, he cuts away everything that doesn't look like the picture that he wants to make.

Carving a woodblock is more like sculpting than drawing. The artist shaves the wood along the grain. The wavy lines that you see in the printed image are the growth rings.

A steelcut uses the same technique, the difference

being that the picture is carved into a steel plate instead of wood. Because steel is smooth, you can distinguish a steelcut from a woodcut by the lack of wavy lines.

In the printing process, the surface of the woodblock or steel plate is inked by means of a roller that is coated with ink. In the old days of linotype printing, the woodblock or steel plate was inserted into the lead plate on the printing press, so that text and pictures were printed on the sheets at the same time. This is how old books, magazines, and newspapers were printed.

The printed picture was a mirror image of the carved picture: that is, the image was reversed. This means that whenever you see writing in a picture – such as the name on a vessel – the letters had to be carved backwards.

Illustrated Newspapers

From the early 1800's, books were illustrated with woodcuts and, later, with steelcuts. But the publications that took the greatest advantage of these illustrating processes were newspapers.

Whereas daily newspapers printed only text for local consumption, illustrated weekly newspapers printed pictures to accompany their stories for broad distribution. These illustrated newspapers sent their artists to various locales in order to sketch scenes of real life. Often the artist who produced the rough sketch was not the same artist who carved the wood or steel. Usually, the sketch artist would make a detailed drawing in the studio, then a carver made the cut in the workshop.

In the United States, the two most widely circulated illustrated newspapers were *Harper's Weekly* (1857 to 1916) and *Frank Leslie's Illustrated Newspaper* (1855 to 1922). Another illustrated newspaper of interest to shipwreck researchers was *Gleason's Pictorial* (1851 to 1854), which became *Ballou's Pictorial* (1854 to 1859). The *Illustrated London News* (1842 to 1993) was the British equivalent.

None of these newspapers was indexed. The only way to ascertain which vessels and shipwrecks were illustrated in their pages was to scan each and every page of each and every issue. I did this in the mid-1980's. It took me two years to complete the project.

The main branch of the Free Library of Philadelphia had complete sets of *Harper's* and *Leslie's*, and partial sets of *Gleason's* and *Ballou's*. *Harper's* was available on microfilm; the others were available in hardcopy. The main branch was located in center city where parking was at a premium or nonexistent. From my home in northeast Philly, it took an hour to ride the trackless trolley and elevated train to City Hall, then walk a mile to the aged library building. In addition to daily hours, the Main Branch was open until 9 o'clock on Wednesday evenings.

Unless I was traveling, every Wednesday night I quit writing at 5 o'clock, took the bus and el downtown, ate a sandwich during the commute, then scanned newspapers for three hours until closing time. I was exhausted and bleary eyed when I arrived home at 10 o'clock.

First I went through *Harper's* on microfilm. I photocopied every picture of a vessel or shipwreck that was relevant to the eastern seaboard. I kept a list of pictures that were of secondary interest. Despite the antique microfilm readers, which constantly broke down and on which the pages had to be advanced by means of a hand crank, the microfilm work proceeded fairly quickly. Occasionally I spent all day Saturday at the library, but I found it excessively wearing to scan microfilm for eight hours straight. Three-hour snippets were more conducive to maintaining alertness.

For *Leslie's*, *Gleason's*, and *Ballou's* I had to flip every dirty and delicate page. I was allowed to see only one year at a time, so I had to keep returning to the circulation desk to submit call slips. The hardcopies were kept in the stacks in the basement. The library was missing several years' worth of *Gleason's* and *Ballou's*. I tracked them down to the college library at Villanova,

Picture Sources

and had to drive there in order to see the hardcopies.

After two years of research, I also had to locate and purchase original issues in order to have high-quality woodcuts for reproduction in my Popular Dive Guide Series. I found vendors that specialized in the sale of old newspapers and magazines. I visited some shops in person. To other vendors I submitted lists of the issues that I wanted to purchase, then bought whatever they had in stock.

These vendors obtained their stock from public libraries that unloaded their hardcopies after microfilming them. Microfilm takes less space than tall stacks of outsized newspapers, and microfilm was more durable. I am certain that many old newspapers were trashed instead of sold, but these enterprising vendors did historians a great service by buying and warehousing the discards.

I spent thousands of dollars on buying the issues that contained the pictures that I wanted.

I also scanned every issue of *Scientific American* from 1845 to 1920.

Oddball Picture Sources

Pictures are where you find them. In the previous section you read about how I found pictures in old newspapers and magazines. There is no telling how many other newspapers and magazines published pictures of vessels and shipwrecks. You could research that avenue forever.

After exhausting the easy sources, you must go after sources that are more obscure. For example, in the early 1980's I wrote to the original owners of the *Choapa* and the *Tolten*, both of which sank during World War Two. J. Lauritzen, the Danish company, was still in business, and in their files they had beautiful photographs of the vessels when they were fresh off the ways. They sent me copies of each under their original names, *Helga* and *Lotta*.

That is only one example among many. Unfortunately for maritime historians, most of the old-time shipbuilders and owners have long since gone out of business. Some may have donated their company records to local museums, but most of their records were trashed. You just never know until you ask . . .

Leave no stone unturned. Consider this prime example. In the mid-1990's, Anne Wilcox, the librarian at the Independence Seaport Museum, received a call from Sharon Reese about a number of vessel pictures that she found in a trunk in her attic. The pictures were not captioned. Reese wondered if anyone at the museum could identify them. Wilcox told her that no one on the staff had that kind of expertise. She suggested that I might be able to help.

Wilcox called me and explained the situation. I was intrigued, so I called Reese for more details. Shortly after the turn of the century, her grandfather had bought the Philadelphia office of the famous East Coast salvage company, Merritt-Chapman & Scott. Reese inherited the family heirlooms. In cleaning out her attic, she came across three boxes of glass negatives, two of which contained pictures of vessels in various states of distress.

Now I was really intrigued. We made an appointment to meet at her house so I could view the negatives. She lived about an hour away. I took a backlit slide sorter with me. What Reese thought were glass negatives were actually glass lantern slides. When I told her this, she recalled that she had also found an antique projector in the trunk. She brought it out; it proved to be a glass lantern slide projector.

I projected the images on a white plaster wall. I recognized many of the pictures right off the bat. I had seen them in museums; I even had prints of some of them in my collection. I called out the names of the vessels that I recognized.

Others I knew by sight but could not remember the names. These latter wrecks were beached sailing vessels that had been successfully refloated. I had seen pictures of them, but had never studied them because they did not fit my research agenda.

Picture Sources 241

The projected enlargements enabled me to read the name on the bow or the stern of some of the vessels. Reese was astonished.

I returned another day with an armful of books in which I knew many of the pictures had been published. All in all, I identified scores of vessels. What I found astonishing was that some of the pictures closely resembled pictures that I owned or had seen, but either the waves were crashing in a different location or the subject angle was slightly askew.

I realized that the photographer did exactly what I have done when shooting a rare subject. He took a number of exposures from different distances and angles. Only one picture wound up in a museum. Reese had pictures of the same subject that the same photographer took on the same day, but which were different shots in the series, and which until now had been lost. This was the case with the *City of Edinburgh*.

Reese let me borrow the pictures that I could use to illustrate forthcoming books in my Popular Dive Guide Series. I didn't have the equipment to copy glass lantern slides, so I took them to a camera shop and had their lab make full-size copy negatives and print enlargements.

I once found a sepia print of the *Oregon* in an antique shop. There was no credit line, and I have never seen this picture in any source or publication.

Vessels and shipwrecks may be found in antique art prints, such as those that were produced by Currier & Ives.

I once found a stamp store that was selling a sheet of ten poster stamps of the *Northern Pacific*. A poster stamp is a non-postage stamp that can be licked and glued to anything for decoration.

I have stumbled on pictures in museums that the librarians did not know were in the collection.

I have seen side-scan sonar images that accurately portrayed shipwrecks the way they exist on the bottom.

You may find pictures of foreign-built vessels in museums that are located in the country in which the vessel was constructed. The possibilities here are endless, as there are thousands of small museums spread throughout the world.

I have obtained a number of pictures from private collectors: individuals who have accumulated pictures from obscure sources of their own.

I obtained pictures of the *Moonstone* direct from the sailor who snapped them: survivor Alvin Smith, who served aboard her during World War Two.

Erik Heyl made scale drawings of steamships that were based upon paintings that he found in museums across the country. He published these drawings, along with statistics and historical information, in *Early American Steamers*, which ran to six volumes that were published between 1952 and 1969.

Before and after the turn of the twentieth century, Samuel Ward Stanton made pencil sketches and pen and ink drawings of hundreds of vessels. The contemporary books in which they were published are out of print and hard to find. In the 1970's, the Steamship Historical Society of America published the drawings in a series of eight booklets. These booklets are still in print.

Antique books often published pictures of vessels, especially antique books with a maritime theme. By haunting libraries and museums, and browsing through the books on their shelves, you never know what pictures you might find.

If you can't find a picture of a vessel under the name that it carried at the time it sank, look for a picture of it under a previous name. If you still don't have any luck, look for a picture of a sister ship. Any likeness is better than none at all.

This is just a smattering of sources from which a shipwreck researcher may obtain pictures of vessels. Seek, and ye may find.

Ownership Conundrum

After determining that my usual sources did not have any pictures of the *Chilore*, a wreck that lay at the

Picture Sources

mouth of the Chesapeake Bay, I started looking for alternative sources. I found a picture at the Kirn Library in Norfolk, but the image was soft and indistinct. I wanted a better picture.

I broadened my search by making phone calls to museums in surrounding States. Eventually I found a museum in Baltimore, Maryland that had a picture of the *Chilore*. (I don't remember the name and I didn't record it.) According to the librarian, the museum had obtained the picture from the Kirn Library. She explained the procedure for ordering a print, quoted the cost, and told me that if I wanted to publish the picture I would have to pay an additional fee for "reproduction rights."

I asked why I had to pay reproduction rights to the museum when the Kirn Library owned the original image. She said the picture was now part of the museum's collection, and if I got the picture from the museum, then I had to pay the museum for the right to publish the picture.

This didn't make sense to me. I asked something like, "So that means that when I buy the picture from *you* it becomes part of *my* collection. Then *I* own the copyright and can sell reproduction rights."

There was a silence on the phone while she digested my line of reasoning. I suspect that she saw the flaw in her argument, but could not accept the logical conclusion because it was not to her advantage to do so. She adopted the attitude that the succession of ownership stopped with the museum. Further argument proved useless.

This incident begs the question: who owns a picture when it exists in more than one collection?

Perhaps we should commence to provide the answer by going farther back: who owns a picture in the first place.

The corollary to this question is: how is ownership transferred from the original owner to a succeeding owner?

Copyright Law

According to U.S. copyright law, a picture is copyrighted in the name of its creator at the moment of its creation. This simple law applies to textual works as well. In other words, any photograph that I take with my camera is automatically copyrighted in my name at the instant I press the shutter release. The analogous situation holds true for my short stories, articles, and books: they are automatically copyrighted in my name as soon as I write them, or portions of them.

Transfer of ownership cannot be made passively; that is, it cannot be assumed by another entity or individual without my express written permission. Lacking such permission, ownership continues to reside with me as the creator.

I never sell the rights to my pictures or written works. I sell the *usage* of them. This usage may be in the form of "first North American serial rights" if I sell a short story or article to a magazine or newspaper. Or it could be "one time rights" if I sell the work a second time, or a third time, or any number of times. In any case, the buyer may publish the work only once for the fee that we negotiated. If he wants to publish the work again, we negotiate another fee.

The same is true for photographs, although generally one sells only "one time rights" instead of "first North American serial rights," as the latter term generally applies to written works.

No matter how many times I sell a photograph, I retain the copyright – unless I sell "all rights." Photographers rarely do this because it transfers the copyright to the buyer, and the photographer is never allowed to sell the picture again. The sale of "all rights" commands a significantly higher fee: often thousands of dollars. This may be done when, say, a picture is sold for advertising purposes, and the advertiser doesn't want the picture to show up in a multitude of places. The advertiser wants exclusivity; he wants the picture to be associated with a product or with the company. He definitely doesn't want the picture to be used by a competitor.

Transfer of title is an affirmative action on which both parties must agree in writing. The high fee is what makes it worth the photographer's while to sell all rights, because he can no longer sell one time rights.

Copyright Image

Although I have been using the word "picture" with regard to copyright registration, many people don't have a clear understanding of what is meant by the word.

Picture refers to the original image: a photograph, a drawing, a work of art, and so on. With respect to copyright, a picture does not mean a print or photocopy or lithograph that is made from the original image. It means the image itself.

For example, if I make a print from my original negative, and you take a picture of that print, you haven't *created* anything. You have *copied* something. You have copied my original image by photographic means. The same is true if you trace the picture, or make a freehand drawing that is based on my original image.

That *image* is copyrighted in my name because I am the creator. You cannot assume a new copyright by dint of reproducing that image by any means, in any form.

The image is my property; it is intellectual property. A copyright is protection for intellectual property.

Copyright Protection

If a copyright is ever questioned, the copyright owner may be called upon to prove his ownership. This can be done in a number of ways.

For writers, the simplest and least expensive way to establish priority is to place a manuscript in an envelope, seal the flap, and mail the envelope to himself. The postmark functions as the date. The writer keeps the envelope sealed unless it needs to be unsealed in a court of law.

For photographers, the approximate time of creation can be demonstrated by the film processor's date stamp on the back of a print or on the mount of a slide.

Another way to copyright a photograph is to publish it. The publication date establishes the time frame.

The surest way to establish copyright is to submit the work to the Register of Copyrights at the Library of Congress. Writers may submit photocopied manuscripts or published volumes. Photographers may submit duplicates of an image. The one-page form is easy to fill out.

The problem with this system is the expense. Presently the copyright fee is $45 per manuscript, book, or picture; although short stories, articles, and pictures may be submitted in groups for a single fee.

Remember that any work is automatically copyrighted at the time of its creation. Copyrighting a work by registering it with the Library of Congress does two things: it certifies the date of submission and therefore establishes the creator's priority in an official and legal manner; and it entitles the copyright holder to recover legal expenses from an infringer in the event of a suit for copyright infringement.

Copyright Limitation

Like patents, copyrights do not last forever. On October 19, 1976, the copyright law was changed in order to grant longer protection to owners of copyrights. The new limitation is for the life of the creator plus fifty years. In other words, for half a century after my death, my heirs will own the copyrights for every book I have written and for every picture I have taken.

Prior to 1976, the law granted copyright protection for 28 years after a work's creation. At the end of 28 years, a copyright owner could file for an extension for an additional 28 years. No more extensions were permitted. Thus, before 1976, the longest amount of time for which any work could be protected by copyright was 56 years.

An extension request was an affirmative process. If no extension request was submitted or payment made, the copyright expired automatically after the initial 28 years.

Once a copyright expires, the work falls into the public domain. This means that anyone has the legal right to publish the work without the permission of the previous copyright owner. The expiration of copyright is irrevocable; that is, the work cannot be copyrighted ever again, not even by the original copyright owner. Prior to 1976, if the original copyright owner failed to file for an extension before the date of expiration, he lost for all time his opportunity to do so.

A work that exists in the public domain may not be privatized: once in the public domain, forever in the public domain. Anyone may exploit a public domain work for any use whatsoever. No permission is required.

This is why you now see so much classic literature being reprinted. Anyone can publish the Sherlock Holmes stories of Arthur Conan Doyle because they are in the public domain. Thousands of other books from the first half of the twentieth century are being reprinted for the very same reason. And because there is no longer any copyright on these works, publishers do not have to pay royalties to the authors or their heirs.

Public Domain

Any pictures that were made with taxpayers' money are automatically placed in the public domain by government fiat. This means photographs, drawings, artwork – literally everything.

For example, during World War Two, the U.S. Coast Guard photographed merchant vessels upon arrival and departure from U.S. ports. These pictures are commonly found in general circulation. On the negatives were written the vessel's name and nationality, the date on which the picture was taken, and whether the vessel was arriving or departing (distinguished by writing IN or OUT on the negative).

These pictures *started* in the public domain. The public paid for them, so the public owns them. As I noted above, public domain pictures may not be privatized. They always were and always will be in the public domain, and no intimidating treatment can make them otherwise.

Navy blimps photographed merchant vessels at sea. These pictures are also in the public domain. Numerous other examples abound. For example, the National Archives possesses tens of thousands of pictures that were taken by military photographers throughout the years. Some were combat photographers in the various services. The individual photographers don't own these pictures because they were paid by the government to take them. I used such pictures on the covers of *Lonely Conflict*, my autobiographical novel of the Vietnam war.

With very few exceptions, nearly every picture that is archived in the Library of Congress, the Naval Photographic Center, the National Archives, or any other public archival facility, is in the public domain.

Any private picture that was taken on or after October 19, 1976 is still in copyright, even if its copyright was not registered.

Pre-1976 copyrights are expiring on a daily basis. All unregistered pictures that were taken on or before October 18, 1976 fell into the public domain no later than October 19, 2004.

If a picture was registered for copyright on October 18, 1976, its copyright expired on October 18, 2004. If the copyright was renewed on time, protection was extended for an additional 28 years: to October 18, 2032.

In other words, unless a copyright owner renewed a copyright that was originally registered before or on October 18, 1976, that picture is now in the public domain.

As this book goes to press in July 2008, the most recent pre-1976 picture that is still protected by copyright must have been registered for copyright in 1952, and must have had its copyright renewed in 1980. Otherwise it has now fallen into the public domain.

I venture to speculate that extremely few pictures have been submitted for copyright renewal.

Picture Sources

A picture that was not registered to begin with cannot have its automatic copyright renewed. Its copyright expired automatically after 28 years.

The Library of Congress keeps records of all copyright registrations. When in doubt about the status of a copyright, consult with the Register of Copyrights.

Primary Contacts

National Archives (Archives One)
700 Pennsylvania Avenue, NW
Washington, DC 20408-0001
Phone: 202-501-5400 / 866-325-7208
Fax: 202-501-7154
E-mail: inquire@nara.gov
Website: http://www.archives.gov

National Archives (Archives Two)
8601 Adelphi Road
College Park, Maryland 20740-6001
Phone: 301-837-2000 / 866-272-6272
Fax: 301-837-0483
E-mail: inquire@nara.gov
Website: http://www.archives.gov

Naval Historical Center
805 Kidder Breese SE
Washington Navy Yard, DC 20374-5060
Website: http://www.history.navy.mil/index.html

> Operational Archives
> Building 57, Third Floor
> Phone: 202-433-3224
> Fax: 202-433-2833
>
> Ships History Branch
> Building 200, First Floor
> Phone: 202-433-3643
>
> Navy Department Library
> Building 44, First Floor
> Phone: 202-433-4132
> Fax: 202-433-9553

Primary Contacts

>Naval Photographic Center
>Building 108, Second Floor
>Phone: 202-433-2765

Judge Advocate General
200 Stovall Street
Alexandria, Virginia 22332-2400
Phone: 301-713-6875
Website: http://www.jag.navy.mil/

Washington National Records Center
4205 Suitland Road
Suitland, Maryland 20746-8001
Phone: 301-778-1510
Fax: 301-778-1561
E-mail: suitland.reference@nara.gov
Website: http://www.archives.gov/dc-metro/suitland/facility-info.html

Historian's Office, CG-09224
U.S. Coast Guard Headquarters
2100 Second Street, SW
Washington, DC 20593-0001
Phone: 202-372-4651 / 202-372-4653
Fax: 202-372-4984
E-mail: link on website
Website: http://www.uscg.mil/history/

Library of Congress
101 Independence Avenue, SE
Washington, DC 20540
Phone (visitor information): 202-707-8000
E-mail (visitor information): vso@loc.gov
Phone (general reference desk): 202-707-5840
Website: http://www.loc.gov/index/html

>Thomas Jefferson Building
>1st Street, SE, between Independence Avenue and East Capitol Street
>Main Reading Room phone: 202-707-3399

John Adams Building
2nd Street, SE, between Independence Avenue
   and East Capitol Street

James Madison Building
Independence Avenue, SE, between 1st Street
   and 2nd Street

Photoduplication Service
Phone: 202-707-5640
Fax: 202-707-1771

Smithsonian Institution Archives
900 Jefferson Drive, SW
   Mailing address:
      Smithsonian Institution
      P.O. Box 37012
      SIB 153, MRC 010
      Washington, DC 20013-7012
Phone: 202-357-1420
Website: http://www.siarchives.si.edu

Independence Seaport Museum
(formerly Philadelphia Maritime Museum)
211 South Columbus Boulevard at Walnut Street
Philadelphia, Pennsylvania 19106
Phone (museum): 215-925-5439
Phone (library): 215-413-8640 / 215-413-8639
Fax (library): 215-925-6713
E-mail: library@phillyseaport.org
Website: http://www.phillyseaport.org

The Mariners' Museum
100 Museum Drive (moving autumn 2008)
Newport News, Virginia 23606-3759
Phone (museum): 757-596-2222 / 800-581-7245
Phone (library): 757-591-7782
Fax (library): 757-591-7310
E-mail: library@mariner.org
Website: http://www.mariner.org

Primary Contacts

Mystic Seaport
75 Greenmansville Avenue
P.O. Box 6000
Mystic, Connecticut 06355-0990
Phone (museum): 860-572-5315 / 888-973-2767
Phone (library): 860-572-5367
E-mail: library.email@mysticseaport.org
E-mail: collections@mysticseaport.org
Website: http://www.mysticseaport.org

Steamship Historical Society of America
1029 Waterman Street
East Providence, Rhode Island 02914
Phone: 401-274-0805
Fax: 401-274-0836
E-mail: info@sshsa.org
Website: http://www.sshsa.org

Peabody Essex Museum
Phillips Library
161 Essex Street
Salem, Massachusetts 01970
Phone (museum): 978-745-9500 / 866-745-1876
Phone (library): 800-745-4054 extension 3053
Fax (library): 978-741-9012
E-mail: research@pem.org
Website: http://pem.org

National Maritime Museum
Reference Librarian
SF Maritime NHP Library
Building E, Fort Mason Center
San Francisco, CA 94123
Phone (headquarters): 415-561-6662
Fax (headquarters): 415-561-6660
Phone (library): 415-561-7030
Fax (library): 415-561-3540
E-mail: link on website
Website: http://www.maritime.org

Primary Contacts

South Street Seaport Museum
Melville Library
207 Front Street
New York, New York 10038
Mailing address for research and photo requests:
    Rights and Reproductions
    Registrar's Office
    South Street Seaport Museum
    12 Fulton Street
    New York, NY 10038
Phone: 212-748-8746
E-mail: mnora@southstreet.org
Website: http://www.southstreetseaportmuseum.org

Hart Nautical Collections
Massachusetts Institute of Technology
MIT Museum Building N51
265 Massachusetts Avenue
Cambridge, Massachusetts 02139
Phone: 617-253-5927
Fax: 617-253-8994
E-mail: museuminfo@mit.edu
Website: http://web.mit.edu/museum/collections/
            research.html

Maine Maritime Museum Library
243 Washington Street
Bath, Maine 04530
Phone: 207-443-1316
Fax: 207-443-1316
E-mail: library@maritimeme.org
Website: http://www.mainemaritimemuseum.org

Penobscot Marine Museum
Stephen Phillips Memorial Library
9 Church Street, P.O. Box 498
Searsport, Maine 04974-0498
Phone: 207-548-2529 extension 213
Fax: 207-548-2520
E-mail: library@penobscotmarinemuseum.org

Primary Contacts 255

Website: http://www.penobscotmarinemuseum.org/
index.html

Outer Banks History Center
1 Festival Park Boulevard, P.O. Box 250
Manteo, North Carolina 27954
Phone: 252-473-2655
Fax: 252-473-1483
E-mail: obhc@ncmail.net
Website: http://www.obhistorycenter.net/index.htm

North Carolina Office of State Archaeology
Underwater Archaeology Branch
Fort Fisher
P.O. Box 58
Kure Beach, North Carolina 28449
Phone: 910-458-9042
Fax: 910-458-4093
E-mail: uab@ncmail.net
Website: http://www.arch.dcr.state.nc.us/ncarch/
underwater/underwater.htm

State Department of Cultural Resources
Division of Archives and History
Archives and Records Section
109 East Jones Street
Raleigh, North Carolina 27601
Mailing address:
    North Carolina State Archives
    4614 Mail Service Center
    Raleigh, NC 27699-4614
Phone: 919-807-7310
Fax: 919-733-1354
E-mail: archives@ncmail.net
Website: http://www.ah.dcr.state.nc.us/

South Carolina Institute of Archaeology and
    Anthropology
1321 Pendleton Street
Columbia, South Carolina 29208
Phone: 803-777-8170
Fax: 803-254-1338
E-mail: amerc@sc.edu
Website: http://www.cas.sc.edu/sciaa/

U.S. Naval Institute
Beach Hall
291 Wood Road
Annapolis, MD 21402
Phone: 410-268-6110
Fax: 410-269-7940
Phone (security department): 410-293-1000
E-mail (naval heritage): mripley@usni.org
E-mail (photo archive): photoservice@usni.org
Website: http://www.usni.org

Submarine Force Library and Museum Association
One Chrystal Lake Road
        Mailing address:
                Box 571
                Naval Submarine Base New London
                Groton, Connecticut 06349-5571
Phone: 860-694-3174 / 860-448-0893 / 800-343-0079
Fax: 860-405-0568
E-mail (office): admin@submarinemuseum.org
Website: http://www.submarinemuseum.org/

Historical Collections of the Great Lakes
(formerly Institute for Great Lakes Research)
Bowling Green State University
Jerome Library, Sixth Floor
Bowling Green, Ohio 43403
Phone: 419-372-9612
Fax: 419-372-9600
E-mail: rgraham@bgnet.bgsu.edu
Website: http://www.bgsu.edu/colleges/library/hcgl

Primary Contacts

Great Lakes Historical Society
Inland Seas Maritime Museum
480 Main Street
Vermillion, Ohio 44089-0435
Phone: 440-967-3467 / 800-893-1485
Fax: 440-967-1519
E-mail: glhs1@inlandseas.org
Website: http://www.inlandseas.org

Canal Park Marine Museum
U.S. Army Corps of Engineers
Duluth Area Office
600 Lake Avenue South
Duluth, Minnesota 55802
Phone (information): 218-727-2497
Phone (office): 218-720-5260
Website: http://www.lre.usace.army.mil/where/
    behindthecastle/exhibitcenters/
    canalparkandmuseum/

Wisconsin Marine Historical Society
Marine Room
Milwaukee Public Library
814 West Wisconsin Avenue
Milwaukee, Wisconsin 53233-2385
Phone: 414-286-3074
Fax: 414-286-2137
E-mail: info@wmhs.org
Website: http://www.wmhs.org

Wisconsin Maritime Museum
75 Maritime Drive
Manitowoc, Wisconsin 54220
Phone: 920-684-0218 / 866-724-2356
Fax: 920-684-0219
Website:
    http://www.wisconsinmaritime.org/library.htm

258 Primary Contacts

Library and Archives Canada
395 Wellington Street
Ottawa, Ontario
Canada K1A 0N4
Phone: 613-996-5115 / 866-578-7777
Fax: 613-995-6274
E-mail: links on website
Website: http://collectionscanada.ca/

National Maritime Museum
The Caird Library
Park Row
Greenwich, London
SE10 9NF
England
Phone (museum switchboard): +44 (0)20-8858-4422
Fax (general): +44 (0)20 8312-6632
Phone (library items): +44 (0)20 8312 6516
E-mail (library items): library@nmm.ac.uk
Phone (manuscript items): +44 (0)20 8312-6669
E-mail (manuscript items): manuscripts@nmm.ac.uk
Phone (charts and maps): +44 (0)20 8312 6757
E-mail (charts and maps): bdthyn@nmm.ac.uk
Phone (picture library): +44 (0)20 8312 6631/6704
Fax (picture library): +44 (0)20 8312 6533
E-mail (picture library): picturelibrary@nmm.ac.uk
E-mail (historic photographs):
    plansandphotos@nmm.ac.uk
Website: http://www.nmm.ac.uk/index.php

Merseyside Maritime Museum
Albert Dock
Liverpool
L3 4AQ
England
Phone: 0151 478 4499
International phone: +44 151 478 4499
E-mail: link on website
Website: http://www.liverpoolmuseum.org.uk

Index

Act of Congress: 94
Adams Building: 150, 152, 156, 252
Akers, Gina: 124
Allard, Dean: 135
Amer, Chris: 177
American Bureau of Ships: 36
American Maritime Cases: 28-29
American Yacht List: 38
Anacostia River: 119
Andrea Doria: 186
Angelo, Michael: 166-167
"Annotated List of Treasure Maps in the Library of Congress, An": 154
Annual Report of the United States Life Saving Service: 24-26, 41, 163, 196
Annual Report to the Secretary of the Navy: 122
Anti-Submarine Warfare records: 123
Architectural Research Room: 110, 111
Archives One: 67-68, 70 (picture)
Archives Two: 67-68, 106-107 (picture)
archivist (defined): 69, 91
Armed Guard Engagement Reports: 75
ASA (defined): 222
Asa H. Purvere: 59-60
Atlantic Divers: 192
Atlas of Treasure Maps: 39
Augean stables: 104
Automated Wreck and Obstruction Information System (AWOIS): 29, 30-31, 155
Baleen: 64
Ballou's Pictorial: 237-238
Bath Iron Works: 175
Bath Marine Museum: 175
Beeson's Maritime Directory: 179
Beeson's (Sailors) Marine Hand Book: 180
Belatty, Captain: 202

Berman, Bruce D.: 17, 194-195
Blanton, J.O.: 42
Blue Book of American Shipping: 180
Boston Globe: 57, 59
Boston Public Library: 58-59
Bowling Green State University: 189
Breese, Denny: 125-126
Bright, Dave: 185-186
Brown, Laura: 171
Brunette: 78
Bulkoil: 143
Bureau of Marine Inspection and Navigation: 75
Bureau of Navigation: 23
call slip: 79-82
Canadian Coastal and Inland Steam Vessels 1809-1930: 27-28
Canadian List of Shipping: 179
Canal Park Marine Museum: 213, 257
cargo manifest: 117-118
Cartographic Research Room: 110, 111
Casey, Robert: 131
Cavalcante, Bernard: 123-124, 126
Central Research Room: 84-86
Certificate of Enrollment: 78-79, 82, 83, 195
Charles, Joan: 40-42
Chesapeake Bay: 117, 243
Chicago Tribune: 57
Chilore: 242-243
Choapa: 239
Christopher Newport University: 170
City of Edinburgh: 241
classified documents: 94-95
Coast Guard, U.S.: 25-26, 78, 112, 176, 247
Coast Guard Historian's Office, U.S.: 148-149, 198-199, 231-232, 251
Coast Guard War Casualty Section – World War Two, Records of the U.S.: 75
Coffin, Michael J.: 201
Cohen, Mark: 130
Congress: 25

Index

Congressional Record: 156
Coffman, F.L.: 39
Cold War: 31, 118
Congress: 94, 129
Constitution of the United States: 70, 90
control F: 62
Copy Card: 89
copyright: 244-249
Coyote: 60, 61-62, 63
Crosson, Michael F.: 202
Currier & Ives: 241
Cussler, Clive: 125
Customs House records: 116-117, 190
Davey, Phil: 28
deck log: 76, 200
Declaration of Independence: 70, 90
declassification: 94-95
Defense Mapping Agency: 31
Delaware: 63
DelCorio, Lynn: 192
Department of Defense: 178
"Descriptive List of Treasure Maps and Charts, A": 154
Dictionary of American Naval Fighting Ships: 36-37, 123, 200
Dictionary of Disasters at Sea During the Age of Steam 1869-1962: 26-27
Division of Naval History: 158
Division of Transportation: 158
Dora: 83
Dough, Wynne: 176
Down Deep: 192
Doyle, Arthur Conan: 247
Dudley, Bill: 135-138
Early American Steamers: 242
Eastern Sea Frontier, War Diary of: 75, 123
East Providence, Rhode Island: 172
eBay: 236
Ebco Host Research Databases: 58
Eldredge collection, Elwin: 168-169
e-mail: 191-192

Encyclopedia of American Shipwrecks: 17-19, 78, 194-195
Ewen, Bill: 172
Ewen, Sue: 172
F.C. Pendleton: 23-24
Federal Bureau of Investigation: 139
Feltner, Charles E.: 43
Feltner, Jeri Baron: 43
Fifth Naval District: 124
Finney, Ed: 232
Fish, John Perry: 39
Fisherman's Wharf: 173
flimsy (defined): 91
Flint, Willard: 189
Flynn, Kathy: 173
Fort Fisher State Park: 176
Fort Meade, Maryland: 150
Fourth Naval District: 114, 115
Frankfurt: 155
Frank Leslie's Illustrated Newspaper: 237-238
Fraser, Megan: 167
Freedom of Information Act: 147
Free Library of Philadelphia: 52-53, 58, 238
Fuhrer's U-boats in American Waters, The: 159
General Sherman: 182-183, 187
Gentian report: 125-127
Geodetic and Coast Survey maps: 176
Germany: 20, 39
Gladstone, Eugene: 153
Glasgow University Archives: 193
Gleason's Pictorial: 237-238
Google: 50, 61, 63, 236
Graham, Bob: 179
grain: 210
Great Lakes Diving Guide, The: 43
Great Lakes Historical Society: 179-180, 213, 257
Great Lakes Maritime History: Bibliography and Sources of Information: 43
Great Lakes Red Book: 179, 180
Great Lakes Wreck Charts: 43

Index

Greenwood's Guide: 179
Groton (submarine base): 178
Guide to Sunken Ships in American Waters, A: 29
G.W. Blunt White Library: 170
Haberlein, Chuck: 232
Hamilton: 40
Harding Ledge: 64
Harper's Weekly: 237-238
Hart Nautical Collections: 174-175, 215, 254
Haviland, Jean: 234
Haviland, Ken: 234
Helga: 239
Hepler, Paul: 40
Hercules, labors of: 104
Heyl, Erik: 242
historian (defined): 91
Historical Collections of the Great Lakes: 178-179, 189, 213, 256
History of U.S. Lightships, A: 189
Hocking, Charles: 26-27
Holdcamper, Forrest R.: 22
Hollowak, Tom: 172
Holmes, Sherlock: 247
Hopalong Cassidy: 235
House, Anne: 171-172
Hudson Canyon: 40
Hudson River: 40
Hulburt, Jon: 77-78
Hulburt, Judy: 77-78
Hunt's Universal Yacht List: 38
Illustrated London News: 237
Independence Seaport Museum: 12, 20, 21, 161, 165-167, 169, 170, 240, 252
Institute of Great Lakes Research: 178
insurance: 196-197
Insurance Company of North America: 12, 197
Internet: 56-65, 182-191
Internet Newspaper Providers: 57-59, 64-65
In the Wake of the Andrea Doria: 153
ISO (defined): 222

James Madison Building: 150, 152, 154-156, 252
Jane, Fred T.: 37
Jane's Fighting Ship: 37
Jefferson Building: 150, 151, 152, 153 (picture), 154, 252
Jefferson, Thomas: 151
JPEG (defined): 225
John Adams Building: 150, 152, 156, 252
John Hastie Company: 192-193
John Morgan: 117-118
Johnson, Paul: 201-202
Joseph Conrad Library: 174
J. Porter Shaw Library: 173-174
Judge Advocate General: 142-147, 251
junkyard dog complex: 14
Kaplan, H.R.: 29
Kenny, Joseph: 201-202
King Philip: 64
Kirn Library: 243
Knox, Frank (Secretary of the Navy): 20
Kohl, Cris: 42-43
L-8: 199-200
Labadie, C. Patrick: 213
Lady Elgin: 197
Lake Underwriters: 179
Landover, Maryland: 150
Lauritzen, J.: 239
Law Library Reading Room: 155
Lawrence, Richard: 176
librarian (defined): 157
Library and Archives Canada: 181, 258
Library of Congress: 29, 50-52, 149-157, 214, 222, 231, 246, 248-249, 251-252
Life Saving Service: 24-26, 100-101, 176
Lighthouse Establishment: 23
Lipfert, Nathan: 161-162
List of Merchant Vessels of the United States: 22-24, 36, 79, 163, 168, 171, 179, 194
Lloyd, Kathy: 125, 128-130, 131, 132, 136
Lloyd's Casualty Weekly: 21-22

Index

Lloyd's of London: 26-27, 33
Lloyd's Register of American Yachts: 38
Lloyd's Register of Ships: 32-35, 36, 79, 161, 163, 164, 168, 170, 171, 179, 194-195
Lloyd's Register of Yachts: 38
Lloyd's Register Wreck Returns: 21
Lloyd's Weekly Casualty Reports: 21-22
Lloyd's Weekly Shipping Index: 20-21, 163, 194
Lloyd's Wreck Returns: 168
Lonely Conflict: 248
Long Island Maritime Museum: 217
Lonsdale, Adrian: 29
Lore, Marie: 174
Los Angeles Times: 57
Lotta: 239
Lusitania: 28
Lytle, William C.: 22, 28
Macedonia: 40
Madison Building: 150, 152, 154-156, 252
Maine, an Account of her Destruction in Havana Harbor, The: 153
Maine Maritime Museum: 161-162, 175, 214, 254
Manchee, Pete: cover, 2
manifest, cargo: 117-118
Manitowoc Shipbuilding Company: 181
Manning's Yacht Register: 38
Manuscript Reading Room: 155
Marine Engineering: 171
Marine Merchant: 198
Marine Review: 179-180
Mariners' Chronicle, The: 16
Mariners' Museum, The: 12, 20, 21, 161, 168-170, 213, 252
Maritime Law Association: 28
maritime museum (defined): 159
maritime museum library (defined): 159-160
Maritime Museums of North America, Including Canada: 45
marker tab (defined): 92
Mars: 63

Maser, Drew: 12, 197
Maxter Metals: 135-136, 138
Meimbresse, Bob: 192
Mercantile Navy List: 38
Merchant Steam Vessels of the United States 1790-1868: 22
Merchant Vessels of the United States, List of: 22-24, 36
Merchant Yachts of the United States: 38
Merritt-Chapman & Scott: 170, 241
Merseyside County Museum: 214, 258
Microfilm Reading Room: 154
Microfilm Research Room: 105-106, 110, 112-113
Mid Atlantic Shipwreck Accounts to 1899: 41
Mid-Atlantic Shipwreck Accounts II to 1914: 41
Milligan, Joe: 78, 203
Mills, John M: 27
Milwaukee Public Library: 180
Milwaukee Sentinel: 180
Ministry of Truth: 187
Miraflores: 193
Mississippi River: 193
Mitchell, Billy: 155
Mitchell, C. Bradford: 22
Mohave: 63
Mohawk: 229
Monitor: 187-188
Montana: 117
Moonstone: 242
Motion Picture Research Room: 110, 113
Moyer, John: 192
Mud Hole: 40
Mueller, Dottie: 164-165
Murphy: 143
museum (defined): 159
Myronus: 201-202
Mystic Seaport Museum: 12, 20, 161, 170-171, 189, 214, 253
National Archives: 11, 25, 26, 29, 66-118, 123, 130, 132-133, 136-137, 140, 142, 148, 152, 154, 156-157, 163, 172, 178, 181, 190, 195-196, 199, 200,

Index

203, 213-214, 215, 226-231, 248, 250
National Library of Canada: 181
National Mall: 158
National Marine Sanctuary Program: 187
National Maritime Museum (London): 181, 214, 258
National Maritime Museum (San Francisco): 173-174, 214, 253
National Oceanic and Atmospheric Administration (NOAA): 30, 187-188
National Ocean Service (NOS): 30
National Park Service: 173
Nautical Research Group: 185
Naval Academy, U.S.: 177-178
Naval Academy Security Department: 178
Naval Historical Center: 36-37, 119, 250-251
Naval History: 177
Naval Institute, U.S.: 177-178, 214, 256
Naval Photographic Center: 121, 214, 215, 231-233, 248, 251
Naval Records Collection of the Office of Naval Records and Library – Subject Files 1911-1927: 75-76
Navy, U.S.: 20
Navy Department Library: 121-122, 250
Navy/Maritime Team: 73, 75, 103-104, 112
Navy Memorial, U.S.: 70
Navy Sea Systems Command: 134
Navy Wreck List: 29, 155
New Jersey: 201
New Jersey Delaware Pennsylvania Shipwreck Accounts 1705 to 1950: 42
Newport News Ship Building and Dry Dock Company: 12, 161
NewspaperArchive.com: 57
Newton, John: 42
New York: 63
New York Maritime Register: 19-20, 21, 163, 168, 170, 194
New York Public Library: 25
New York Ship Building Company: 12, 161
New York Times: 40, 48-49, 50, 57, 59, 195

1984: 187
noise: 210
Non-Submarine Contacts: 31-32
North Carolina Office of State Archaeology: 215, 217, 255
North Carolina Shipwreck Accounts 1709 to 1950: 42
North Carolina State Archives: 176
North Carolina State Department of Cultural Resources: 177, 215, 217, 255
Northern Pacific: 241
Oceanographic Atlas of the Carolina Continental Margin, An: 42
Official Records of the Union and Confederate Navies in the War of the Rebellion: 42, 43-44
100 Best Great Lakes Shipwrecks, Volume I, The: 43
100 Best Great Lakes Shipwrecks, Volume II, The: 43
Operational Archives: 121, 123-124, 250
Oregon: 241
Orwell, George: 187
Orzech, Otto: 137-138
Ostfriesland: 155
Outer Banks History Center: 176, 215, 217, 255
Peabody Essex Museum: 172-173, 215-216, 253
Penobscot Marine Museum: 175, 214, 254-255
Pentagon: 119
Perils of the Port of New York, The: 40
Peterson, Gene: 192-193
Philadelphia, Free Library of: 52-53, 58, 238
Philadelphia Maritime Museum: 12, 163-165
Phillips Library: 172-173
Photograph Reading Room: 156
picture (defined): 245
Ping-Yang River: 183
Pilke, Orrin: 42
pixelation: 210
Popular Dive Guide Series: 136, 159, 239, 241
poster stamp: 241
Potomac River: 141
Pottstown: 63
Princess Royal: 183

Index

Princess Royale: 182-183
Proceedings: 177
Prints Reading Room: 156
ProQuest: 57, 58
Public Archives of Canada: 181
public domain: 247-248
puller (defined): 69
pull times: 102-105
Quartermaster's Department: 23
Raleigh, North Carolina: 177
Rattray, Jeannette Edwards: 40
RAW (defined): 226
Readers' Guide to Periodical Literature, The: 10
Record of the American Bureau of Ships: 36, 79, 161, 163, 168, 170, 171, 189, 194-195
Records of the U.S. Coast Guard War Casualty Section – World War Two: 75
redacting: 144-145
Reference Service Slip (also see call slip): 80
regenerator: 89
Regional Archives: 114, 115-116
Register of Copyrights: 246, 249
Reese, Sharon: 240-241
reinsurance: 196-197
Reports and Analyses of U.S. and Allied Merchant Ship Losses: 75
research assistant (defined): 68-69
researcher identification card: 72-73
Revenue Cutter Service: 23, 25
Rieseberg, Lieutenant Harry E.: 39
Rilley, Harry E.: 127, 130-131
Romance: 63
R.P. Resor: 39
Russian submarines: 31
San Diego: 132-138
San Francisco Maritime National Historical Park: 173
Santiago: 78
Schulte, Matt: 172
Schwartz, Allyson: 130
Scientific American: 239

Seamans, Nike: 77-78
Seamans, Trueman: 77-78
Seamen's Church Institute: 174, 214
Secretary of the Navy, Annual Report to: 122
Sheard, Brad: 84
Sherman: 183
Ship Ashore!: 40
Shipmasters Association Directory: 180
Ships History Branch: 37, 121, 122-123, 196, 250
Shipwreck Heresies: 144
Shipwrecks of New York: 217
Shipwrecks of North Carolina: 18, 125
Shipwrecks of Rhode Island and Connecticut: 201
Shipwrecks of South Carolina and Georgia: 42
Shore, Hellen: 176
shuttle bus: 76-77
Sigsbee, Charles: 153
Smith, Alvin: 242
Smith's Guide to Maritime Museums of North America – Part 1: Canadian Maritime Provinces, New England/Mid-Atlantic: 45
Smith's Guide to Maritime Museums of North America – Part 2: Southern Gulf Coast: 45
Smith's Guide to Maritime Museums of North America – Part 3: Mid-West/Canada/West Coast including Hawaii: 45
Smithsonian Institution: 158, 215, 252
Sound Research Room: 110
South Carolina Institute of Archaeology and Anthropology: 177, 215, 217, 256
South Street Seaport Museum: 174, 214, 254
Specter, Arlen: 131
Spence, E. Lee: 42
Spence's List: 42
Spicer, Angie: 116-117
Stachura, Irene: 174
Stanton, Samuel Ward: 242
Steamboat Inspection Service: 77-78
Steamship Historical Society of America: 23, 27, 171-172, 213, 242, 253

Index

steelcut (defined): 236
Stephen Phillips Memorial Library: 175
Still Picture Branch: 75, 118, 227
Still Picture Research Room: 110, 227, 228, 230
St. Mary: 193
Suffolk County Historical Society: 217
Submarine Force Library and Museum: 162-163, 178, 199-200, 215, 217, 256
suggestion boxes: 104-105
Sumner: 118
Swan Hunter & Wigham: 193
Talbot Booth's Merchant Ships: 38
Tennesee: 201
Tenth Fleet: 123, 140
Textual Research Room: 110
Thomas A. Scott (wreck company): 12, 161, 170
Thomas Jefferson Building: 150, 151, 152, 153 (picture), 154, 251
Tientsin: 182
TIFF (defined): 226
Tobin, Paul: 127, 131-132
Tolten: 239
Track of the Gray Wolf: 81, 124, 128-130, 132
Treasury Department: 23, 201
Trimble, Jim: 118, 229
U-432: 193
"U-boat Operations in the Western Atlantic During World War I": 127-128
U-boats: 124, 155
Ultra decrypts: 140
Underwater Archaeology Branch of the North Carolina Office of State Archaeology: 176
Underwriters' Registry for Iron Vessels: 38
University of Maryland: 172
Unfinished Voyages: 39
U.S. Naval Academy: 177-178
U.S. Naval Institute: 177-178
U.S.S. San Diego: the Last Armored Cruiser: 132-134
Vanderbilt Museum: 217
Vandereedt, John: 117

Video Research Room: 110
Villanova: 238
Virginia (Confederate ironclad): 44
Virginia (U.S. battleship): 201
Virginia and Maryland Shipwreck Accounts 1623 to 1950: 42
von Doenhoff, Richard A.: 11, 127, 130-131
Walker, Mike: 123-124, 126
W.A. Marshall: 64
War Diary of the Eastern Sea Frontier: 75, 123
Washington National Records Center: 142-144, 145, 251
Washington Navy Yard (map): 120
Washington Post: 57
Wellfleet Pleasant Hill Cemetery: 59
Wheeler, Peter: 130-131
Wikipedia: 184-185
Wilcox, Anne: 164-166, 240
Winter Quarter Shoal Light Vessel: 114
Wisconsin Marine Historical Society: 180, 213, 257
Wisconsin Maritime Museum: 180-181, 213, 257
woodcut (defined): 236
World's Fighting Ships, The: 37-38
World Trade Centers: 119
"Wreck Charts and Information Lists": 154
Wreck Information List: 29, 155
x-ray: 70-71
Zerby, Barry: 11

Books by the Author

The Popular Dive Guide Series
Shipwrecks of Massachusetts: North
Shipwrecks of Massachusetts: South
Shipwrecks of Rhode Island and Connecticut
Shipwrecks of New York
Shipwrecks of New Jersey (1988)
Shipwrecks of New Jersey: North
Shipwrecks of New Jersey: Central
Shipwrecks of New Jersey: South
Shipwrecks of Delaware and Maryland (1990 Edition)
Shipwrecks of Delaware and Maryland (2002 Edition)
Shipwrecks of Virginia
Shipwrecks of North Carolina: from the Diamond Shoals North
Shipwrecks of North Carolina: from Hatteras Inlet South
Shipwrecks of South Carolina and Georgia

Shipwreck and Nautical History
Andrea Doria: Dive to an Era
Deep, Dark, and Dangerous: Adventures and Reflections on the Andrea Doria
Great Lakes Shipwrecks: a Photographic Odyssey
The Fuhrer's U-boats in American Waters
Ironclad Legacy: Battles of the USS Monitor
The Lusitania Controversies: Atrocity of War and a Wreck-Diving History (Book One)
The Lusitania Controversies: Dangerous Descents into Shipwrecks and Law (Book Two)
The Nautical Cyclopedia
Shadow Divers Exposed: the Real Saga of the U-869
Shipwreck Heresies
The Shipwreck Research Handbook
Stolen Heritage: the Grand Theft of the Hamilton and Scourge
Track of the Gray Wolf
USS San Diego: the Last Armored Cruiser
Wreck Diving Adventures

Books by the Author

Dive Training
Primary Wreck Diving Guide
Advanced Wreck Diving Guide
The Advanced Wreck Diving Handbook
Ultimate Wreck Diving Guide
The Technical Diving Handbook

Nonfiction
Wilderness Canoeing

Science Fiction
A Different Universe
A Different Dimension
A Different Continuum
Entropy
A Journey to the Center of the Earth
The Mold
Return to Mars
Silent Autumn
The Time Dragons Trilogy
   A Time for Dragons
   Dragons Past
   No Future for Dragons

Sci-Fi Action/Adventure Novels
Memory Lane
Mind Set
The Peking Papers

Supernatural Horror Novel
The Lurking: Curse of the Jersey Devil

Vietnam Novel
Lonely Conflict

Videotape or DVD
The Battle for the USS Monitor

Visit the GGP website for availability of titles:
http://www.ggentile.com

Two Unforgettable Volumes

There is more to a book than its title. There is the subtitle.

A subtitle is an explanatory device which describes the topic of a book more fully than its title. A case in point is *The Lusitania Controversies*. At first glance the title implies the sole subject of the *Lusitania*. But each of the two volumes possesses a subtitle which explains in greater detail the global premise of which the *Lusitania* is but a part.

Together, both volumes present the entire history of wreck-diving, from its meager beginnings in the 1950's to the advent of technical diving in the 1990's.

Book One is subtitled *Atrocity of War and a Wreck-Diving History*. One quarter of the volume is devoted to the construction, career, sinking, and aftermath of the *Lusitania*. Three quarters are devoted to the history of wreck-diving and to autobiographical experiences of the author, who became an essential element in wreck-diving and a pioneer in technical diving. Coverage extends to 1979, and includes a section on the author's first *Doria* trip, in 1974.

Book Two is subtitled *Dangerous Descents into Shipwrecks and Law*. This volume continues the history of wreck-diving from 1980; describes numerous dives on ever-deeper shipwrecks; a number of incredible penetrations into the vast interior of the *Andrea Doria*, including the recovery of two bodies; and details the beginning of mixed-gas diving to the point at which an expedition to the *Lusitania* became practical. The volume concludes with a detailed description of the 1994 *Lusitania* expedition (of which the author was a part) and subsequent legal activities.

The two volumes of *The Lusitania Controversies* are larger than the sum of their parts. They comprise biographical content with incredible underwater adventures: some hair-raising, others deadly, all exciting: a fascinating excursion into the real world of wreck-diving and the evolution of the activity.

www.ingramcontent.com/pod-product-compliance
Lightning Source LLC
Chambersburg PA
CBHW050133170426
43197CB00011B/1822